NEW JERSEY

Also in this Series

Arizona, Malcolm L. Comeaux

Colorado, Mel Griffiths and Lynnell Rubright

Hawaii, Joseph R. Morgan

Maryland, James E. DiLisio

Michigan, Lawrence M. Sommers

Missouri, Milton D. Rafferty

Texas, Terry G. Jordan, with John L. Bean, Jr., and William M. Holmes

Wyoming, Robert Harold Brown

Forthcoming Through 1984

Alaska, Roger W. Pearson and Donald F. Lynch

Mississippi, Jesse O. McKee

North Carolina, Ole Gade and H. Daniel Stillwell

South Carolina, Charles F. Kovacik and John J. Winberry

Utah, Clifford B. Craig

All books in this series are available in paperback and hardcover.

GEOGRAPHIES OF THE UNITED STATES

Ingolf Vogeler, General Editor

New Jersey: A Geography
Charles A. Stansfield, Jr.

New Jersey. The name evokes many images, most of which are narrow stereotypes that fall short of reality. For example, though New Jersey's salient cultural characteristic is its high population density—the highest in the United States and higher than that of Britain—there is a surprising amount of open space in the state. Areas of the pinelands remain virtually unexplored, vast bogs are nearly impenetrable, and lush forests on the Appalachian ridges and holly-decked beaches on the ocean invite the city-weary urbanite.

This geographic study of New Jersey, a multidimensional portrait of the state, incorporates three major themes: (1) the state's cultural diversity, an amalgam dating from colonial days, of many varied ethnic, national, and racial groups; (2) its bipolar orientation to two neighboring giant metropolitan areas, New York and Philadelphia, again a factor that dates to the time of the Revolution; and (3) an economy heavily influenced by the state's accessibility to major metropolitan centers and its well-developed corridor functions. Dr. Stansfield depicts New Jersey as a state others should watch: How it controls suburban sprawl, environmental deterioration, and the internal competition among agricultural, suburban, industrial, and recreational uses of land and water resources offers a model for the rest of the United States. Newark's Mayor Gibson observed of his city, "I don't know where America's cities are going, but I think Newark will get there first." It also might be fairly concluded, writes Dr. Stansfield, that wherever the United States is heading, New Jersey could get there first.

Charles A. Stansfield, Jr., is professor of geography at Glassboro State College. He is the president of the New Jersey Council for Geographic Education and is coauthor (with C. E. Zimolzak) of *The Human Landscape* (Second Edition, 1983) and *World Regions: Changing Interactions* (1982).

NEW JERSEY

A GEOGRAPHY

Charles A. Stansfield, Jr.

Westview Press / Boulder, Colorado

Geographies of the United States

Copyright © 1983 by Westview Press, Inc.

Published in 1983 in the United States of America by
  Westview Press, Inc.
  5500 Central Avenue
  Boulder, Colorado 80301
  Frederick A. Praeger, President and Publisher

Library of Congress Cataloging in Publication Data
Stansfield, Charles A.
  New Jersey, a geography.
  (Geographies of the United States)
  Bibliography: p.
  Includes index.
  1. New Jersey—Description and travel. 2. New Jersey—Historical geography. I. Title. II. Series.
F134.S8 1983   974.9   83-6636
ISBN 0-89158-957-0
ISBN 0-86531-491-8 (pbk.)

Printed and bound in the United States of America

For my parents, with happy memories of
those golden days at the Jersey shore

CONTENTS

FIGURES

TABLES

ACKNOWLEDGMENTS

Many persons—teachers, colleagues, students, family, and fellow New Jerseyans—have made their mark on my thinking and thus on this book. Foremost among my many stimulating colleagues at Glassboro State College are Professors Wade Currier and Chester Zimolzak. Wade Currier shared his specialized knowledge of the Pinelands, his expertise in the interpretation of aerial photography, and his experiences as both professor of metropolitan planning and longtime chairman of the Gloucester County Planning Board. He also copied prints, maps, and photographs for use in this book; the resulting illustrations attest to his skill and aesthetic judgment. Chester Zimolzak shared his zest for learning about New Jersey, accompanying me on several field trips and advising me on maps.

Marvin Creamer, now professor emeritus of geography at Glassboro, not only hired me to teach *in* New Jersey, but *about* New Jersey as well; his appreciation of his native state is contagious. Herbert Richardson involved me in his research project in southern New Jersey and taught me to appreciate architecture in the landscape. Robert Harper, also of Glassboro's history faculty, gracefully shared his insights as well. President Mark M. Chamberlain and Dean Alan B. Donovan supplied timely research support, which they know I appreciate. Richard Scott of the Bureau of the Budget, the White House, supplied aerial views of the shore area. Professors Peirce Lewis, Jean Gottmann, and the late John Rickert each helped "peel the scales from my eyes" so that I could begin to really *see* the cultural landscape, to enjoy it, and to comprehend it. I am in their intellectual debt.

I hope that the many interested, and interesting, students at Glassboro will forgive my mentioning only a few of them by name as particularly stimulating scholars. Kevin Patrick, a fellow railroad buff, enlightened me on New Jersey's fascinating transportation geography; Don Evans helped demonstrate "Galactic City"; and Emilio Cruz provided insights into northeastern New Jersey's changing racial and ethnic distributions. Emilio Cruz designed and drafted the original maps in this book; his talent is matched only by my gratitude. Ken Lacovara did the original map for Figure 1.3.

The professional staff of Savitz Library at Glassboro State College were most helpful and generous with their time and assistance. Dr. Sandor Szilassy, director; Clara Kirner, curator of the Frank H. Stewart Collection; and Ethel Traub merit my special thanks.

My wife, Diane, and our children—Lisa, Wayne, and Paul—cheerfully accompanied me on many field trips that in their more innocent days they believed to be vacations. They patiently did without my attention when I was "booking." Diane typed the manuscript, gently criticized it, and generally aided and abetted. Janice Bittle prepared the tables.

The manuscript never would have been transformed into a book without the patient guidance and friendly counsel of Dr. Ingolf Vogeler, series editor, and Lynne Rienner, associate publisher and editorial director at Westview Press. Jeanne Remington was project supervisor at Westview Press, and Libby Barstow was copy editor. Their professional judgment and advice were invaluable and are much appreciated.

Charles A. Stansfield, Jr.

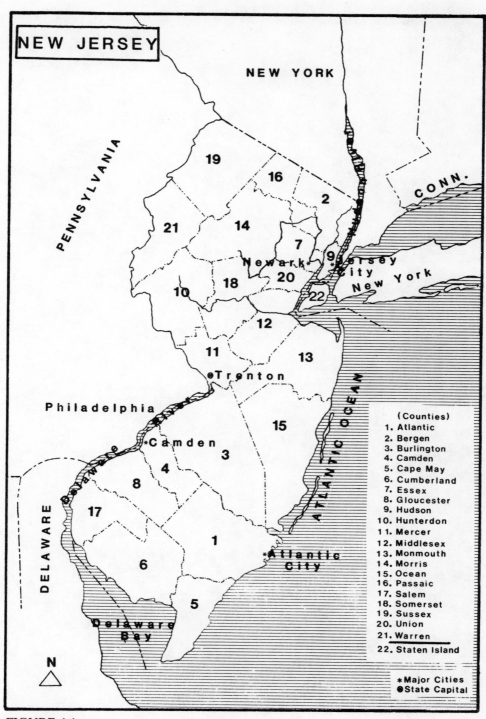

FIGURE 1.1.

CHAPTER 1

INTRODUCTION

SOME BASIC THEMES

New Jersey: The name evokes many images, but these commonly lack a positive focus and frequently fail to represent reality. However, the real New Jersey will become apparent to those who seek it out. Through 200 years of description of New Jersey—by geographers, journalists, historians, and social scientists as well as by astute travelers and perceptive citizens—three general themes are repeated that accurately depict the state.

The first is that New Jersey is culturally diverse—an amalgam of varied ethnic, national, and racial groups. From its colonial origins, New Jersey has had a heterogeneous culture that reflected no particular or distinctive proto-American culture and thus reflected in fact the new, definitively American culture. In many respects—geographic, economic, demographic, and historic—New Jersey is not just representative of the evolving American cultural landscape, but is perhaps the quintessence of the American experience, the American process, and the American dream.

The second observation in common is that of New Jersey's bipolar orientation to its neighboring giant metropolitan centers, New York and Philadelphia (see Figure 1.1). The image of New Jersey as "a barrel tapped at both ends," attributed to Benjamin Franklin, is a widely understood one. New Jersey has somehow stopped short of developing its own cosmopolitan, powerful metropolis on the scale of its two dominant neighbors. It seemed at one time that the state was perversely doomed to play suburb: an array of satellites without a central star to call their own. In the present phase of deconcentration of many (if, indeed, not all) urban functions, New Jersey may come into its own as New York and Philadelphia effectively decentralize and disperse into New Jersey, as well as further into New York State and Pennsylvania.

An important corollary of New Jersey's intermediate position between New York and Philadelphia has been its corridor function. A prevalent image of New Jersey—that of a transportation-dominated landscape with the New Jersey Turnpike's clamorous traffic rushing between the Newark Airport and the huge port facilities of Newark and Elizabeth—is an accurate if nearsighted view of the state. Since colonial times New Jersey has functioned as a corridor, and that function has been an important part of its economic and cultural life. Mobility and dispersal, suburbanization and exurbanization are typical of New Jersey and have been so throughout its history, just as they are prevalent themes in the contemporary United States.

A third fundamental observation about New Jersey and New Jerseyans is that the entire state's economy is heavily influenced by its accessibility to major metropolitan centers and its well-developed corridor function. The earliest geographers of the United States, for example, observed that New Jersey's agriculture produced a wide variety of crops and animal products, much

FIGURE 1.2. *Nighttime Census Map.* On viewing nighttime satellite photos showing cities as brilliant spots of light against the darker countryside, census officials realized that a satellite photo was very like a negative of the census dot-map of population distribution. This map negative highlights the continuous interlinkage of the northeastern megalopolis much as it might appear to astronauts seeing it at night. (U.S. Bureau of the Census)

of it destined for delivery as high-priced fresh produce to nearby urban markets. Likewise, New Jersey industry has been strongly influenced by the high density of transport facilities in the "corridor" and the proximity of huge markets, both industrial and consumer. The evolution of the northeastern seaboard *megalopolis*, that constellation of great cities growing toward one another along their interconnecting transport arteries, has enhanced the relative centrality of New Jersey. The state is midway within the southern New Hampshire–northern Virginia megalopolis, shown as the continuous bright area along the eastern coast in Figure 1.2. The heavily industrialized nature of New Jersey is thus based primarily upon its "situational resource" rather than on minerals or richly productive agricultural resources. Relative location has been, and continues to be, New Jersey's prime asset.

VARIATIONS ON THE THEMES

New Jerseyans—patriots, partisans, journalists, and scholars—tend to find themselves on the defensive when discussing the state. More than a century ago, a popular book included such a defense of New Jersey:

Although New Jersey, ever since her admission into the Union, has been the butt for the sarcasm and wit of those who live outside her borders, the gallant little state has much to be proud of. Her history is rich in instances of heroism, especially during the Revolutionary period. Her prosperity is far greater than that of many noisier and more excitable communities . . . her territory includes every variety of scenery, from the picturesque hills and lakes of her northern regions to the broad sandwastes of her southern counties. Those interested in the statistics of industry will find much that is worthy of notice in her iron-works and other great manufacturing establishments, while those who seek the indolent delights of summer enjoyment cannot fail to be charmed with her famous and fashionable sea-side resorts. (Bryant 1874, 47)

Geographer Peter Wacker felt obliged to ask the rhetorical question as to why New Jersey should be of interest to scholars, answering with the observation that if New Jersey were an independent country of comparable population, or even another state, the question would not arise (Wacker 1975, 2). Popular historian and geographer John Cunningham observed that New Jerseyans rate the state highly as a place to live, indicating that the poor image of New Jersey is mostly generated, and swallowed, outside rather than inside the state (Cunningham 1978, 11).

This apparently poor, or at least blurred, image may be traced to the lack of a single, centralized, New Jersey-based government until near the end of the colonial period. Historically, New Jersey was not one colony but rather was referred to as "The Jerseys"; the division of East Jersey and West Jersey was remarkably close to the contemporary *functional region* boundary between a metropolitan New York orientation and a metropolitan Philadelphia orientation.

In addition, the lack of a distinctively "Jersey" culture is a situation not unconnected with New Jersey's role in developing and displaying the majority American culture. There is little in the state that is unexpected, unusual, or flamboyant. An obvious, though generally unremarked, corollary of this is that New Jersey's human landscape is typically American and therefore unexceptional within the national context. New Jersey shares with Pennsylvania an important role as cultural source or *hearth* for much of American culture.

A final and immediately relevant factor in New Jersey's notoriously unfocused image is the prevalence of externally based metropolitan news media whose writers and commentators apparently attempt to gain reputations as sophisticates by sneering at the suburbs, particularly New Jersey. New Jersey is a predominantly urban state of over 7 million people without a single commercial VHF television station based within it until 1983. (Delaware is the only other similarly deprived state.)

No region or area as large as a state would be expected to be homogeneous in its physical, economic, or cultural geography. Partisans of all states tend to emphasize the variety within their state and note the superlatives. New Jersey, though, seems to have more than its share of paradoxes, exceptions, and curiosities, considering that only four states (Rhode Island, Delaware, Connecticut, and Hawaii) are smaller in territory. New Jersey's salient cultural characteristic is its high population density—at 979 people per sq mi (378 per sq km), the highest in the United States (see Figure 1.3). The national average is only 64 per sq mi (24 per sq km), and few states even approach New Jersey in density (see Table 1.1). Only Massachusetts has a higher percentage of its population living in metropolitan areas, and only California and Connecticut match New Jersey's figure. New Jersey's per capita income is fifth highest in the nation, outranked only by Alaska, Connecticut, Maryland, and Nevada. New Jersey is close to average in its proportion of black population and precisely average in Spanish-origin population percentage (Table 1.1). While in some of the older industrial cities of northern New Jersey the population density approaches 40,000 per sq mi (15,440 per sq km), large tracts of the Pine Barrens are virtually

4

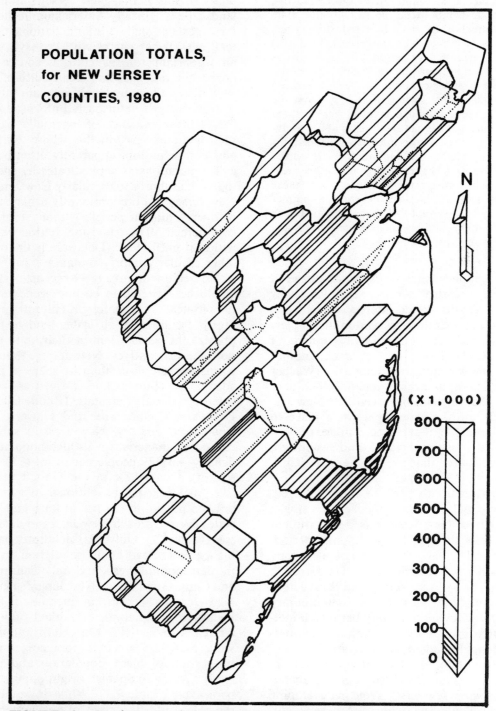

POPULATION TOTALS,
for NEW JERSEY
COUNTIES, 1980

N

(X 1,000)

800
700
600
500
400
300
200
100
0

FIGURE 1.3. *Population Totals, by Counties.* A striking view of New Jersey's population distribution (and political geography) is this three-dimensional county outline map: the north-oriented nature of the state's population is evident.

TABLE 1.1
Representative Statistics: New Jersey in Comparison with Its Neighbors and Leading States in Statistical Categories

	Total Area in 1000s Square Miles	Rank Order	Persons Per Square Mile of Land Area 1980	Rank Order	Per Capita Income, 1977
United States	3,618.5	--	64	--	$5,751
New Jersey	7.8	46	979	1	6,492
Near Neighbors					
New York	49.6	30	367	6	5,849
Pennsylvania	45.3	33	264	8	5,622
Delaware	2.1	49	300	7	5,883
Megalopolitan Region Neighbors					
Connecticut	5.0	48	639	4	6,564
Rhode Island	1.2	50	903	2	5,589
Massachusetts	8.3	45	733	3	5,826
Maryland	10.6	42	426	5	6,561
Virginia	40.8	36	134	16	5,883
Other Sample States					
Florida	58.6	22	180	11	5,761
Michigan	58.2	23	163	12	6,130
California	158.7	3	151	14	6,487
Alaska	589.8	1	1	20	9,170

TABLE 1.1 continued on page 6.

TABLE 1.1, continued

	% Black 1980	% Spanish Origin 1980	Percent of Land in Farms 1978	Percentage of Population Living in Metropolitan Areas (1978)	
United States	11.5	5.3	46	73	U.S.
New Jersey	10.8	5.3	22	92	N.J.
Near Neighbors					
New York	12.5	8.1	32	88	N.Y.
Pennsylvania	8.7	1.1	30	80	Pa.
Delaware	13.4	1.2	53	68	Del.
Megalopolitan					
Region Neighbors					
Connecticut	6.9	2.6	16	92	Conn.
Rhode Island	2.7	0.8	11	91	R.I.
Massachusetts	3.3	1.5	14	96	Mass.
Maryland	20.7	0.8	43	85	Md.
Virginia	15.9	1.1	39	66	Va.
Other Sample States					
Florida	15.5	7.9	39	86	Fla.
Michigan	11.2	1.1	31	81	Mich.
California	7.8	15.9	33	92	Calif.
Alaska	4.3	1.4	*	45	Alaska

Source: U.S. Census of Population, 1980; U.S. Census of Agriculture, 1978.

Formula to convert sq mi to sq km is: 1 square mile equals 2.59 sq kilometers.

*Statistic rounds to zero.

empty. Some Pinelands rural townships have population densities of less than 20 per sq mi (7.7 per sq km). New Jersey's population increased by only 2.7 percent from 1970 to 1980, far below the U.S. average of 11.4 percent, but respectably above those of its two largest neighbors. Pennsylvania barely grew at 0.6 percent, and New York suffered a loss of 3.8 percent (U.S. Bureau of the Census, *Census of Population*, 1980). Another paradox is that the license plates of this heavily industrial state brag "Garden State." Perhaps best known for its seashore resorts, New Jersey includes a section of the Appalachians (High Point, naturally the highest point, is 1,803 ft or 549 m high) that is also a mountain resort area. In a state known for its suburbs and industrial satellites of out-of-state big cities, Camden and Newark have attained a kind of grim notoriety among urbanists as "worst cases in the nation."

The corridor function of New Jersey means that many travelers are merely transients on their way to or from an out-of-state metropolis. The very scale of the demand for transport facilities in the corridor eliminates any possibility of scenic, lightly traveled roads through bucolic countryside. "Corridor vision" may delude the corridor user into thinking that all of New Jersey must be like the congested corridor at its metropolitan extremes. In fact, New Jersey is 40 percent forested, a higher proportion in forest than is found in Minnesota or Alaska and about the same percentage as California.

"Garden State" is as much nostalgic as descriptive: a quick look through an atlas shows that "Manufacturing State" might be more appropriate. New Jersey's *value added* by manufacturing (*value added* is the difference between the value of the raw materials or components and the value of the finished or shipped manufactured product) outranks every other state with but six exceptions. Only California, Illinois, Michigan, New York, Ohio, and Pennsylvania outproduce New Jersey in manufacturing, and New Jersey produces more

goods by this measure than the states of Alaska, Delaware, Hawaii, Idaho, Maine, Montana, Nevada, New Hampshire, New Mexico, North Dakota, Rhode Island, South Dakota, Utah, Vermont, and Wyoming together! Considering its population size, New Jersey's economy is more dominated by manufacturing than three large states that outproduce it in total value. New Jersey's population, only 31 percent of California's, produces 44 percent of California's value added; similarly, New Jersey, with but 41 percent of New York's population, produces 52 percent of New York's value-added total. New Jersey also produces slightly more than Pennsylvania's output in relation to population.

If New Jersey were an independent nation in the world community, it would have more people than Denmark, Finland, Switzerland, Norway, Ireland, New Zealand, Bolivia, Haiti, Guatemala, Angola, or Tunisia. New Jersey's population is larger than any of ninety-five independent countries.

Related to New Jersey's highly industrialized and urbanized character is its relatively high income level. If this is expressed as an average income per capita, New Jersey as an independent country would have a higher average than that of the United States. In fact, it would be higher than every independent state in the world with the exception of some oil-rich, relatively lightly populated, Persian Gulf states (Kuwait, Qatar, United Arab Emirates, and Saudi Arabia—the only one of these that also exceeds New Jersey's population), Nauru (about 10,000 people on an island composed mostly of phosphate rock exported for fertilizer), and Switzerland.

For all its urban-industrial superlatives, New Jersey manages to be a frontier. It is clearly on the inner frontier where Americans are grappling with the intensifying problems of how to deal with a changing, perhaps diminishing, resource base and how to shift toward reliance on long-distance imports. It is a frontier in developing new strategies of pollution control and waste management. For much of its history, it has occupied a place on the frontiers of decentralization of urban populations and functions.

Finally, New Jersey is among the leaders in the ongoing human reassessment of the problems and potentials of the physical landscape. Kenneth Gibson, the mayor of Newark—the state's largest city and one with painfully obvious urban problems—has remarked, "I don't know where America's cities are going, but I think Newark will get there first." Geographers might as reasonably conclude that, wherever the United States is heading, New Jersey could get there first.

THE "CITY OF NEW JERSEY"

In addition to ample evidences in the cultural landscape of New Jersey that it is a preeminently metropolitan state, statistics show that almost the entire area of the state is officially part of metropolitan systems.

Metropolitan areas have been recognized by the U.S. Bureau of the Census since the late 1940s. The standard metropolitan statistical areas (SMSAs) consisted of one or more counties (there was a slightly different definition in New England where counties have less significance). If more than one county, these counties had to be contiguous, and the SMSA had to be characterized by a significant volume of *daily interaction*—commuting, shopping, and social-leisure travel within the area. There had to be a central city or cluster of cities with more than 50,000 population. There was also a maximum percentage of total population that could be engaged in agriculture.

Prior to the 1980 census, by the SMSA definition all but four of New Jersey's twenty-one counties were part of metropolitan or consolidated areas (see Figure 1.4). The four nonmetropolitan counties—

Cape May, Hunterdon, Ocean, and Sussex—were all peripheral to the main axis of the northeastern megalopolis and relatively remote from the two major metropolitan centers of New York and Philadelphia. The interstate nature of New Jersey's metropolitan population is obvious on the census map. Of the seventeen metropolitan counties in the state, fifteen were parts of interstate metropolitan areas or "consolidated" areas (groupings of SMSAs in strongly interrelated areas, as around New York or Chicago). Two SMSA counties in New Jersey—Atlantic and Cumberland—stood alone without significant interstate daily interaction in 1970.

New standards of metropolitan statistical areas (MSAs) have been determined by the Bureau of the Census for use with data from the 1980 census. These new standards have been proposed to make the definition more flexible in recognition of the very high degree of daily interaction now common over greater distances than before. Counties once considered remote from metropolitan areas, and thus unlikely candidates for metropolitan status, are now interlinked with the urban centers and their nearer suburbs, a phenomenon discussed in more detail in Chapter 9.

The effect of the new definitions of metropolitan statistical areas will be to increase New Jersey's metropolitan counties from seventeen to twenty. Although the Census Bureau anticipates that about sixty-two present SMSA counties across the nation will not qualify as MSAs under the revised standards, no New Jersey county will be demoted. On the other hand, according to the Census Bureau, Hunterdon, Ocean, and Sussex counties will probably qualify for inclusion in the New York consolidated MSA.

Only Cape May County will not be officially "metropolitan" among New Jersey's counties. Even so, it is hardly a rural county. Although Cape May County contains only 1.1 percent of New Jersey's total population in 3.5 percent of the state's

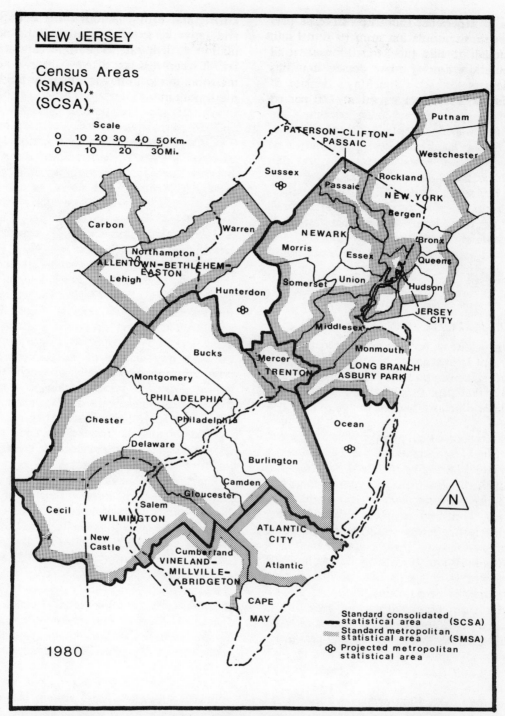

NEW JERSEY

**Census Areas
(SMSA)**.
(SCSA).

Scale

0   10 20 30 40 50Km.
0   10   20   30Mi.

Standard consolidated
statistical area (SCSA)
Standard metropolitan
statistical area (SMSA)
Projected metropolitan
statistical area

1980

FIGURE 1.4. *Census-Designated Metropolitan Regions.* The very high degree of interstate interaction is clear on these official census regions involving New Jersey counties. With the application of new definitions to the 1980 census data, only Cape May County remains outside a consolidated or metropolitan region.

area, it experienced an impressive 38 percent gain in population from 1970 to 1980. Although it has the second-lowest total population among New Jersey counties (Salem is lowest), Cape May's density of population (312 per sq mi or 120 per sq km) is above that of four other counties, and only two counties outpaced its population growth rate. The time cannot be far off when this last of New Jersey's non-metropolitan counties is officially labeled metropolitan.

CHAPTER 2

EARLY SETTLEMENT

INFLUENCE OF AMERINDIANS

Patterns of Aboriginal Settlement

The impact of the Amerindians upon New Jersey was relatively light, in the consciousness of most contemporary Jerseyans. Actually the presence of the Indians was of marked importance to the early non-Indian settlers, and through them, some traces remain today in the cultural landscape. There is archaelogical evidence that Amerindians had occupied New Jersey about 8,000 years ago, but Indian traditions repeated to the first Europeans indicated that the tribes present when the Europeans arrived had migrated in from the north only a few centuries before. That there were very few Indians in New Jersey at the time of European discovery is a unanimous opinion among scholars. Estimates of population size range from 2,500 to 10,000, with 6,000 the most generally repeated "guesstimate."

These aboriginal New Jerseyans referred to themselves as the Lenni Lenape, "original people." The Europeans called them the Delawares, after the river so named by Europeans. There were three bands or subdivisions of Lenni Lenape within the present state. The most warlike, the Minsi, whose totem was the wolf, occupied the north. The Unami, whose sign was the turtle, were located in the central part of what became New Jersey, and the Unalachtigo, with their turkey totem, occupied the south. Their population density, low by modern standards, apparently was about average for the east coast but lower than that estimated for coastal Massachusetts, Rhode Island, or Virginia.

The lasting significance of the Lenni Lenape lies in their continuing influence on the natural environment, particularly upon vegetation, and their contributions to the colonial culture. The Lenape had developed a statewide network of trails, many portions of which are followed by modern roads. There is now some uncertainty about the once-widespread assumption that the primary use of the trails was to migrate seasonally to the seashore to gorge on shellfish, although there are eyewitness accounts of these seasonal migrations in the early colonial period. If the trails were used more generally for travel for hunting expeditions, trade, and joint ceremonies, then the huge shell middens left on the coast may have resulted from shorter-range migrations of coastal bands. Some middens (refuse piles of discarded shells and other debris) were over 100 ft (30.5 m) long and 10 to 12 ft (3 to 3.6 m) high. The trails were footpaths only 3 to 5 ft (0.9 to 1.5 m) wide, as the Lenape customarily traveled single file. The more frequently used paths were smooth and well beaten; lesser-used ones were marked by piles of stones or marked trees. The Indian paths tended to be rather circuitous routes that reflected supreme sensitivity to topography. They followed drainage divides where possible, as the Indians preferred dry paths with few stream crossings.

The Minisink Trail, for example, followed the terminal moraine as much as possible. When streams were crossed, the Indians preferred shallow water with firm footing as fords.

Modern road engineers need not be as sensitive to terrain and drainage, with their capability of bridge building and gradient smoothing, but large portions of contemporary highways still follow the Indian trails. This is not necessarily in conscious imitation, but rather because the same topographic factors that influenced Indian paths—ease of usage with minimal "costs" in crossing streams—led to their adoption by early non-Indian settlers. The present concrete ribbons follow the old routes because these link early settlements, many of which have evolved into large urban places. Parts of state routes 9, 10, 22, 27, and 47 follow Indian paths for these reasons, providing good examples of *route succession*—a situation in which successive cultures and transport technologies use essentially the same routes for much the same reasons.

Agricultural Practices

Indian agriculture featured a pattern of clearing land (sometimes merely by girdling trees to defoliate them so sunlight could reach the crops), using it until diminishing crops indicated declining fertility, then abandoning it at least temporarily in favor of a new clearing. In effect, the Indians had worked out a long-term crop rotation in which the "fields" lay unused for long periods. This meant that the "Indian old-fields" (much prized by early colonists who thus were spared the full labor of clearing land and were given good clues as to relative fertility of land) were fairly widespread, given the very small numbers of Indians present.

The Lenape also affected the land and its vegetation by their common practice of burning the woods to drive game during hunts, to make travel easier, and to encourage the kind of vegetation preferred by white-tailed deer, their favorite game.

Just as contemporary hunters recognize that deer, as well as rabbits and gamebirds, are more likely to frequent abandoned fields or burned-over areas than mature forests, so the Indians knew that low, scrubby, secondary growth made better browse for deer. The burned-over area also provided more berries for both game and people. Repeated burnings seem to favor pines over oaks, so that the Pine Barrens may be a relic of Indian burnings, supplemented by more modern burnings, accidents, and arson. A fortuitous accident of repeated Indian burnings was that a surprising amount of land was already cleared of trees, so that the "taking up of the land" by European-culture colonists was made easier.

Finally, the Indians communicated their knowledge about a wide variety of foods to the Europeans. The first European-culture settlers, coming from a society far removed from its own neolithic ancestors, needed guidance from the Amerindians in most effectively utilizing the wild foods and other materials available to them. The Indians had developed a wide range of cultivated plants and gathered others in the wild. Corn, of course, was the major crop; the Indians planted several different varieties including popcorn, flint corn, and sweet corn. They also knew the cultivation of kidney and lima beans, pumpkin, Jerusalem artichoke, sunflower, and tobacco. Wild rice was harvested (and possibly even sown) by Indians, who also gathered chestnuts, walnuts, butternuts, hickories, and hazelnuts. They gathered wild crabapples, strawberries, and blackberries; they used maple sugar and sassafras for flavor, along with American licorice. They ate mulberries and cranberries. They made huckleberry (domesticated as blueberry) cornmeal cakes, so that when we eat blueberry muffins, we are enjoying a traditional Indian treat. The Europeans quickly developed a taste for most of these foods. Corn, blueberries, cranberries, sugar maples, and strawberries—all Indian gifts—are today commercial farm products in New Jersey.

Place-names

The place-names of New Jersey have been greatly enriched by the many surviving Lenape place-names, even if the non-Indians commonly misapplied them, misunderstood them, and misspelled them. Hackensack, Cohansey, Repaupo, Manasquan, Wickatunk, Hopatcong, Wanaque, Totowa, Mahwah, and Musconetcong are but a few of the intriguing place-names bequeathed, directly or inadvertently, by the Lenape.

Removal of the Lenape

The "vanishing American," described in late-nineteenth-century western lore, by then had already vanished from New Jersey. Two centuries ago the Lenape had already sold, or had been dispossessed of, all their land. In 1758 the colonial government determined that all outstanding claims of Indians were to be settled by a government purchase of land specifically to accommodate the remaining Lenape. The money was to be raised by lotteries, and so, by 1762, the nation's first officially constituted Indian reservation came into being. The site was 3,284 acres (1,330 ha) of land in Burlington County. Characteristic of later Indian reservations throughout the country, the land chosen for this first one was considered undesirable by the victorious non-Indians—a portion of the outer coastal plain. The land was, however, to be tax free and to be held in trust for the Lenape for all time; the Indians were forbidden to lease or sell it. The Lenape also retained fishing and hunting rights on any unenclosed land throughout the colony. The reservation, named Brotherton (now Indian Mills), was provided with European-style houses, a school, store, meeting house, and grist mill. Though a quite generous settlement by the standards of the time, and well intentioned, the Brotherton settlement was a failure. Three-quarters of the sixty-three adults at Brotherton later voted to accept an invitation to join another Indian group near Oneida Lake, New York. Thus,

the first reservation was sold, and the proceeds used to transport the Lenape to Oneida and provide them with farm implements, clothing, and household goods. In 1822, forty descendants of the Brotherton group moved on to Green Bay (then Michigan Territory, now Wisconsin) to land purchased for them by the New Jersey state government from the Menomonee Indians. This transaction severed the last ties of New Jersey with its first people.

EAST JERSEY AND WEST JERSEY

New Jersey had a badly confused start as a colony; indeed, New Jersey's separate existence from the colony of New York was in question at times. Vaguely worded deeds, leases, trusts, and charges to royal governors led to such a murky set of boundaries that a long, bitter dispute with New York was not settled until late in the colonial period with regard to the 50-mile (80-kilometer) land boundary. The exact location of the Hudson River boundary was finally agreed on in 1834. The internal boundary of East Jersey and West Jersey took even longer to resolve, so that New Jersey has had more than its share of boundary disputes.

Early Explorations

The first European to record the general area of the future state of New Jersey was John Cabot, an Italian working for the English, who sailed along the coast in 1498. In 1524, Giovanni da Verrazano, an Italian working for the French, anchored off Sandy Hook and explored the Raritan Bay–Lower New York Bay areas by small boat without actually landing. European excitement at these discoveries must be rated as rather low, for the next effort at exploration did not follow until 1609, when Henry Hudson, on behalf of the Dutch, sailed the *Half Moon* into New York Bay, sent small craft as far as Newark Bay, and generally was impressed. One of Hudson's officers, Robert Juet, wrote of Raritan Bay and the Navesink Highlands, "This is a very good land to fall with and a pleasant land to see" (Wacker 1975, 19). The fishing was good, the qualities of the timber and wild fruits were pleasing, and, this time, permanent settlement was to follow.

Establishment of New Netherland

The Dutch claim to New Netherland, approximately from Long Island Sound to Delaware Bay, was based on Henry Hudson's explorations in their behalf in 1609. There were probably a few Dutch fur traders in present-day Bergen and Hudson counties, as well as Manhattan, by 1615. In 1626, the Dutch purchase of Manhattan made that island their permanent base. The colony of New Netherland was to be a money-making effort of the Dutch West India Company, which expected to profit from the fur trade. No large agricultural settlements were envisioned, just fortified trading posts, with perhaps enough food production for self-sufficiency. The company's efforts were focused on the Hudson Valley; two short-lived settlements were attempted at Burlington Island (1626) and Fort Nassau (1626) on Big Timber Creek in the Delaware Valley (see Figure 2.1). Settlement on the west bank of the Hudson was more successful.

The first European attempts at settlement in New Jersey (which did not become "New Jersey" until 1664) were so small that they indicate a certain lack of enthusiasm on the part of those expected to do the work—the rank and file of European colonists. It was all very well for investors comfortable in Amsterdam to dream of quick profits from furs and precious metals. (Henry Hudson's men had taken note of the Lenni Lenape habit of wearing copper jewelry, and Hudson's English aide, Robert Juet, had written optimistically of "probable" copper and silver mines in the interior. There was no evidence of silver mines, but it did tend to encourage one's financial backers to fund another voyage.) There was a very obvious shortage, however, of men and women actually willing to undertake the hard work of establishing permanent settlements. Undoubtedly, this sparse supply of volunteers was related to the feudal ambitions of the Dutch, who seem to have expected hard work to reward one's masters, not oneself. There were only about thirty people in the abortive Burlington Island settlement of 1626. By 1630, the settlement had been abandoned; the settlers may have walked back to Manhattan.

A determination in 1629 to encourage more agricultural settlement was unfortunately shortsighted. A *patroon* (patron) was to pay the full passage and initial costs of establishing fifty settlers on a large plot of land; after four years of successful settlement, the land would be the patroon's. The settlers would be, for practical purposes, serfs. Their earnings would belong to the patroon, who also had power over their behavior. There was a definite shortage of emigrants under that scheme. One Michael Pauw, who never left Amsterdam, registered a patroonship across the Hudson from New Amsterdam. Pavonia ("land of the peacocks"—from a wordplay on his family name) was located in present Hoboken and Jersey City. There were never fifty settlers in Pavonia, which was thus surrendered back to the company within a few years. The tiny population of Dutch on the west bank of the Hudson apparently lived in fear of Lenni Lenape aggression. They decided on a preemptive strike, murdering about eighty Lenape, including infants, near Pavonia in 1643. Indian reprisals for this unprovoked atrocity lasted nearly two years and flickered on and off until 1655. In 1660 the Dutch decided that consolidated, fortified settlements in the hostile frontier would be safer, and they founded Bergen, New Jersey's first real town. The settlement at Bergen, in what is now Jersey City, was also America's first example of the "Philadelphia Square" type of urban planning. Since Bergen was laid out some twenty years earlier than Philadelphia, Philadelphia Squares should rightly be called Bergen Squares (see, for example, Wacker 1975, 389–390).

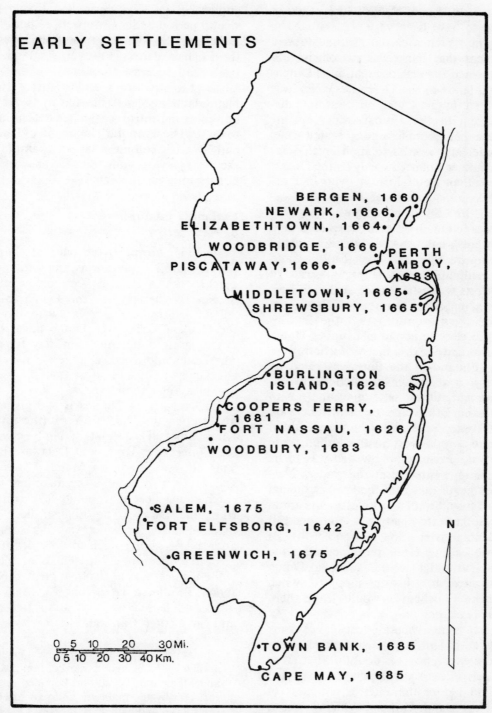

EARLY SETTLEMENTS

BERGEN, 1660
NEWARK, 1666.
ELIZABETHTOWN, 1664.
WOODBRIDGE, 1666. PERTH
PISCATAWAY, 1666. AMBOY, 1683
MIDDLETOWN, 1665.
SHREWSBURY, 1665.

BURLINGTON ISLAND, 1626
COOPERS FERRY, 1681
FORT NASSAU, 1626
WOODBURY, 1683

SALEM, 1675
FORT ELFSBORG, 1642
GREENWICH, 1675

0 5 10 20 30 Mi.
0 5 10 20 30 40 Km.

TOWN BANK, 1685
CAPE MAY, 1685

N

FIGURE 2.1. *Early Settlements in New Jersey.* Although the very earliest European settlements rank in age with those of other Middle Atlantic colonies, much of the future state was essentially empty for more than a century afterwards, particularly the northwestern ridges and the Pinelands-Seashore areas.

Dutch settlement of New Jersey cannot be said to have been very successful. The Dutch had such a casual attitude toward settlement that there was no official objection when Swedish occupation of Dutch-claimed lands in the Delaware Valley was attempted. In fact Dutch businessmen, dissatisfied with the almost imperceptible progress being made under Dutch rule, persuaded the Swedes to sponsor colonies that would be financed partly by the Dutch. No less than Peter Minuit, who had negotiated the purchase of Manhattan, organized the "Swedish" colony. New Sweden was founded by a mixture of Dutch and Swedish colonists, who were delivered to Delaware Bay by Dutch captains and crews sailing Swedish ships. A series of crude forts was established, including Fort Elfsborg in Salem County, which was so plagued by mosquitoes that the Swedes were not slow to abandon it under Dutch pressure. The Swedes, many of whom were Finns (Finland at the time was ruled by Sweden), were under instructions to encourage agricultural settlement and not to disturb the Dutch and English traders on the Delaware River, but to undersell them and gain a monopoly in the Indian trade by cutting prices. New Sweden was to be New Jersey's first discount trader. New Sweden never quite got the level of official support from Sweden or investment capital from Holland that had been envisioned; it lasted only from 1638 to 1655. Most of the Swedes and Finns remained after the official surrender to the superior Dutch forces, apparently just as happy to switch allegiance to whoever would leave them reasonably alone.

There is no accurate census of New Jersey as a Dutch-Swedish-Finnish colonization effort, but it is doubtful that more than a few thousand Europeans occupied the land before the English conquest of New Netherland. Earlier English claims to the general area, based on Cabot's explorations on Britain's behalf, had not been followed by military action to oust the Dutch and Swedes. England was preoc-cupied by its Civil War and Commonwealth period under Cromwell; so both the Dutch and Swedes had cheerfully ignored the English claim. However, England already had successful colonies on the Atlantic seaboard north and south of New Netherland and had the naval power to dominate the entire coast when determined to do so. The temporary incursion of Dutch and Swedish colonies was an example of the mice playing while the cat was working out its internal problems.

England's Establishment of New Jersey

In 1664, however, the pace of claims, counterclaims, explorations, and settlement quickened. An English fleet took control of New Netherland, as the Dutch called all of their claim from Delaware Bay to the Hudson Valley (the Dutch never had any separate designation for New Jersey). The Dutch and Swedish settlers chose new allegiance to England rather than the much less pleasant alternative.

England's King Charles II had given to his brother, the Duke of York (the future King James II), a tract of land between the Connecticut River and Delaware Bay. This gift was made on March 12, 1664, and within two months the duke had dispatched the fleet that would take control from the Dutch. The English fleet demanded surrender, which was forthcoming after a face-saving week to consider it.

In the meantime, the Duke of York, while his fleet was at sea, had created New Jersey. In a lease dated June 23, 1664, the duke had leased to Lord John Berkeley and Sir George Carteret,

all that part of land adjacent to New England and lying and being westward of Long Island and Manhattan Island and bounded on the east part by the main sea and part of Hudson's River and hath upon the west Delaware Bay or River and extendoth southward to the main ocean as far as Cape May at the mouth of the Delaware Bay and to the northward as far as the northernmost branch of the said bay or river of Delaware which is in forty one degrees and forty minutes of latitude and crosseth over thence in a straight line to Hudson's River in forty one degrees of latitude which said tract of land is hereafter to be called by the name or names of New Caesarea or New Jersey. (Wacker 1975, 225)

The name honors Carteret's heroic defense of the Isle of Jersey in the English Channel when Royalists there were attacked by Cromwell's forces during the English Civil War. *Jersey* was a corruption of *Caesarea*—the island had been named for Julius Caesar to commemorate his invasion of Britain.

Several problems were created through this deed. The duke had already given orders to Richard Nicolls to overcome the Dutch, govern the territory from the Connecticut to the Delaware, and above all, encourage English settlement. Settlement was a high priority for two reasons. The small, fur-trade-oriented Swedish and Dutch colonies had demonstrated that sparse, trade-oriented settlements could not effectively hold the land. Obviously, too, the mere possession of huge tracts of land was no way to wealth—the land had to be productive to generate income for landlords and for the government tax coffers. So a dense, agricultural settlement was to be encouraged for motives of practical defense and income production. Governor Nicolls took this charge seriously. As the Duke of York was also Duke of Albany, and the York title had been honored in the naming of former New Amsterdam, Nicolls designated the land west of the Hudson as Albania and encouraged settlement. To quickly begin exploiting land, the basic resource of Albania, Nicolls decided to recruit some settlers from other American colonies rather than rely on the much slower arrival of pioneers from across the Atlantic. He circulated through the other colonies the information that Albania offered a degree of self-government, self-taxation, and a limited range of religious freedom (any variety of Protestant Christ-

tian was welcome). Settlement was to be of the New England "town" style—a nucleus of families living in an agricultural village and supporting a church and other social institutions. Each family would have a generous town lot and outlying acreage as well. Nicolls stipulated that prospective settlers also must arrange to purchase the land of their official grants from the Indians. Two Puritan groups from Long Island made the first purchases and arrived on their "patents" the next spring.

Apparently no one, including Governor Nicolls, was told of the duke's lease to Berkeley and Carteret until more than a year afterwards. The news seems to have arrived with Philip Carteret, appointed governor of their proprietary colony by Berkeley and his distant relative, George Carteret. Albania, that happy land of self-government and self-taxation, had never really existed, legally. This mess was an early indication of the Duke of York's incompetence and arrogance, a combination that later lost him his throne after four disastrous years as James II. The colony of New Jersey thus started with a wholly unnecessary confusion of land titles, citizen rights, and taxing powers. The news that the ex-Albanians, now New Jerseyans, were to pay the proprietors an annual rent was most unwelcome. The proprietors did have the sense to declare a five-year "tax holiday" to let their new tenants get started—the first rents were not due until 1670. One of the new settlements was named Elizabethtown to honor Mrs. George Carteret.

That some of the fifty new arrivals with Carteret from "old" Jersey—the Isle of Jersey—were Roman Catholic may or may not have had an effect on the Puritans' enthusiasm for New Jersey. The next year, 1666, another group of Puritans, this time from Connecticut, founded Newark (the "new ark of the covenant"). They were followed by groups from other New England colonies who founded Woodbridge and Piscataway (see Figure 2.1). New Jersey was thus getting off to a good start, despite the duke's bumbling and the festering problem of taxation and land rents.

Disputes over Government and Borders

Then Governor Carteret, operating under what amounted to New Jersey's first constitution—"The Concessions and Agreements of the Lords Proprietors"— called an Assembly at Elizabethtown in 1668. A number of settlers who had deeds from Nicolls and the Indians rather than the proprietors argued that the proprietors did not have the power of government. The "revolution of 1672" resulted when settlers from Newark, Elizabethtown, Woodbridge, Piscataway, and Bergen held a revolutionary assembly at Elizabethtown that deposed Philip Carteret, who promptly sailed for England. King Charles upheld the proprietors over the holders of Nicolls's patents. The Dutch briefly regained New York and New Jersey in 1673; New York, by now following a pattern, quickly surrendered before anyone was injured. England regained control, again peacefully, the next year.

If all of this activity in northern New Jersey was confusing, the situation along the Delaware Bay and Delaware River, the only other part of New Jersey to have any non-Indian settlement so far, was worse. Lord Berkeley was rich in land, but very short of cash. Deeply in debt, he wished to sell his half of New Jersey. Berkeley and Carteret agreed to a split between the east and west halves of the grant in 1676, ending the former ownership in common. The English Quakers eagerly bought Berkeley's share of the colony, hoping to establish a refuge there for their persecuted members. John Fenwick was the purchaser, but he was really a front man for Edward Byllynge, for whom Fenwick held the land in trust (Byllynge legally could not own property at the time due to a bankruptcy). Fenwick and Byllynge quarreled, and William Penn arbitrated the dispute; he awarded one-tenth of the land to Fenwick and nine-tenths to Byllynge, who by that time was

so deeply in debt that his land was turned over to trustees, including William Penn. Fenwick, who had settled Salem, New Jersey, also fell deeply in debt and sold much of his tenth to Penn and associates; so it came to be that West Jersey, not Pennsylvania, was Penn's first Quaker colony. There still was no clear idea as to exactly where and how the East Jersey lands of Carteret were separated from the West Jersey lands of Berkeley-Fenwick-Byllynge-Penn. A boundary was to be drawn from a point on Little Egg Harbor on the seashore to the most northerly point on the Delaware River within New Jersey. The problem was that no one knew exactly where the most northern point in New Jersey was located, as that involved the land border with New York. The intent was to evenly divide New Jersey, which at the time apparently included Staten Island. Because the maps of the time were grossly inaccurate and conflicted with one another, there were several surveying attempts at an East Jersey–West Jersey boundary.

The mutual boundary was first surveyed as the Keith Line of 1687 (see Figure 2.2). The more easterly Lawrence Line, based on the same starting point, was surveyed at the behest of the East Jersey proprietors to correct the admitted inaccuracies of the earlier survey. West Jersey, however, insisted that the *true* boundary was even farther to the east. The controversy dragged on until 1855 when the New Jersey Supreme Court ruled that the Lawrence Line was the boundary. In the meantime, the boundary area tended to be avoided by settlers fearful of losing a deed challenge.

Aside from the serious problems of actually determining the east-west separation line, the basic idea of the line made sense. The boundary ran through the least densely settled part of the twin colony, recognizing that the only really settled parts of New Jersey then were in the neighborhoods of Delaware Bay and the Delaware River (West Jersey) and the Hudson shores, Newark Bay, Raritan Bay, and Monmouth (East Jersey). The East Jersey–West Jersey

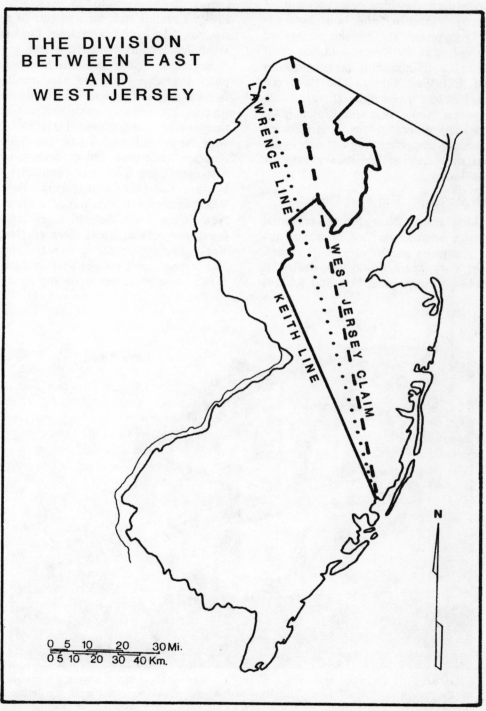

THE DIVISION
BETWEEN EAST
AND
WEST JERSEY

LAWRENCE LINE

WEST JERSEY CLAIM

KEITH LINE

N

0 5 10 20 30 Mi.
0 5 10 20 30 40 Km.

FIGURE 2.2.

boundary is significant in that it reflected far more than the historical accident of dual proprietorship. The boundary explicitly recognized the bipolar nature of early non-Indian settlement and was itself related to the different cultural geographies of East and West Jersey. The Lawrence Line is close to a modern *functional boundary* between New York and Philadelphia metropolitan spheres; as such, it remains of interest in understanding contemporary cultural, economic, and political geography of New Jersey.

Merger Attempts and Port Disputes

Nothing about New Jersey's colonial experience seems simple or straightforward. The gross incompetence of James, Duke of York, again was demonstrated in 1674 when he appointed Edmund Andros to govern both New York and New Jersey, though no one seems to have told Governor Philip Carteret that he was out of a job. Andros, who jailed both John Fenwick in West Jersey and Philip Carteret in East Jersey, became so monumentally unpopular that eventually he was recalled to face charges in England. In the meantime, Andros had followed royal instructions to merge both New York and New Jersey with New England, so that both Jerseys, between 1674 and 1689, were governed first from New York and then later from Boston. The event that "saved" East and West Jersey from this forced merger into New England was the immensely deserved overthrow of James II, former Duke of York. The "glorious revolution" put an end to the grand merger and enabled Andros's enemies to insist on his recall.

FIGURE 2.3. *Perth Amboy—The Governor's Mansion.* Dual capitals were a heritage of the "twin colonies." Until the Revolution, the royal governor and legislature migrated back and forth from East Jersey's capital, Perth Amboy, to Burlington, capital of West Jersey. The process did encourage a better road across the "waist" of New Jersey. The ghost of William Franklin, last royal governor, is alleged to haunt the mansion, now being restored by the state.

In the intervening years, the separation of East New Jersey and West New Jersey had progressed to the point that each proprietary colony had its own capital. West Jersey's capital, chosen as such in 1677, was Burlington, on the Delaware, about 16 mi (25 km) northeast from Philadelphia. In 1682, East Jersey chose Perth Amboy at the mouth of the Raritan, a location that should have developed into a major port without the interference of New York.

New Jersey seems to have been rather consistently and persistently harassed by New York. New York repeatedly suggested that East New Jersey be merged with the colony of New York without, naturally, any consultation with East Jerseyans. The city of New York continually maneuvered to deny New Jersey any customs stations, an action that prevented Jersey ports from receiving foreign ships and crippled their potential as rivals to New York City. The governor of New York and the mayor of New York City managed to obtain quo warranto proceedings in London against East and West New Jersey's proprietors. In this legal proceeding, the proprietors were forced to demonstrate *why* they had the right to any free ports. King James directed the governor of New York to press the legal action against the Jerseys. Governor Thomas Dungan took steps to seize vessels at Perth Amboy that had not called first at New York to pay customs duties. The proprietors of East New Jersey decided to ask for customs houses at Perth Amboy and other Jersey ports in order to circumvent New York's trade monopoly (see Table 2.1).

In 1682, the province of East Jersey was put up at public auction, and William Penn headed a successful syndicate of twelve people in purchasing the province and then promptly offering plots for sale. For a while,

TABLE 2.1
The Early Effect of New York and Philadelphia's Status as Customs Ports on New Jersey's International Trade

	1769	
	Total Value (in pounds sterling)	
Colony	Imports	Exports
New Jersey	1,991	2,532
New York	188,976	231,906
Pennsylvania	399,821	410,757

Source: Historical Statistics of the United States, Colonial Times to 1957 (Washington, D.C.: Bureau of the Census, 1961).

In 1769, New Jersey's population numbered about 135,000, about 50 percent of New York's and about 35 percent of Pennsylvania's.

in the confusion following the overthrow of James II, East Jersey was ruled by a deputy governor who did not bother to leave England, and West Jersey had two successive illegal governors.

Appointment of a Royal Governor

Widespread resentment against the proprietor's feudal exercise of political power led to so many riots and "abuses" of government officials that the proprietors petitioned Queen Anne to appoint a royal governor, make East and West Jersey one royal colony, and guarantee the proprietors' land holdings in return. The proprietors had had enough of trying to rule the notoriously unruly Jerseyans and wanted only to sit back and enjoy their income from selling or leasing land. The queen agreed, combining the two Jerseys into one royal colony but recognizing their dual nature by ordering the Assembly to alternate its sessions between Burlington and Perth Amboy. Queen Anne also forbade anyone in New Jersey to own a printing press, reasoning that newspapers spread rebellion and New Jersey had amply demonstrated its revolutionary tendencies.

The first royal governor of New York and New Jersey (the two had been combined again, effectively, much to the disgust of Jerseyans) was, not by coincidence, a distant cousin of the queen. She probably was just as happy to send him off to America: Lord Edward Cornbury took no pains to hide his enthusiasm for dressing as a woman, complete with wig and heavy makeup, and in 1702, when he became governor of New York and New Jersey, public displays of that nature tended to cause comment. Lord Cornbury received written instructions to transmit, "by the first opportunity, a map with the exact description of our whole territory under your government and of the several plantations (towns and townships) that are upon it" (Wacker 1975, 223). The governor was also directed to send back yearly abstracts of birth and death records, so that London would have a continuous census of the colonies and, with luck, an accurate map for the first time.

In 1738, New Jersey finally was assigned a governor all its own; this first exclusively New Jersey royal governor was a native son of the colony, Lewis Morris. He was no more popular than most governors of New Jersey had been, and at least one Assembly managed to pass no bills at all that were acceptable to the governor. The last royal governor, Ben Franklin's son William, ironically was one of the most popular and was merely confined to a more or less polite house arrest at the onset of the Revolution.

From Colony to State

East and West Jersey, joined as one royal colony in 1702, were never again separate for administrative purposes: the royal colony became the state of New Jersey. However, the heirs and descendants of the proprietors of East and West Jersey retained their land rights when surrendering their right to govern. To this day, any odd piece of land found to be untitled, through faulty surveying in the past, is the property of the proprietors. The proprietors, meeting annually at their respective seats—Burlington (West Jersey proprietors) or Perth Amboy (East Jersey proprietors), share any proceeds from such land sales, which in most other states would benefit the government.

OTHER BOUNDARY PROBLEMS

Although the troublesome land boundary with New York, along with the internal division into East and West Jersey, receives the most historical commentary, the other boundaries of New Jersey have occasioned interstate disputes as well. Even the federal government disagrees with New Jersey's claim to jurisdiction over water areas in lower Delaware Bay and Raritan Bay. Some statistical sources list New jersey's total area as 8,204 sq mi (21,248 sq km), while others quote it as 7,836 sq mi (20,295 sq km). The difference is the coastal-waters

23

FIGURE 2.4. *Detail from a 1726 Map of the East Coast.* This map of the area *from New York to the Carolinas* was produced by the famous Homanns firm in Nurnberg, Germany. Although more decorative than accurate, it does show the "Two Jerseys" and clearly places Staten Island in New Jersey. (Courtesy of the Frank H. Stewart Collection, Savitz Library, Glassboro State College)

area that the federal and state governments both claim, about 368 sq mi (953 sq km). New Jersey enforces its laws within the disputed area without interference from the federal government.

The Staten Island Dispute

Staten Island was in dispute between New Jersey and New York from the early colonial period until 1834. In 1681 Governor Philip Carteret, on behalf of the East Jersey proprietors, wrote to the governor of New York, demanding the surrender of Staten Island to New Jersey (Boyer 1915, 60). The problem was vague wording of the description of New York's territory in the bay; an early grant stated that the boundaries of New York should include "All small islands in adjacent waters." New Jersey contended that Staten Island was not particularly small (60 sq mi or 155 sq km) and that the main channel of the Hudson should be the logical boundary as stated in the original deed to New Jersey (see Figure 2.4). New York's lust for territory was compounded by its desire to control completely the trade of the Hudson and contiguous waters to the exclusion of New Jersey, as evidenced also by New York's attempted monopoly of customs ports. New York claimed not only Staten Island but *all* waters between the states, "including shores, roads (open anchorages or roadsteads) and harbors within the natural territorial waters of New Jersey" (Boyer 1915, 60). This assertion of control right up to New Jersey's mean high-tide line meant that New York would have exclusive navigation rights. In fact, New York granted Robert Livingston an exclusive charter for steam navigation and refused such rights to New Jerseyan John Stevens. New York

sought to prohibit New Jersey shore (riparian) landowners from building wharfs or jetties out into New York-claimed waters. Allegedly, the compromise worked out in 1834 was that New York kept Staten Island and New Jersey got control over its territorial waters to the midpoint of the Hudson River, Arthur Kill, and Kill Van Kull.

The Delaware Boundary

Although the Pennsylvania–New Jersey boundary seems always to have been free of controversy, the Delaware boundary has been troublesome. This dispute dates to William Penn's acquisition of the "three lower counties" to ensure that Pennsylvania's access to the sea and Delaware River navigation would be unchallenged by either Maryland or New Jersey. The Duke of York's charter in August 1682 gave to Penn ". . . all that tract of land lying within the compass of a circle of twelve miles above the said town [New Castle, actually, the tower of the courthouse there] and all the islands in the said river and soil thereof lying north of southernmost part of said circle" (Boyer 1915, 65). These territorial rights included fishing rights and were not settled finally until 1905 (mostly in Delaware's favor).

Thus, on both the Delaware and Hudson estuaries, New Jersey's control over navigation was challenged by the two powerful colonies neighboring it. The aim was to establish thriving ports in Pennsylvania, its onetime territory, Delaware, and in New York in order to exercise exclusive port monopolies relative to New Jersey's trade that naturally was oriented to one or the other great port region. Both larger neighbors repeatedly attempted to secure all the port trade to themselves.

CHAPTER 3

THE PHYSICAL SETTING

New Jersey is a transitional state between the New England–New York region and the upper South, in its physical geography as well as its cultural geography. In both landforms and climate, New Jersey exhibits the gradation and intermingling of the physical characteristics of the states to the north, west, and south.

The physical setting of the state has been an important, if passive, consideration in the patterns of human settlement and economic development. The differing character of the state's regions shows the significance of landforms and underlying geology, climate, drainage, and the geologic-topographic-climatic interactions apparent in soil and natural-vegetation development.

New Jersey can be described as a sizable peninsula of land lying between the Hudson and Delaware rivers. This peninsular quality is better appreciated on a map emphasizing the Delaware River boundary with Pennsylvania than it would be in a satellite view, as the Delaware Valley is not particularly impressive as a peninsular boundary until the section below Trenton (see Figure 3.1). Nonetheless, New Jersey's only land boundary—that with New York State—forms only about 12 percent of the total boundary of the state. This peninsula combines a section of the Appalachian Highlands and Piedmont with a large area of Coastal Plain; the state is about 40 percent Appalachians and Piedmont and 60 percent Coastal Plain (see Figure 3.2). The basic shape of New Jersey resembles

a highly stylized **S** or a lightning bolt done with short, thick strokes of a pen. The northwestern, upper limb of this lightning bolt is in the Appalachian Highlands and Piedmont, and the lower, southeastern section is in the Atlantic Coastal Plain.

LANDFORMS

The boundaries of New Jersey's landform regions run generally northeast-southwest, so that the prevailing "grain" of the topography approximately parallels the oceanic coastlines. In this, as in so many other aspects, New Jersey is a microcosm of the contiguous forty-eight states in general.

Valley and Ridge Province

The northwesternmost portion of New Jersey's Appalachian region is occupied by a relatively narrow segment of the Valley and Ridge Province. This province of the Appalachians runs from New York State to Alabama and is generally wider to the south. This is a region of sedimentary and metamorphic rock that includes New Jersey's highest point. The Valley and Ridge Province is quite sparsely populated and is a major recreational asset to New Jersey, as it includes New Jersey's share of the Delaware Water Gap National Recreation Area, Stokes State Forest, and High Point State Park.

Kittatinny Mountain, roughly paralleling the upper Delaware Valley for some 35 mi (56 km) between the Delaware Water Gap and the New York state line, is com-

FIGURE 3.1.

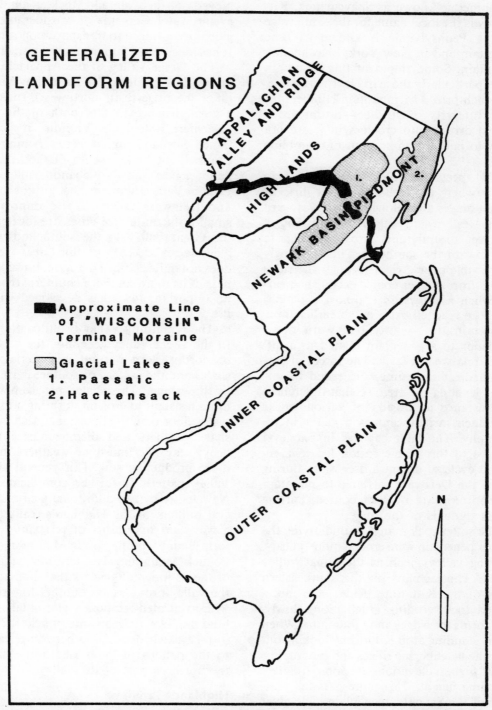

GENERALIZED LANDFORM REGIONS

APPALACHIAN VALLEY AND RIDGE

HIGHLANDS

PIEDMONT

NEWARK BASIN

1.

2.

Approximate Line of "WISCONSIN" Terminal Moraine

Glacial Lakes
1. Passaic
2. Hackensack

INNER COASTAL PLAIN

OUTER COASTAL PLAIN

N

FIGURE 3.2. *Generalized Landform Regions.* The basic "grain" of New Jersey's topography runs northeast-southwest, following the major axis of the Appalachian system.

posed of a hard, erosion-resistant quartzite conglomerate known as Shawangunk. Kittatinny is the local name for the same ridge that in Pennsylvania is known as Blue Mountain and in New York, Shawangunk Mountain. Some slopes of this mountain ridge, particularly those in New York State, are much prized by mountain climbers for their integrity of surface—pitons (rock spikes) driven into crevices in it are not likely to pull out on account of crumbling rock.

The spectacular Delaware Water Gap occurs where the Delaware River turns at a right angle; after flowing southwestward on the western side of the Kittatinny Ridge, the river abruptly cuts across the ridge to flow toward the southeast. This seemingly improbable course right through the ridge results from a river course established earlier when a *peneplain* ("almost a plain") had been reached. At a much earlier time, erosion in the vicinity had worn down highlands to a peneplain related to a different relative sea level. The forces of erosion had, at that time, succeeded in virtually leveling the area, so that differences in resistance to erosion of various rocks were then insignificant as a factor in topography. The later changes in sea level relative to this whole region led to a renewed cycle of downward erosion, during which the Delaware was able to maintain its approximate present course, cutting across the axis of the ridge.

The softer rock materials underlying the former peneplain were eroded more quickly, creating valleys such as the Great Valley of the Appalachians on the southeastern flank of the Kittatinny Ridge; the more-rugged rock, eroding much more slowly, now forms the ridges and mountains. When one is standing atop Kittatinny looking out over the neighboring ridges and mountains, all the highest elevations are approximately the same height. This represents the remnant of the Schooley peneplain. The great water gap has a local relief difference of about 1,100 ft (335 m). Few gaps of this scale interrupt the Appalachian ridges; if

not comparable to passes in the Sierra Nevada or the Colorado Rockies, the Delaware Water Gap was of considerable regional importance to transportation routes. It has long been a famous tourist attraction.

The Great Valley of the Appalachians, known in New Jersey as Kittatinny Valley (after the ridge to its northwest), runs for a great distance to the south in the Appalachian system. In Virginia, it is the famed Shenandoah; in Pennsylvania, the Cumberland Valley, south of the Susquehanna River, and the Lebanon Valley and Lehigh Valley between the Susquehanna and Delaware rivers. While important, small-to-medium size cities are located in the Great Valley to the south and west, New Jersey's sector of the Great Valley does not quite achieve the agricultural lushness of its more southern counterparts, and no important town has developed within it.

The Kittatinny Valley is quite complex. In the Great Valley generally, the western or northwestern portion is underlain by shales and the eastern or southeastern part by limestone. The shales are somewhat more resistant to erosion, forming a higher valley floor than the limestone. Also, while shale weathers and disintegrates into a heavy clay, the limestone weathers into a more productive soil. This general Great Valley pattern is further complicated in New Jersey by two additional factors. Several outliers of the Highlands, caused by a westward overthrust of resistant rocks, form Jenny Jump, South Mountain, and Pohuck Mountain. The terminal moraine of the continental glaciers that cuts across the valley provides yet another low ridge, with associated temporary glacial lakes behind it. The rich organic muck soils of former lake beds add another complication to the pattern of landforms and soils in the northern part of the valley.

Highlands Province

The Highlands Province, which flanks the Valley and Ridge Province on the southeast, represents an extension of the rugged,

crystalline rocks of the New England Upland, which crosses New Jersey, extends
into eastern Pennsylvania, and finally terminates near Reading, Pennsylvania. The
Highlands Province in New Jersey is about
25 mi (40 km) wide in its northern and
central sections, narrowing to about 10 mi
(16 km) wide at the Pennsylvania border.

Although the Highlands only range about
500 to 600 ft (152 to 182 m) above their
long, narrow valleys, there are few east-
west passes through them; they are far more
rugged than their height may imply, and
local relief is great. The Highlands merit
the title "mountains" in terms of their
effect on settlement and transport route
patterns; in fact, the northeastern sector is
known as the Ramapo Mountains. The
valleys that slice through the Highlands,
following New Jersey's familiar northeast-
southwest grain, are the results of the erosion of somewhat-softer, less-resistant rock
materials, generally limestones and shales.
The Highlands' southeastern boundary is
sharply defined by a *fault line,* a fracture
in the earth's crust that here also is the
line between unlike rock types.

Piedmont Province

The Piedmont ("foot of the mountains")
Province in New Jersey differs from the
classic Piedmont to the south in Pennsylvania and on down the east flank of the
Appalachians into Georgia. That Piedmont
commonly features hard crystalline rocks
(igneous and metamorphic) whose contact
with the much less resistant sedimentaries
of the Atlantic Coastal Plain forms the
famed *fall line.* There, streams and rivers
tumbling off the resistant crystalline rocks,
which they are eroding slowly and with
difficulty, onto the soft, readily eroded,
coastal-plain sedimentaries form a line of
rapids and waterfalls. This fall line has
become the site of many cities as it combines two economic advantages at that
location. Unless—and until—the navigational barrier is circumvented by engineering works, the fall line represents the
furthest-inland penetration of ocean ship-

ping. The fall line also is frequently a good
location for waterpower development, giving it an early, industrial-site advantage at
many places.

New Jersey's Piedmont is of a different
nature; it consists of primarily sedimentary
rocks rather than crystalline ones. It is also
known as the Newark Basin, one of a series
of sedimentary basins, dating to the Trias-
sic-Jurassic geologic period, that occur from
the Carolinas to Canada. This province is
extremely complex geologically, as the
sandstones and shales of the Newark Basin
are interspersed with basalt ridges forming
the First and Second Watchung ridges and
the Packanach and Hook mountains. Molten rock or magma that was intruded (in-
jected) into the sedimentaries, later tilted
by tectonic activity, and then exposed at
the surface by erosion forms the Palisades
along the Hudson, the Sourland Mountains,
and the Cushetunk Mountain (see Figure
3.3). In between these more-rugged crystalline rocks, the softer sandstones and
shales have eroded to lower levels, high-
lighting the ridges. The First Watchung
Mountain reaches elevations over 800 ft
(243 m) near Paterson, and the Palisades
rise gradually from a low ridge at Hoboken
to over 500 ft (152 m) at the New York
state line.

The rocks of the Piedmont have been
used extensively as building material and
in highway-construction and beach-ero-
sion-control projects. Most of the shales
and sandstones of the Newark Basin are
reddish or medium brown in color, which
is reflected in the local soils. In addition,
a dark chocolate brown sandstone has been
quarried extensively; it was a popular facing
stone for late Victorian houses—"brown-
stones"—in New York and Philadelphia
as well as New Jersey cities. The basalts
and diabases of the basin are known as
traprock; crushed materials from these
ridges form a major part of many highways
and concrete structures of the region. The
scenic Palisades were being literally demolished by the demand for construction
materials until a conservation-minded

FIGURE 3.3. This 1844 woodcut dramatizes the famed Palisades, sills of diabase intruded into the sedimentary rocks of the Newark Basin. (*Early Woodcut Views of New York and New Jersey.* New York: Dover Publications, 1975, p. 76)

women's club instigated a successful drive to preserve the Palisades as public parkland. Portions of the "rescued" Palisades, however, are mere facades or false fronts behind which quarrying in unprotected areas continues to remove rocks. Substantial chunks of the Palisades formation line the Jersey shore as seawalls and jetties.

Glaciation

The Valley and Ridge, Highlands, and Piedmont (Newark Basin) provinces all have been extensively and profoundly affected by continental glaciation. During the Pleistocene (approximately the last million years) great sheets of ice moved slowly, erratically outward from major centers of ice accumulation in a crescent around present Hudson Bay, Canada. Seasonally advancing, then stagnating, the ice sheets were highly efficient agents of erosion. The moving ice was capable of transporting boulders the size of small cars as well as materials ranging down to finely ground "rock flour." The ice sheet gouged out chunks of bedrock, scraped surfaces bare, grooved solid rock by dragging rock chunks across it, and generally stripped surfaces near its centers of origin. At its furthest extent outward from the core of ice accumulation, however, the ice became an agent of deposition. There it dropped, in characteristically unsorted layers and ridges of debris, the soil and rock materials it had been transporting. Glacial deposition frequently produces ridges of debris, *moraines,* that lie across preexisting valleys and ridges at right angles; this is a "calling card" of glacial action—no other agent of erosion and deposition is capable of so directly interrupting normal drainage patterns. The terminal moraine that represents the furthest advance of the continental Pleistocene glaciers (shown in Figure 3.2) cuts across the grain of New Jersey's topography from the mouth of the Raritan, swinging north through Union and Morris counties to the vicinity of Morristown, then running east-west to the Delaware Valley near Belvedere. The final retreat of the last glacier (the Wisconsin glaciation) occurred about 15,000 years ago, practically yesterday on a geologic time scale. (In retreat, a glacier is melting back faster than it is advancing from accumulating pressure at its source.)

The glacier's effect was great.The inexorable, if halting, advance of the glacier over the surfaces of New Jersey north of the terminal moraine scraped bare the uplands and deposited debris in the valleys. Because the morainal materials often run at right angles to stream valleys, drainage is "deranged" by glacial deposition, creating lakes where stream valleys are blocked. Many lakes in the northern Highlands Province, such as Lake Hopatcong, the largest such glacial lake remaining, were formed at the end of the glacial period. Two large glacial lakes that were only temporary have left their imprint on contemporary New Jersey drainage and soils (see Figure 3.2). Glacial Lake Hackensack formed where the moraine blocked the exit of that river; the legacy of that glacial lake is the Hackensack Meadows, nearly 20,000 acres (8,100 ha) of tidal marsh at the upper end of Newark Bay. Another great glacial lake, Lake Passaic, formed between the Second (inner) Watchung Ridge and the Highlands to the northwest. The clay deposited in the bottom of that temporary lake, together with the deranged drainage of the area, results in the Great Swamp, now a national wildlife refuge, and in a series of smaller swamps.

The Fall Line and the Coastal Plain

A small protrusion of the southeastern Pennsylvania Piedmont of hard crystalline materials extends across the Delaware a short distance into New Jersey at Trenton. The Delaware River's difficulty in eroding through this piedmont-type rock forms the rapids that are the inland limit to Delaware navigation and make Trenton the northernmost true fall-line city.

South of New Jersey the Atlantic Coastal Plain is wider; north of New Jersey the coastal plain appears only as Staten and Long islands, part of Cape Cod, and the offshore islands like Nantucket, Martha's Vineyard, and Block Island. From Cape Cod to Georgia the combined width of the Atlantic Coastal Plain and its submerged section is about 200 mi (321 km), but the proportion of drowned versus dry land changes steadily from north to south. Northeast of New Jersey, the *continental shelf,* the submerged continuation of the coastal plain, forms almost the entire width of this sedimentary, almost flat-lying feature. South of New Jersey, the coastal plain widens as its submerged counterpart, the shelf, correspondingly narrows. Cape Cod and its neighboring offshore islands, Long Island, Staten Island, and a small slice of New Jersey near Perth Amboy are the only parts of the Atlantic Coastal Plain to have been glaciated, although glacial debris was deposited on the shelf itself, helping to create the shallow fishing banks off New England.

The sedimentary strata, or layers, under the coastal plain all dip (plunge further beneath the surface, or from the horizontal) toward the sea, to the southeast. The New Jersey portion of the coastal plain, as is true of the plain in general, is former sea bottom. Part of the New Jersey coastal plain was still submerged as late as the beginning of the Pleistocene epoch. Geologically, this is the youngest part of the state, and the very gently dipping sedimentary strata with few observable relief differences are rather poorly drained. The underlying strata dip from horizontal at only about 5 or 6 ft per mi (1 to 1.1 m per km). These sedimentary strata continue beneath the continental shelf until the shelf abruptly terminates at the continental slope, the actual geologic boundary of the continent. The continental shelf off New Jersey is about 80 to 100 mi (128 to 160 km) wide; the outer edge of the shelf at the beginning of the slope is at a depth of about 500 to 600 ft (152 to 182 m). Thus the very gentle slope seaward of the coastal plain is continued, as the shelf submerges from sea level to 500 or 600 ft over 80 to 100 mi (128 to 160 km).

The Atlantic Coastal Plain Province is separated into inner and outer coastal plain on the basis of the age of sediments, their degree of consolidation, and the qualities of the soils that have developed on them. The inner coastal plain, about 15 percent of the state, is composed of somewhat better consolidated, older sediments of the Cretaceous and Tertiary periods exposed at the surface. The outer coastal plain (outward from the bulk of the landmass) has even younger and more poorly consolidated materials exposed at the surface. The inner-coastal-plain materials have more water-retaining clay; the outer-plain materials are more porous with more sand and gravels. The entire plain widens from about 25 mi (40 km) wide south of Raritan Bay to about 60 mi (96 km) wide between the lower Delaware Valley and the ocean. The boundary between the inner and outer coastal plains is marked by a low, much-eroded cuesta, or ridge, formed by the erosion of a tilted or dipping stratum of sedimentary materials. This cuesta is better defined to the north and east; it corresponds approximately to the drainage divide between the Delaware and Raritan systems to the west and north and to streams flowing directly to the Atlantic to the east. The highest points of the coastal plain are only about 400 ft (121 m) above sea level, and nearly half the plain is below 100 ft (30 m) in elevation. The Navesink Highlands, part of the lower Atlantic Coastal Plain fronting on Sandy Hook Bay, rise only 276 ft (84 m), but their steep rise from an otherwise low shoreline makes them appear more dramatic (see Figure 3.4).

From Sandy Hook to Cape May the New Jersey shoreline is characterized by sandbars, marsh and lagoon development, and, above all, by an offshore, alongshore

"conveyor belt" for sand formed by a combination of shallow water, abundant sand, ocean waves, and ocean currents. Some of the nation's finest sand beaches lie along this shoreline, conveniently close to the recreational demand generated within the nearby metropolitan areas. The combination of this magnificent, if rather mobile and transitory, recreational asset with excellent accessibility to the great cities presents some interesting problems for attempts to stabilize an inherently unstable, mobile shoreline. From approximately Barnegat Inlet northward, the alongshore current is moving north. From Barnegat Inlet southward, the alongshore current is moving south. The presence of this natural conveyor belt of sand means that—if unhampered by people's jetties, seawalls, sand-pumping operations, and the like—the beach one stands on this year is composed of some different sand (along with some of the same) than it was formed of last year, even though the sand may look all the same. The alongshore current moves and distributes sand largely by influencing the angle at which the forward rush of water moves up the slope of the beach. The forward crash of waves up the beach, the *swash,* comes in at an angle different from a right angle to the slope, along most of this shoreline. South of Barnegat Inlet, the swash, moving some sand as it goes, comes in from an angle north of a right angle; north of Barnegat Inlet, the tendency is for the swash to move in from an angle south of a right angle. The drain of seawater back down the slope of the beach, the *backwash,* is always at a right angle to the slope of the beach, for the same reason that water always drains downhill. This combination of swash and backwash serves to move sand along the shoreline. Storms, especially those coinciding with high tides, combine with currents and the low resistance of sand to erosion to continually reshape this coastline, opening and closing inlets between the barrier beaches, shifting inlets, widening or narrowing sandbars, creating islands, and destroying islands (see

FIGURE 3.4. *The Twin Lights Atop Navesink Highlands.* The highest point directly on saltwater south of Maine, the Highlands of Navesink have been a prominent landmark for centuries. This 1874 print shows some of the resort development catering to New Yorkers who sailed across Raritan Bay by steamboat. (William Cullen Bryant, ed. *Picturesque America.* New York: D. Appleton and Co., 1874, p. 177)

Figure 3.5). Once property rights are established and buildings erected, people take an active interest in this highly mobile coastline and attempt to stabilize it, with varying—but in the long run, always temporary—success.

THE SEASHORE ENVIRONMENT

The ocean shoreline, with its complicated intermingling of land and water, sandbar and marsh, inlet and backbay, is New Jersey's cultural environmental counterpart of California's San Andreas fault. In both instances, in the past natural forces have rearranged physical features, including the coastline itself, destroyed property on a wholesale basis, and even, tragically, taken lives. In both cases, everyone knows for certain that past tragedies will be repeated; only the timing of future occurrences is uncertain.

Why don't people collectively, as a society, learn from past errors in evaluating the possibilities of the physical environment? There is ample evidence that they do not learn. People insist on building and rebuilding homes, schools, and hospitals literally on top of the same fault line that gave birth to the 1906 San Francisco earthquake. Although the destructive power of storms, especially hurricanes, combined

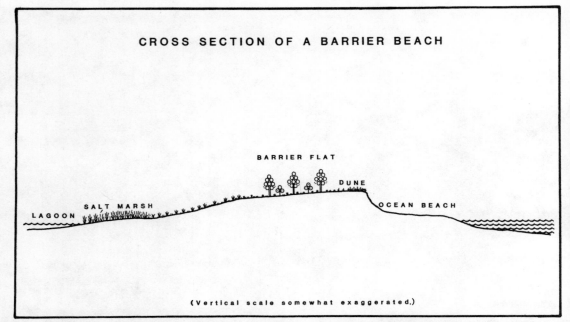

CROSS SECTION OF A BARRIER BEACH

BARRIER FLAT

DUNE

SALT MARSH

LAGOON

OCEAN BEACH

(Vertical scale somewhat exaggerated.)

FIGURE 3.5.   The seashore, including some of New Jersey's most appealing landscapes, is also a hazardous zone for long-term occupance. Storm waves and high tides can open or close inlets between the barrier beaches overnight, and the beaches are continuously subject to erosion and reshaping. Ill-considered removal of dunes and filling of marshes can increase the likelihood of storm damage.

with high tides, is not as precisely predictable in geographic location as a fault line, its inevitability along every portion of coastline *sometime* in the future matches the inevitability of earthquakes. New Jersey is an unlikely location for a major earthquake, and its ocean shoreline is less frequented by hurricanes than the Gulf coast and the vicinity of Cape Hatteras, but its shoreline is, nonetheless, a series of disasters waiting to happen. True, the alongshore current and storm waves have been shaping and reshaping the shoreline continuously, and hurricanes surely hit the coastal areas long before their permanent human settlement, but human activities over the last century have greatly accelerated the erosion of parts of the coastline and also greatly increased the probability of serious damage to any structures on the offshore sandbars.

New Jersey's seacoast, from Bay Head to Wildwood Crest, is fringed by offshore

sandbars or barrier beaches. Cape May was at one time separated from the mainland by a tidal channel that has since silted in to become a tidal creek, incompletely severing the cape from the mainland (Cape May is technically an island again, thanks to the Cape May Canal, part of the Intracoastal Waterway for small craft). North of Bay Head, the barrier beaches almost disappear. They are visible only as sandy barriers across river and creek mouths that convert saltwater lagoons into brackish water and as the elongated sandspit of Sandy Hook, which forms the northernmost New Jersey offshore-bar development. The northern shore has been subjected to severe erosion, resulting in beaches that are short and steep in comparison to those characteristic of the south shore. The characteristic profile of a barrier beach is shown in Figure 3.5. The inlets between the barrier beaches, with their combination of shifting channels and sometimes strong currents,

FIGURE 3.6. *The Entrance to Cold Spring Harbor, Cape May.* The long jetties built to protect the entrance to Cold Spring Harbor have interrupted the conveyor belt of sand powered by the alongshore currents, southbound at this point. Sand accumulates to the north of the jetties (Wildwood Crest) but is not replaced to the south, eroding the beaches of Cape May. (Courtesy of Dick Scott)

are often treacherous even for small boats. A maze of low, marshy islands and tidal flats, interwoven with tidal channels, makes the entrances to small rivers such as the Great Egg Harbor River and the Mullica River difficult for the uninitiated to navigate. The fringe of marshes tends to be wider toward the south. Fewer than 7 mi (11 km) of the seacoast have been preserved in a more or less natural state for public enjoyment.

CLIMATE

For a relatively small state, New Jersey has a remarkably varied, and variable, climate (U.S. Department of Agriculture 1941; U.S. Department of Commerce 1959). Only 166 mi (267 km) long at its extreme north-south extent and with a maximum width of 65 mi (104 km), New Jersey is a very small area for a climatological study;

yet there is a considerable range of temperatures, winter and summer, from north to south and from seacoast to mountains. The north-to-south differences have an obvious latitudinal relationship; however, the north-south temperature variations are greater in New Jersey than its relatively minor latitudinal extent (less than 2½ degrees of latitude) would suggest. New Jersey's is a *continental climate,* or rather a range of variations of a continental-type climate. The coastal location has comparatively little influence on climate, as this is primarily a *lee* shore, one dominated by offshore winds except in the immediate vicinity of the shore. The effect of continentality is to intensify seasonal extremes in temperatures compared to an oceanic or *maritime climate* at the same latitude. Every county in New Jersey has at least one official weather station that has reported summer maxima over 100°F (37°C), and every county has recorded minimum temperatures below 0°F (−17.8°C). The present statewide records are 110°F (43°C) at Runyon, Middlesex County, and −34° (−36°C) at Rivervale, Bergen County.

While these hundred-plus-degree extremes are found in every county and are not all that uncommon within any one year, the regional tendency is for the southern-shore area to be milder in winter and warmer in summer and to have a much longer growing season than the northwestern mountains. Temperature differences from northwest to southeast are greatest in winter, least in summer (see Figure 3.7). July temperature averages along the seashore are above 74°F (23°C) and in the mountains of the northwest, below 70°F (21°C). In winter, though, the difference in average temperatures increases. January averages of over 34°F (1°C) in Cape May contrast with figures below 26°F (−3.3°C) in the extreme northwest.

The average length of frost-free season varies from over 200 days along the Delaware Bay and Atlantic coastlines to 140 days in the northern Valley and Ridge Province. Thus the marine influence upon New Jersey's basically continental climate is enough to significantly moderate the climate of the extreme southern part of the state, which is influenced by water bodies both to the west and southwest (the Delaware Bay and estuary) and the east (the Atlantic).

New Jersey is far wetter than most of the United States and, indeed, most of the world. Almost every part of the state receives at least 40 in. (101 cm) of precipitation in the average year, while about two-thirds of the state, primarily the northern and eastern Atlantic Coastal Plain and northern sectors of the Highlands and Piedmont, receives over 45 in. (114 cm) per year (see Figure 3.7). Precipitation is well distributed throughout the year with an annual average of 120 days with precipitation. The fall months average about 8 days each of measurable precipitation; the other months have some precipitation on

between 9 and 12 days each. The northern part of the state is somewhat cloudier, at 50 percent of possible sunshine received compared to the south's 60 percent.

This abundant moisture, with a prolonged drought occurring an average of once in fifteen years, is related to New Jersey's location relative to storm tracks. Frequent storms move eastward across the southern Great Lakes, swing northeastward across New York State, and move toward the Atlantic paralleling the St. Lawrence Valley. Northern New Jersey is influenced by these storms, which are joined by a storm track running from the upper South across Pennsylvania and merging with the Great Lakes storm track over New York State. Another major storm track lies along the Atlantic coast from Georgia to New England. This seems to be related to the warm temperatures of the Gulf Stream in that the higher temperatures there induce a trough of lower atmospheric pressure that can help channel storms along the coast. The coastal storm track lies closest to the coast in January, and New Jerseyans have learned to be wary of winter storms approaching from the south along the coast. Heavy snowfalls can result from these northbound storms, as the water vapor available to be condensed is quite high.

GEOLOGICAL RESOURCES

The mineral variety of the Garden State is impressive, if little recognized beyond the community of geology scholars. Although New Jersey is not generally considered an important mining state, mining played a significant role in its early settlement, and New Jersey remains the only source in the United States for a few exotic minerals. Copper was mined by the Dutch in what is now Warren County in 1644; the colonial iron industry started in 1674. New Jersey long had the nation's most-important zinc mine, and the state is the sole producer of greensand marl (glauconite), a material now used in water softeners and long famous as a fertilizer.

37

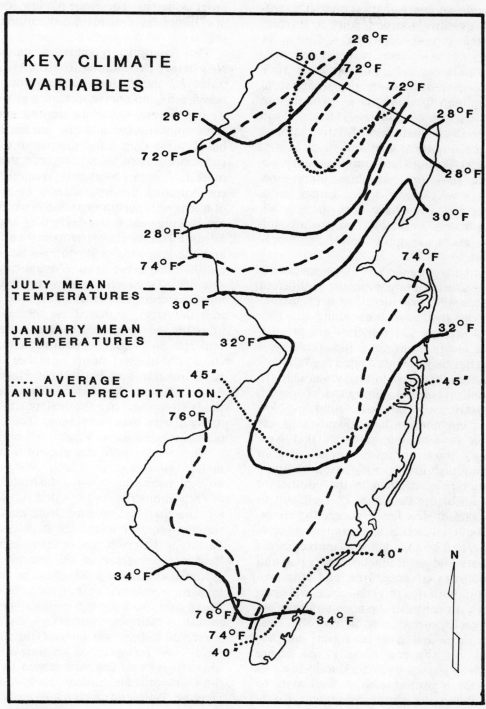

FIGURE 3.7.

Relatively few minerals in the state are *economic minerals,* that is, present in sufficient quantity and/or quality to warrant profitable mining. However, the complex geology of New Jersey, with its sedimentary, metamorphic, and igneous rock types—some of them ranging in age from Precambrian to Quaternary—produces an intriguing list of minerals. Metals found include small quantities of native (almost pure, uncombined) gold and silver as well as copper. Precious and semiprecious stones such as ruby, opal, sapphire, tourmaline, zircon, smoky quartz, spinel, garnet, beryl, citrine, and agate have been located, all, unfortunately, in quality and quantity too low to excite any but collectors, or "rockhounds."

Franklin, New Jersey, is an incredibly prolific source of rare minerals; 33 different minerals were first identified here, including some that have been found nowhere else. A further 139 minerals are present; only a few of them are commercially valuable, but they include some very "showy" specimens that glow in ultraviolet light, to the delight of museum goers. Nineteen radioactive minerals are found in New Jersey, but none in large quantity.

It is in economic minerals that New Jersey's more common image—low in glamour, high in workaday practicability—is better reflected than in the oddities of Franklin or the Palisades. It is difficult to keep track of New Jersey's operating mines, as production tends to begin, cease, rejuvenate, and be abandoned as market prices fluctuate and as production costs rise and technologies advance. Iron and zinc production both fit this on-again, off-again pattern. In contrast, the nonglamorous but vital geologic resources of traprock, glass sand, clays, and greensand marl are produced virtually continuously (see Figure 3.8). New Jersey even produces minerals from the seawater: a large plant at Cape May Point, the extreme southern tip of the state, extracts magnesium from the sea. As a magnesium oxide, the material finds use in heat-resistant furnace brick and as the key ingredient in a popular remedy for upset stomachs. The value of New Jersey's raw minerals is about $200 million per year.

The economically marginal nature of New Jersey's remaining iron ores is illustrated by the nation's first venture into *beneficiating* an ore (processing a low-quality ore to concentrate the desired mineral prior to shipment and use in furnaces), based at the Odgen mine, where the magnetite ore was of such low grade that the mine had been abandoned. A method of concentrating the iron content by means of a magnetic separator through which the crushed ore passed was devised by Thomas Edison. The mine was reopened in 1890, and the magnetic separator worked well, but the process proved uneconomic in that instance. The basic principles are used with more success elsewhere today. The early iron industry was based on coastal-plain limonite, or "bog ore." Other economic minerals no longer in production include slate in Sussex County, graphite near Bloomingdale, and barite near Hopewell. Some titanium is dredged from coastal sands (ilminite), but the real potential of mineral wealth in New Jersey lies in the possibilities of oil and gas offshore.

New Jersey, until the present, has had no local sources of fossil fuels. This proved no real handicap to its industrialization, as early industrialists exploited the woods for charcoal for smelting iron and used waterpower, such as the Great Falls of the Passaic at Paterson, for other enterprises. Coal was brought from the nearby Pennsylvania anthracite fields, first by canals, then by a network of railroads; this was the primary fuel for the middle phases of industrialization in New Jersey. As petroleum and natural gas became the desired fuels, New Jersey relied on long-distance imports. Natural gas now comes in from the Gulf coast and midcontinent areas by pipeline. Petroleum arriving by both pipeline and tankers supplies two of the nation's largest concentrations of oil refineries—the Delaware Valley, shared with Pennsylvania

PROPERTY OF SAMUEL HILLIARD,
PROPRIETOR OF THE CELEBRATED GLASS SAND PITS, MAURICE RIVER, NEAR MILLVILLE, N.J.

FIGURE 3.8. *Glass-sand Pits in South Jersey, Circa 1876.* One of the few New Jersey mineral resources that continues to be commercially important, high-quality silica sand still supports a glass industry. (D. J. Stewart, compiler, *Combination Atlas Map of Cumberland County, New Jersey.* Philadelphia: D. J. Stewart, 1876, p. 26)

and Delaware, and the northeastern New Jersey complex around Rahway, Linden, and Elizabeth.

The combination of the Organization of Petroleum Exporting Countries (OPEC) price increases of the 1970s and the evolving technology of underwater drilling and production led to considerable interest in the possibilities of offshore oil and gas. The continental shelf and slope are, after all, sedimentary, and the steeply rising prices of both oil and gas justified serious exploration. The U.S. Department of the Interior offered 154 tracts for lease in 1976. These tracts were located off the east coast from south of Long Island to Cape Charles,

Virginia. Twelve oil companies or consortiums successfully bid over $1 billion in this initial sale of leases. "Shows" of hydrocarbons, some of them indicating possible wells, were found about 100 mi (160 km) east/southeast of Atlantic City, continuing southwestward to about 100 mi off Ocean City, Maryland (Zimolzak and Stansfield 1979, 460). In late 1981, the fourth sale in the area was held, one in which the oil industry was asked in advance to indicate areas of high, medium, or low interest. Interest was highest in the deep-water tracts along the continental slope over a potentially oil-bearing buried reef that lies at depths between 600 and 6,000 ft (182–1820 m). Areas near shore held little interest. Government and private estimates of the size of the reserves run from a low of 1.8 billion bbl of oil and 5.3 trillion cu ft (150.08 billion cu m) of natural gas to nearly 5 billion bbl of oil and 14 trillion cu ft (396.438 billion cu m) of gas. Test wells indicate far greater probability of commercially exploitable natural gas than oil. So far, the U.S. Department of the Interior has been the major beneficiary of the hunt for oil and gas. December 1981 lease sales alone netted almost $322 million. Interested companies included Arco, Amoco, Chevron, Gulf, Mobil, Shell, and Exxon. Although the reserve estimates may seem high, there is slight chance that these fields will produce enough to even meet New Jersey's domestic needs.

SOILS AND NATURAL VEGETATION

Soil is a complex and—literally—vital topic; the overwhelming bulk of the human food supply depends on the qualities of the top 6 to 10 in. (15 to 25 cm) of soil carpeting the best agricultural lands. Soil is almost continuously variable in details of its various characteristics. The physical and chemical qualities of soils reflect a large number of causes and modifiers; soil is primarily influenced by *parent material* (the rocks underlying the soil, whose disintegration contributes soil materials), climate, vegetation cover, animal activities (from earthworms and insects to people and their domestic animals), slope, drainage, and above all, perhaps, time. Time to develop a balance among all the other inputs is critical to soils. New Jersey's complex solid geology, direct and indirect experience of glaciation, generally abundant precipitation, and relatively long history of use by people have all contributed to an exceedingly complex soils pattern.

In general, there is a correlation of physiographic provinces of New Jersey with soil utility. Most of the outer coastal plain

would be classed as poor to very poor, because it is practically pure sand. There is little clay in the well-drained sands, and these soils tend to be quite acid in reaction. Poorly drained lowland areas, such as the floodplains of sluggish rivers, have deep accumulations of decaying organic materials and are sometimes used for cranberry or blueberry cultivation. The soils of the inner coastal plain are generally better and have a good mixture of sand, clay, and silt. The reddish shales and sandstones of the Piedmont are generally superior and contain some of the best soils in the state and in the United States. The traprock ridges usually weather to excellent soils, at least when not overlain by glacial debris. South of the terminal moraine, Highlands soils are generally quite good and are farmed whenever the slope is not excessive, as in the fertile Musconetcong Valley. The Kittatinny Valley has good soil where adequately drained, and the narrow terraces of the Delaware Valley above the gap are desirable too. Some areas of recently drained swamp or lake bed, north of the terminal moraine, make superb soil for vegetable cultivation. Thus New Jersey's soils range from highly productive to unusable. Where people have been cultivating, draining, fertilizing, and otherwise reshaping soil the longest, as in the inner coastal plain, Piedmont, and the valleys of the southern Highlands and Valley and Ridge, their activities have become important modifiers and improvers of the natural soil qualities.

As in its geologic and soil varieties, New Jersey is characterized by a complex natural-vegetation pattern. The present patterns of vegetation, even forest vegetation, do not accurately represent "natural" conditions, that is, the vegetation that would appear without any human interference. Except in the most remote, inaccessible areas, people have cut down forests for timber or charcoal-fired iron or glass furnaces, cleared land for cultivation, drained swamps, filled in marshes, and introduced a wide variety of exotic plants along with domestic animals that have selectively encouraged or discouraged plant growth. In addition to all these complications, New Jersey's familiar role as a transition state, meeting ground, and melder of both physical and cultural extensions from neighboring regions is apparent in vegetation as well. Some plant species reach their southernmost extent in New Jersey, while a greater number reach their northern extremes in the state.

Three major forest regions are within the state. The Sugar Maple–Mixed Hardwoods association prevails in the Valley and Ridge, Highlands, and Piedmont provinces. The inner coastal plain and those parts of the outer coastal plain with less infertile soils support Mixed Oak forest, and the Oak-Pine forest covers the sandy, low-fertility soils of the region termed the Pine Barrens. Generally, the vegetation of the Valley and Ridge, Highlands, and Piedmont represents southern extensions of northern-type forests, while the Atlantic Coastal Plain has more of an affinity for southern species. White cedars once flourished in the bogs of the Pine Barrens and in the Hackensack Meadows but have long since been overexploited by people because the rot-resistant cedar makes excellent roof and siding shingles. Salt marshes are found around the coastal perimeter of the state from the lower valleys of the Passaic and Hackensack rivers to Salem County's Delaware Bay shores.

THE CULTURAL LANDSCAPE

Cultural landscapes have developed over the entire history of human settlement to the date of observation. As geographer Peirce Lewis has put it, *landscape* is used in its fullest geographical and cultural sense—the composite of *everything* that we see, or can be educated to see, when we look at a particular piece of the world around us (Meinig 1979, 11–32). In a far narrower sense, and as a verb rather than a noun, to *landscape* means to decorate and prettify a relatively small territory— a suburban house lot, a campuslike setting for a corporate headquarters, or even a parkway right-of-way—with shrubs, trees, and flowering plants. This is not the "wrong" definition; it is not even misleading in a broader sense of the word, for rearranging the landscape according to cultural values—"improving" it by shaping it to conform to human ideas of beauty, order, and privacy—is certainly part of the geographer's understanding of landscape. However, *landscape* in the broader sense includes terrain, drainage, natural vegetation, and all the effects of solid geology and climate. And all those parts of the natural world where people have lived in any significant number and for any significant time have been extensively altered, shaped, and used by people. While there are some relatively small portions of the planet that show little, if any, permanent traces of human settlement and activities,

other scenes—such as those in any large city—may seem to be totally cultural, that is, artificial and unrelated to a natural landscape. In fact, there are just as few purely artificial or human-built and shaped landscapes as there are purely physical or natural. The natural-artificial ratio is continuously variable. The keen observer will come to understand the complex interactions of the natural environment and the cultural environment that have produced the cultural landscape and to see that the two sets of factors have influenced one another, blending into the landscapes of New Jersey.

Urban and suburban landscapes may seem obviously cultural or human produced, but the open countryside should not be imagined as the antithesis of cultural landscapes. The countryside of such a long-settled, intensively used, and densely occupied part of the world as New Jersey is not untouched by people—not the forests, the marshes, or the farms. The original, or pre-European, forest cover of New Jersey now exists only in a few isolated acres of land; the largest plot, near East Millstone, is owned by Rutgers University. The rest of the forested area has been influenced, whether obviously or subtly, by the past and present activities of people. People have selectively cut certain desirable species, inadvertently introduced disease and predators, and added exotic animals and

FIGURE 4.1. *The George Washington Bridge, Looking West Toward Fort Lee.* This double-decked bridge across the Hudson, opened in 1931, led to a real estate boom in Bergen County. Note the forested, steep slopes of the Palisades rising abruptly from the New Jersey shore of the Hudson. (Courtesy of Port Authority of New York–New Jersey)

plants from overseas, deliberately and accidentally. Mining, road construction, nonscientific farming, and other activities have induced erosion and lowered or raised *water tables* (the upper limit of water saturation in soil and subsoil). The domestic animals brought in from Europe, from horses and cattle to starlings and honeybees ("English flies" to the Indians), eliminated, encouraged, or otherwise altered the natural vegetation through their direct and indirect activities. Because of their economic wants and cultural prejudices, people have altered natural slopes, dammed streams, created lakes, drained swamps or filled them with rubbish, and even changed climate on a highly localized scale. The clearing of woods, creation of lakes, and plowing of fields can all contribute to changes in the *microclimate*, the climate (especially temperature, humidity, and wind speed) near the ground. The changes in microclimate, even if measured in minute changes in temperature, can be critical to the growth and regeneration of plants, which start in the top few inches of soil and spend their first season, even if trees, very close to the ground.

CRITICAL STAGES

What then did New Jersey's cultural landscape look like in times past? Four critical stages in New Jersey's cultural landscape history have been selected as examples: Pre-European contact, around the

FIGURE 4.2. *A Landscape of Abandonment—The Kill Van Kull.* Backwaters of the aging industrial landscapes of the northeast take on the appearance of a casual junkyard set amongst space-consuming industries such as petroleum tank farms. Many of the New Jersey approaches to Manhattan seem to feature such forlorn landscapes, contributing to the state's "image problem." Clearly, people have reassessed the utility of this landscape. Once this general area was a bucolic resort.

dawn of the seventeenth century; the late colonial era, about 1776; a critical watershed period in the transition to an industrial state in 1840; and the triumph of the era of steam and concentrated industry in densely built, robust central cities, about 1900.

Any landscape portrait, no matter how detailed and clear, is like one frame of a motion picture—it is usually difficult, probably impossible, to understand what is going on and why it is going on in that single frame unless one has seen the preceding part of the film. It is the same with any picture or description of a cultural landscape—full understanding and appreciation require some knowledge and interpretation of what went on before. Imagine an immense, richly detailed, satellite photograph of New Jersey. It would show the gross features of the cultural land-

FIGURE 4.3. *Puerto Rican Flag as Storefront Graffiti, Camden.* The cultural markers in the urban landscape are not always as clear as the Puerto Rican flag paintings across an abandoned storefront, but they are there for the trained eye. Landscapes are successively shaped and reshaped by different generations and by peoples of different cultures.

scape—the clearing of land and its use in agriculture, the roads and other transport facilities, the settlement pattern with its arrangement of buildings and farmsteads, cities, and towns, and perhaps, some indications of environmental problems such as erosion and pollution. The finer details of the cultural landscape would be missing, of course. Something else, of vital importance, would be missing too. Any one such picture of the landscape, whether in the form of a painting, an engraving, a detailed description, a photograph taken at whatever scale and perspective, would fail us as a completely comprehensible picture of any

cultural landscape. Viewers (the readers), through their understanding of New Jersey's changing geography up until the time of that picture, should put the picture in the necessary perspectives of both time and space.

The Pre-European Cultural Landscape

It is sometimes assumed that members of human societies of relatively primitive technological level were necessarily shorter lived and generally less healthy than people of more advanced culture. In the context of the seventeenth-century contacts of Amerindians and Europeans in New Jersey,

FIGURE 4.4. *Scene on the Passaic (1874)*. The great stone viaduct is carrying the Morris Canal across the Passaic River, whose nonnavigability here is evidenced by the rock shelves in it. As population densities change and economies and technologies evolve, the human perception and use of the environment changes, too. Cultural landscapes are always changing, though at varying rates of evolution. (William Cullen Bryant, ed., *Picturesque America*. New York: D. Appleton and Co., 1874, p. 47)

this was not so. According to accounts of early European contacts with New Jersey's Lenape, the Amerindians were at least as tall as the Europeans and were of robust build ("well made" in the terminology of the day).

Before the successful invasion by Europeans, the land that became New Jersey had a rather small population (estimates run from 2,500 to 10,000) of Amerindians living in the Stone Age, technologically. Their imprint on the land was naturally much lighter than that resultant from a larger group of people, equipped with the power of machines and inanimate energy. As would later settlement patterns, those of the Amerindians showed uneven densities that reflected the varying possibilities of the land and other resources for supporting people. The Amerindians' perceptions of the resource base were far narrower than those of contemporary New Jerseyans, reflecting the Amerindians' Stone Age culture. There was relatively little job specialization among the Lenape; virtually every family was engaged in hunting and gathering, agriculture, and production of some craft items.

Only in rocky outcrops and steep cliffs of the mountains and along the marshy shoreline and bays were trees naturally absent. The Lenape had cleared many small openings in the woods to plant their crops. Because they moved their villages periodically as these fields declined in fertility and thus production, there were many "Indian oldfields" (abandoned clearings) that were useful to later European settlers. The villages were sited with care: near a water supply, above flood levels, and facing south to maximize passive solar heating of their homes and to minimize exposure to cold winter winds. The lighter soils of stream valleys were also preferred for ease of hoe agriculture, even though these light, sandy soils were not the most fertile. Both bark canoes and dugouts (log canoes) were used, and an extensive network of trails (really single-file paths) linked villages with a variety of natural environments. Using these trails, the Lenape could visit the seashore for seasonal feasting on fish and shellfish or hunt game in more distant grounds if hunting became unrewarding locally due to overhunting.

The Newark Basin and Highlands, south of the terminal moraine, seem to have had some of the more dense Lenape populations; the rugged ridges and the extensive coastal marshes were less appealing, though doubtless visited for hunting or fishing. The small number and primitive technology of the Lenape should not, however, lead to the conclusion that they left New Jersey untouched for the most part. The Lenape, like Amerindians elsewhere, deliberately set forest fires; much of the Pine Barrens' "natural vegetation" may have resulted from periodic burning, carried out to drive game in desired directions and to increase local populations of wildlife. Wild berries, roots, and nuts are also less plentiful in a mature forest than in a more open woods. Repeated burning made sense to the Lenape, and this habit made a significant impact on the forest, in terms of which plant and tree species thrived, and on animal populations.

The Lenape's semipermanent houses were made of saplings placed upright in the earth, a few feet apart along the walls and bent over at the top to touch one another, either in a circle, giving a domed roof, or in a rectangular plan, producing an arched or gabled roof. If built as a temporary shelter while hunting, this framework was covered by woven grass mats. More permanent dwellings were shingled with bark and perhaps sealed with clay. Smoke-holes were left in the roof. A "great house" for ceremonial purposes formed the focus of the little settlements. A version of a sauna was built on the banks of the stream (the villages were always near running water) with a pit in which heated stones were doused with water to provide steam. After this steambath, the Lenape would dive into the stream to finish cleansing themselves (Wacker 1975, 61–62).

Pre-European New Jersey was a boun-teous place, providing an admirable variety of wild and cultivated food for the Lenape. Lenape women did the cultivating while the men hunted and fished. The brackish and saltwater bays and coasts provided clams and oysters, and the Lenape were adept at building large fish weirs as well as fishing with hooks. Game animals seem to have included anything that lived in New Jersey. Deer were the favorite game, but both early European observations and archeological finds indicate that the Lenape also ate bear, elk, rabbit, groundhog, squir-rel, badger, raccoon, skunk, and dog, as well as a great variety of birds. A harsh variety of tobacco was available if the Lenape chose to finish off a meal with a smoke.

Animals dangerous to people were for-tunately few. Bears were present, but not so plentiful as to be much of a threat, and Schmidt asserted that the most dangerous animal for people was the anopheles mos-quito that carried malaria (Schmidt 1973, 21). Coyotes and an occasional timber wolf doubtless feared people more than the con-verse, and wildcats and mountain lions seem to have been relatively scarce outside the mountainous regions. Rattlesnakes, copperheads, and water moccasins were carefully avoided, especially the very ag-gressive moccasin, which was known to not only attack, but pursue.

Corn, beans, and wild rice kept well in pits in wigwams (houses, not tents), and the Lenape probably kept turkeys and rab-bits penned as a source of fresh meat. All in all, New Jersey must have provided a good food supply to its pre-European in-habitants.

Beyond their impact on natural vege-tation through burning, little remains today of the cultural landscape created by the Lenape. One of their lasting contributions, however, was the store of information on living in the natural environment that they passed on to the Europeans, along with their domesticated plants.

The Late Colonial Period

Because New Jersey was settled late among the American colonies, substantial numbers of Europeans had been present for less than a century in most of the state by the time of the Revolution. Many of the important cities of the future, however, were already a century and more from their founding—Newark, Elizabeth, Bergen (now Jersey City), Woodbridge, Piscataway, and Shrewsbury in the north (East Jersey), and Burlington and Salem, in South (West) Jersey. The Census of 1772 is incomplete, unfortunately, with the southern counties missing, but a reasonable estimate for New Jersey's population on the eve of the Re-volution would be between 90,000 and 120,000. The population of the area had increased over the pre-European Amerin-dian population by between twelvefold and twenty-fivefold, depending on which esti-mates of Amerindian numbers are ac-cepted. As shown on Figure 4.5, only Kit-tatinny Mountain, the northern, glaciated portion of the Highlands, and the Pine Barrens remained outside the *ecumene* (the effectively settled area) by 1776 (Wacker 1975, 126–157).

This great increase in population (though from a very small base) within the twin colonies had an unavoidable impact upon the natural landscape, especially in con-sideration of the drastically higher tech-nological level of the Euro-Americans. The clearing of the land was underway on a scale far above that of the Lenape. The European settler's most important tool was the axe. The Americans of the time lived in the Iron Age, technologically, but theirs was a wood-based society that used metal in much less volume than it used the products of the forest. Houses, furniture, fences, farming equipment, transportation equipment (wagons, coaches, boats), and fuel for household and industrial needs—all consumed wood.

The need for wood itself, though, does not explain the rapid destruction of the

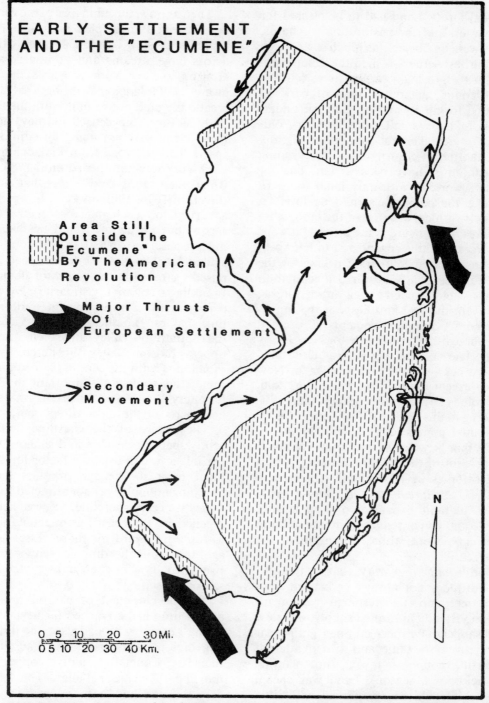

FIGURE 4.5. *Patterns of Early European Penetration.* The northeastern New Jersey bays and channels associated with the Hudson and the Delaware Bay and River for southern New Jersey were the major means of European penetration. The ocean shoreline, with its navigational hazards and the seemingly useless Pinelands to the interior, hosted few early settlements; the exceptions were Cape May and Toms River (indicated by the lower two arrows on the right).

original forest. Land had to be cleared for cultivation and for pasture and orchards. Trees were an obstacle as much as an asset. The earliest settlers copied the Lenape approach to farming—girdling trees (cutting a horizontal, encircling strip of bark off the tree to kill it) and burning off underbrush to clear small areas. Indian "oldfields" were taken full advantage of, too. Still, the job of clearing land, and keeping it clear, must have been a hard one for farmers working with only hand tools. In context, the colonials should be forgiven for their ruthless clearing of the land; what deserves our censure is the attitude toward resources that this engendered in later generations. Charcoal cutters, working for the iron furnaces, early acquired a reputation for a no-holds-barred attack on the forests; they were the real antithesis of the much-later conservation movement.

Although the growth rate for New Jersey in the late colonial period was close to 4 percent per year, the highest ever for New Jersey except for a brief period after 1900, the colony was typical rather than outstanding in this respect (Brush 1958, 25–28). Estimated populations of the colonies indicate that New Jersey accounted for about 5.6 percent of the total in Britain's American colonies in 1700 and 5.4 percent in 1770 (U.S. *Bureau of the Census* 1961, 756). The rapid expansion of New Jersey's people and its consequences to the cultural landscape were, thus, not atypical for America.

The *frontier mentality*, that is, the general attitude, not always verbalized, that land, trees, and other resources were available in virtually unlimited supply, was slow to disappear. Farmers cropped grain year after year on the same land with no attempt at fertilization or fallowing (not planting the field for a season). Land was cheap, and so it could be abandoned with little more regret than some of our contemporaries toss away empty beverage containers. Some farmers, at least, asserted that their land was theirs, to use, abuse, and abandon, if they chose (Schmidt 1973, 61).

Then as now, the main axis of movement lay between Philadelphia and New York. Travel was slow, as few bridges existed across large streams and none across the Hudson to New York or across the Delaware at Philadelphia (bridges at these locations would not be built until the twentieth century). Stagecoach journeys across New Jersey were not noted for comfort or speed. The first road from Philadelphia to New York was not opened until 1764, and it had many fords and ferries that slowed travel. In 1676, William Penn had ordered a survey for a canal across central New Jersey, but no action would be taken on this proposal until 1830. In addition to the Philadelphia-to-New York post road (supposedly created at the behest of Benjamin Franklin as colonial postmaster), New Jersey was part of an important south-north link that ran up the Delaware Valley to the Kittatinny Valley and then into the upper Hudson Valley. Sheltered by the mountains from the coastal plain and Piedmont, this route was important in Revolutionary War times when British troops held parts of the more direct route.

The nature of the coastline, with its gently shelving beaches and shallow, shifting inlets, was a negative factor for settlement prior to the age of mass leisure. Shipping not only was not attracted to New Jersey's ocean shoreline, it was actively repelled by the coast's grim reputation as a ship's graveyard for those vessels swept aground while heading for either of the two great bays at the flanks of the open seacoast itself.

The development of natural resources at this time had advanced far beyond that of the Lenape, who had used the limonite bog ores as body paint and had limited their use of metals to native copper from the upper Delaware Valley. The Schuler copper mine had been opened in 1712, and iron furnaces were "in blast" by the late colonial period in the Highlands (taking advantage of magnetite ore and some hematite) at Morristown, Hanover, Ringwood, Oxford, and Dover. Monmouth,

AMSHIP AMERIQUE. Stranded Sunday, January 7th, 1877, Three Miles North of Long Branch, N.J.   STEAMER RUSLAND. Stranded Sunday Morning, March 18th, 1877, at Long Branch, N.J.

BARNEGAT INLET.

FIGURE 4.6. *Hazards of the Jersey Coast.* These 1878 prints document the continuing hazardous nature of the New Jersey ocean shoreline for shipping. It was a coast to avoid, with no significant ports between the Raritan and Delaware estuaries. The shallow, shifting inlets, such as that at Barnegat, were suitable only for small craft, and in good weather at that. Their recreation functions, indicated in the scene at Barnegat, did not flower until the second half of the nineteenth century. (T. F. Rose, *Historical and Biographical Atlas of the New Jersey Coast.* Philadelphia: Woolman and Rose, 1878, p. 115)

Gloucester, and Burlington counties at that time also boasted iron furnaces, most of these based on limonite or bog ore. New Jersey was already on the way toward becoming a major iron-ore producing state. By 1790, at the first federal census, New Jersey would be mining 10,000 tn (9,070 t) of ore per year.

If the cultural landscape of 1776 was drastically different from that prior to the European invasion of the Lenape's homeland, it was to change even more radically in the decades ahead. New Jersey on the

eve of the American Revolution was in the infancy of the Industrial Revolution. Within sixty years, the state would have railroads, canals, and manufacturing enterprises in the forefront of developing technology, but for now the population was still largely agricultural, and the cities were commercial and crafts centers rather than industrial giants. Although there were plenty of portents for the future in New Jersey's geography of 1776, the locational assets of the state could not be more fully developed until the new nation expanded its com-

52

FIGURE 4.7. In 1844 Trenton was already a prosperous manufacturing center, served by both canal and railroad. Chosen as the state capital in 1790, Trenton was a good choice of a capital location. At the head of navigation on the Delaware River, on the Delaware and Raritan Canal, and astride the rapidly developing New York–Philadelphia corridor, Trenton's location is also a classic example of state capital choices—reasonably central, avoiding regional claims, and in a location expected to prosper as an industrial and commercial as well as administrative center. (*Early Woodcut Views of New York and New Jersey*. New York: Dover Publications, 1975, p. 98)

merce and industry.

French geographer Paul Vidal de la Blache said it well,

A country is a reservoir where potential powers lie asleep, the development of which devolves on the inhabitants. They give them shape while molding them to their use and taste. Thus men establish new relationships between scattered features. For the random effect of local circumstances, they substitute a new and coherent system of interlocking forces. (Translated in Gottmann 1961, 81.)

The Adolescence of Industrial New Jersey: 1840

Around 1840, the cultural landscape of New Jersey began to change with accelerating speed. Everything seemed to be changing; there were new economic and technological rules for decision making in everything from agriculture through mining and transport development to industrial and urban expansion. The year 1840 was a watershed in population growth rates, marking a transition from a period of net out-migration to the new farmlands of the West to net in-migration to operate the proliferating factories. Immigration was surging upward, and cities were beginning to grow explosively. New York City had emerged as the great port of immigration. The rising flood of hopeful, would-be Americans, many of them very poor and some sick as well, had incited strict immigrant screening and regulation by a city not anxious to add still more social welfare costs.

New Jersey, still determined to help *its* ports, especially Perth Amboy, achieve the business that their natural situations seemed to warrant, made sure that immigrants entering through its portals would be treated more leniently. Emigrant agents quickly exploited this considered generosity, diverting streams of future Americans to New Jersey ports and, often, to New Jersey industries.

The immigrants were welcome. They were necessary. Industry was booming in response to New Jersey's location between two great port cities and the state's superior transport facilities. By 1840, both the Morris Canal and Delaware and Raritan Canal were in operation, and both were heavy carriers of Pennsylvania anthracite to the industrial cities of New Jersey and to New York City. The Camden and Amboy Railroad (C and A) had been in operation for seven years between Bordentown and South Amboy. The Camden and Amboy was a spectacular success; it was an unusual railroad in several respects. Partly owned by the state, which condoned the C and A's absolute monopoly of transient trade through the busy corridor (it controlled the parallel Delaware and Raritan Canal as well), the railroad fattened on its heavy traffic. John Quincy Adams survived a crash on the railroad, but many others were less fortunate. Poor maintenance on rolling stock and roadbed both contributed to a high accident rate.

However arrogant the monopolies might have been, they contributed mightily to reshaping the cultural landscape of New Jersey. The state was no longer dependent on its own domestic industrial resources but could attract industry through its increasingly efficient transport interconnections. Most early railroads were built to funnel trade to a particular city; they were intended to serve purely local needs. The Camden and Amboy was intended as a through transient carrier in the northeast urban corridor. In this sense it was a forerunner of the gradually emerging philosophy that railroads should serve whole regions and should interconnect cities rather than develop isolated hinterlands.

Zinc was being exploited at Franklin, along with iron ore. The Morris Canal brought new life to Morris County iron works, and anthracite replaced the timbered-out reliance on charcoal. The state's production of iron ore was over 30,000 tn (27,210 t) annually and climbing.

The mutual advance of northern New Jersey's industrial cities and immigration transformed the cultural landscapes of that part of the state far more profoundly and

54

FIGURE 4.8. *Central Newark (1844).* At this time Newark was already renowned for its quality craftsmanship in leather, textiles, jewelry, carriages, and machinery. The city's seaport was large enough to be a port of entry, and the combination of the Morris Canal and railroads gave the city excellent transport connections. (*Early Woodcut Views of New York and New Jersey.* New York: Dover Publications, 1975, p. 86)

FIGURE 4.9. In 1844 Jersey City was already a railroad terminal for New York, reached by ferry as shown in this woodcut. The interstate dispute over the placement of the boundary had been settled, and the New Jersey shore was the site of several huge freight terminals and marshaling yards. The Cunard Lines' U.S. terminus was here, and the Morris Canal ended in a large barge basin near the present Liberty State Park across from the Statue of Liberty. (*Early Woodcut Views of New York and New Jersey.* New York: Dover Publications, 1975, p. 93)

noticeably than the southern part. New Jersey was becoming a microcosm of the United States—an industrial north that welcomed immigrants and a more slowly developing south that was more agricultural and less attractive to the new arrivals.

The significance of the 1840 cultural landscape is that the basic framework of industrialization and urbanization was in place. The massive frame would fill out over the next century, but the skeleton was established. Coal-fired steam power was firmly established as the dominant energy source, and the state's urban-industrial landscapes would wear a pall of coal smoke for almost a century. The great urban implosion had begun. People were leaving farms in marginal agricultural areas of New Jersey and its neighbors and in Ireland, Britain, Germany, and Scandinavia as well, streaming into the burgeoning industrial cities of New Jersey. The cities then growing were still painfully crowded; for the majority of their citizens, the geography of home, work, shop, and fun was a necessarily compact one, for they could not afford daily transportation to connect workplace and home. Intraurban and suburban rapid, cheap transit lay in the future.

Agriculture was continuing to specialize for urban markets and was advancing to a more scientific understanding of soil management, erosion control, and controlled breeding of both animals and plants. Farmers were benefiting from cheaper transport, via railroads, of fertilizer and farm products, but the rails also greatly expanded the hinterlands of urban market centers, forcing New Jersey farmers to compete with increasingly distant producers.

In the Pinelands, the pattern of isolated nodes of extractive industries continued from the Revolutionary War period and earlier. The old industrial triad of glass sand, charcoal, and iron ore was becoming a duo of glass sand and charcoal: glassmaking and papermaking survived longer than iron making. The iron furnaces, some twenty of them, had boomed in the Re-

volution and War of 1812 but could not compete with Pennsylvania and Morris County iron making fueled by coal. The local paper industry, based on pine and scrub oak, produced a rather coarse, yellowish paper like old-fashioned butcher's paper (the strong yellow tint was contributed by the iron content of the local water supply) that commanded only low prices. The labor force scattered with the successive failure of many Pinelands enterprises, leaving an island of lightly settled wilderness in sharp contrast to the prospering, industrializing cities.

In a sense, the scenery had been shifted, awaiting the next dynamic act of rapid industrialization.

The Triumph of Steam: 1900

The coming to maturity of the age of steam, around 1900, witnessed an associated transformation of New Jersey's landscapes. The railroads were approaching their zenith of power and prosperity, to be reached around 1920. A true, integrated transport *network* had been achieved as local and regional rail systems were standardized in gauge: 4 ft 8½ in. (1.43 m), the "English" gauge or distance between the rails, was accepted as the standard U.S. gauge. Many early locomotives imported from England had been built to those specifications. New Jersey, ever eccentric, had tried to popularize the "Jersey gauge" of 4 ft 10 in. (1.47 m), but lost out. To an astonishing degree, the state of New Jersey reflected the potentials, and the future liabilities, of heavy dependence on railroads. The Camden and Amboy monopoly (approved to avoid domination by Pennsylvania) had been ended; ironically, the right-of-way had been acquired by the Pennsylvania Railroad. Railroads had multiplied as competing lines tapped the Pennsylvania coal fields for the benefit of northeastern New Jersey and New York City and as railroads demonstrated their economic power by transforming the Jersey shore from a near-wilderness spotted with

FIGURE 4.10. It was "the view from Philadelphia" that indeed was important to Camden, a typical industrial satellite of a metropolis, shown here in an 1844 woodcut. The Delaware was not bridged at Philadelphia until 1926, so that the time and cost handicaps of the "Camden ferries" (an early version is shown here) were part of a markedly lower pace of urban expansion in the New Jersey portion of Philadelphia's metropolitan area. (*Early Woodcut Views of New York and New Jersey*. New York: Dover Publications, 1975, p. 90)

FIGURE 4.11. *Summertime Fun: The North Jersey Shore as Represented in an 1870s Engraving.*
The work of an artist more enthusiastic than talented (notice the awkward diver), this print shows
one of the many bathhouses that catered to the needs of the day trippers, brought for just one day
by the railroads. (T. F. Rose, *Historical and Biographical Atlas of the New Jersey Coast.* Philadelphia:
Woolman and Rose, 1878, p. 200)

two or three resort towns into a nearly
continuous strip of urban pleasure factories.

The great cities had begun to expand
outward, following the steel ribbons of both
the commuter railroads and the proliferating electric streetcar lines. Growth was
there, but it was channeled and directed
growth, for the rails could not economically
spread everywhere.

The flood of immigrants had quickened,
its source shifting around the close of the
century toward eastern and southern Europe. The skills level, education level, and
ready adaptability to urban industrial life
changed also. The large component of Brit-

ish immigrants was coming from an already
industrialized society. They were more likely
to have manufacturing experience and skills
than were later immigrants from more-
rural backgrounds. For example, the
post–Civil War expansion of textile industries in North Jersey was accelerated
by large-scale transfers of workers, machinery, and capital. Scottish and Ulster
(northern Ireland) thread manufacturers
established branch plants in New Jersey,
as did English carpet weavers. The high
rate of British and Irish skilled-worker
immigration slowed, though, as the technology of the industry progressed. The
highest human skill was necessary on the

simplest, crudest machines. As the machines became more automatic and more reliable, an operative with less skill and experience could tend the machine. Machinists' skills were still very much in demand, but much of the routine work in the mills was now taken over by the unskilled, recent immigrant who often was handicapped by a temporarily inadequate command of English.

To put it plainly, many immigrants (and multigeneration Americans too, for that matter) were shamefully exploited. In 1900, half of all New Jerseyans of foreign birth lived in Essex, Hudson, and Passaic counties, and most of the rest lived in Middlesex, Union, and Bergen counties; the other fifteen counties—still nonindustrialized rural areas—had "native stock" majorities (Vecoli 1965, 180). "Home work" was a notorious abuse in the garment, cigar, and artificial-flower industries, mostly among north Jersey's immigrant communities. In this system, work was subdivided—the making of buttonholes, for example, was one job and was subcontracted out to households on a "piecework" basis. This meant that household workers, probably including children, were paid by the unit of work completed, rather than by the hour. Some bitter strikes were the result of abuse of labor, particularly in Paterson. In Newark, dangerous working conditions helped that city achieve the unhappy distinction of having the highest death rate among U.S. cities of over 100,000 population (Cunningham 1966b, 90).

Industrialization in South Jersey had its problems, too. A vicious heritage of the iron furnaces and glass works of the Pine Barrens persisted in the glass industry until 1900. In a system operating like that in the Appalachian coalfields of the time, employees of the relatively isolated glass towns were dependent upon the company for housing and provisions in "company towns." Workers were advanced credit in the form of scrip, or private money, that could be spent only in the company store. Prices at the company store just happened

to be above the competition, for there was no competition for the scrip, only for legal currency. By payday, when workers were entitled to be paid in legal currency, their debts to the company would exceed their wages, and so they would see no cash. A "benevolent" company would issue scrip as an advance on wages, and so the circle of indebtedness would continue. Reportedly, the majority of Bridgeton's 7,000 glass workers in 1899 never received cash at all. Workers also were required to live in company houses. This industrial peonage was ended by a series of strikes in 1900 that ended compulsory patronage of company stores. The South Jersey glassworkers, mostly native born, were so resentful against immigrants, who had been used as strike breakers, that local unions set a $500 initiation fee for foreign-born workers and one of $5 for "native Americans" (Vecoli 1965, 91).

Some of the foreign-born workers had their own grudges to settle. Paterson schoolteacher and parttime inventor, John Holland, was working on a more-practical submarine. His first successful effort, the *Fenian Ram*, was financed by the Irish immigrants' Fenian Society, who allegedly intended to use it to sink British warships!

Although notorious as a haven for big business (the state's tax incorporation laws attracted many companies to become New Jersey corporations), New Jersey was among the first states to enact employers' liability for industrial casualties. It was first in encouraging free night schools in which immigrants were taught English and the history of the United States.

The cultural landscape of 1900 was only two generations from that of 1840, which obviously was within living memory, but 1900 was an entire industrial revolution away in technology. A generation in late maturity then had witnessed some of the most profound changes in a cultural landscape observable any time, anywhere. If there was a personification of these changes and the new age they seemed to produce, it was Thomas Alva Edison. Like New

Jersey's other famous citizen, Woodrow Wilson, Edison had migrated to the state as an already successful and mature man. Having sold an improved stock ticker for $40,000, Edison moved to Newark from New York. It was a wise choice for Edison, who was determined to make a living as an inventor. His location requirements included access to the financial center, Manhattan, for financing production of his inventions. He also needed to be in a highly diversified industrial center in order to be able to call upon specialized expertise in any facet of industry. Typically pioneering a future trend, Edison then moved to the cheaper, but still highly accessible, suburbs. He built a new laboratory at Menlo Park, where he perfected, in addition to the phonograph and electric light, his most important contribution—the "invention factory" or research lab. The think tanks of the present day, such as at Princeton, that gather together a team of specialists to focus on specific problems, follow an Edison tradition. In 1887, Edison moved his research labs to West Orange, New Jersey, where they survive as a National Historic Site. (The Menlo Park buildings and contents were removed to Greenfield Village in Dearborn, Michigan, by Henry Ford as a tribute to his friend Edison.) Thanks to Edison's motion-picture projector, the first movie studio in the world was built in West Orange.

Commuting had become a way of life for many by 1900, and New Jersey was becoming the quintessential commuting state. Back in 1874, a popular book had proclaimed,

> Indeed thousands of the businessmen of New York live in the midst of these [New Jersey] picturesque scenes, an hours ride serving to convey them from the turmoil of city occupations to the serene quiet and sylvan charms of rural life. Jersey City and Newark are flourishing cities with populations of their own; but the multitudinous smaller towns and villages within a radius of fifty miles owe their existence to the surplus population of New York. (Bryant 1874, 50)

Literally millions more yearned to "be conveyed from the turmoil" too, and they would be, by the maturation of the automobile, then in its infancy. Individual mobility for the average person was to be the force behind the continued reshaping of the cultural landscape.

NAMES ON THE LAND

The names given to both physical and cultural features on the land reflect the cultural traits and background of the people who provided the names. Names on the land are not a continuously revised catalog of the changing mix of ethnic and cultural contributions and participation in the development of the state, however. Only the first waves of European settlers had the options of naming physical features and settlements, often choosing more or less garbled versions of Amerindian names to supplement those reflecting their own background. Later immigrants arrived in a landscape already labeled; their opportunities to coin place-names usually were limited to more ephemeral or small-scale place-names, such as unofficial neighborhood designations, the names of churches, synagogues, temples, cemeteries, and, of course, individual businesses and service organizations. Although these names are "on the land" too, observable in a personal view of the cultural landscape, they rarely appear on maps.

Two classic studies of place-names used for the minor physical features of small streams established that New Jersey was a transitional state, showing the influences of major cultural hearths to the north-northeast and to the west-southwest (Zelinsky 1955; Kurath 1949). For example, the Dutch usage for stream or channel, *kill*, is most common in the Hudson Valley in New York State, but also is found in the areas of New Jersey where early Dutch settlers had a chance to establish such place-names firmly enough to resist change by later English arrivals. Northwestern New Jersey's Walkill River (the *river* is redundant) and the Arthur Kill and Kill Van Kull channels separating Staten Island from New Jersey are the best-known examples. *Branch*, a small-stream designation common from Maryland to West Virginia, is evident in many such names in the Pinelands, while *brook*, a New England favorite, is more prevalent in old East Jersey, reflecting the New England origins of many early arrivals there.

The names given to settlements reflect New Jersey's rich cultural heritage. Here, names persist as the most obvious contribution of the long-vanished Lenni Lenape. Colonial place-names exhibit nostalgia for the "old country"; a tendency to name one's new home for the old is evident, as well as an understandable flattery of various royalty, patrons, and local officials.

Historical personalities, especially presidents, form another place-name grouping, along with a large number of names indicating economic function, such as mills, ports, and (iron) furnaces. Sprinkled in among the historical, ethnic, Amerindian, patriotic, and physical-characteristic names are those of exotic origin with no apparent relationship to New Jersey or New Jerseyans other than that they sounded interesting to someone.

County names are primarily British colonial namesakes—Camden, Cumberland, Burlington, Essex, Gloucester, Middlesex, Monmouth, Salem, Somerset, and Sussex. Just to prove that place-names borrowed from across the ocean need not reflect the new realities, Sussex—originally "South Province/Kingdom"—ended up in the extreme northwestern corner! Bergen, Hudson, and Cape May (Captain Mey) speak to the Dutch explorers and their heritage. Mercer honors a popular Revolutionary War general; Morris, a colonial governor (the first "native" New Jerseyan to hold that post); and Hunterdon, another early governor. Passaic is the sole Amerindian name among New Jersey's counties, while Atlantic and Ocean share an obvious physical reference.

Amerindian place-names number among the largest single source, and contribute some of the most interesting—Almonesson, Cinnaminson, Macopin, Mantoloking, Matawan, Parsippany, Piscataway, Rancocas, Secaucus, Tuckahoe, and Wickatunk are but a few of the Lenni Lenape heritage. England, Scotland, and Wales are amply represented by Albion, Andover, Barrington, Cardiff, Chatham, Chester, Deptford, Dover, Greenwich, Newark, Paisley, Oxford, Kenilworth, Berkshire Valley, Birmingham, and Runnemede. Perth Amboy is a hybrid of a Scottish name with an Indian one.

Physical descriptions abound in such names as Atlantic Highlands, Bay Head, Cold Spring, Gravelly Run, Great Notch, and Long Valley; *sea, beach, ocean, oak, pine,* and *cedar* form parts of dozens of place-names. The mid-nineteenth-century craze for using "classic" (Greek or Roman, mostly) place-names, very visible in New York State, touched New Jersey but lightly, with Sparta and Troy Hill.

Historical personages are represented by Washington (several times), Berkeley and Carteret (but not John Fenwick), Jefferson, Lafayette, Madison, Monroe (several), and Lincoln. Pioneer Elizabeth Haddon is represented by Haddonfield and Haddon Heights, and William of Orange is celebrated by "the Oranges"—East, South, and West Orange, and just plain Orange. Fittingly, Thomas Edison is represented on maps, as is the great bridge engineer, John Roebling, although by a "company town" built by Roebling. Richard Stockton, one of the state's signatories to the U.S. Constitution, is memorialized by both a town and a state college; another state college, Kean State, commemorates another famous New Jersey political family including the governor elected in 1981, Thomas Kean. President James Garfield, who chose the Jersey shore for his convalescence after his tragic shooting in 1881, is remembered in a northern New Jersey industrial community (although he died despite the supposed curative effects of sea air).

Ethnic and religious groups are well

represented in Baptistown, Quakertown, Quaker Bridge, Englishtown, Frenchtown, Dutch Neck, Cornish, Hibernia, Scotch Plains, Hamburg, Berlin, Cologne, New Russia, and Swedesboro. Less clearly connected with specific immigrant groups are New Egypt and New Lisbon.

Functional place-names abound, such as Glassboro, Millville, Bricktown, Ironia, Indian Mills, Dover Forge, Mine Hill, Copper Hill, Hanover Furnace and Hampton Furnace, Stafford Forge, Merchantville, and Bargaintown. Bivalve is, appropriately, the old port for the greatest single oyster bed in the United States at one time, the Maurice River cove of Delaware Bay. Despite New Jersey's prominence in Revolutionary War battles and maneuvers, only Fort Lee commemorates such an antique military function (Fort Dix began its career as a basic training camp in World War I).

Famous taverns that were stops along stagecoach routes have become part of the landscape of names—Blue Anchor, Cross Keys, Pole Tavern, Seven Stars, White Horse, Black Horse, and Woods Tavern. Bridgeport, Bridgeton, and Bridgeville complement Port Elizabeth, Port Mercer, Port Monmouth, and Port Republic; Egg Harbor was wishful thinking, because a proposed canal that would have justified "harbor" was never built.

Headquarters, too small really to be one for anything sizable, is not far from Sergeantsville. Friendship, Hope, and Tranquillity grace the map, along with Mount Freedom, Mount Hope, Mount Joy, and Mount Pleasant. Penny Pot, Ongs Hat, and Gum Tree Corner make life a little more interesting in South Jersey, while along the seashore, Loveladies appears not to be a command or wish, but a misspelling of a

FIGURE 4.12. *The Windsor Hotel, Cape May.* A wealthy South Jersey glass manufacturer, an admirer of British royalty, named his Cape May hotel after Windsor Castle, assuming that the name would reassure his clientele of royal treatment. Cape May's Victorian seafront survived virtually intact until the 1970s, attracting tourists to an otherwise peripheral location with severely eroded beaches. Although admired from the outside, too few tourists actually stayed in the vintage hotels; the Windsor, vacant for several years, burned in 1979.

town founded by a Captain Lovelady. Double Trouble must have been, for someone, while Cheesequake refers to a "quaking bog"—a soggy landscape like fresh gelatin dessert.

Resorts, especially, like to bask in the reflected glory of famous resorts elsewhere, and so the seashore gives us Avalon, Margate, Miami Beach, and Ventnor. The British seaside resort of Brighton unaccountably becomes a mountain resort in New Jersey, along with Newfoundland and Alpine, atop the northern Palisades.

Modern real estate developers are fond of inventing attractive names for suburban developments, frequently ignoring the absence of some of the physical attributes claimed. Brooklawn and Fair Lawn are names that surely must have helped sell houses, as did Laurel Springs, Spring Lake, and Maplewood. Perhaps the ultimate example of modern image shaping was Camden County's Delaware Township; after the construction there of an immensely successful shopping center, the township voted to change its name to that of the shopping center, Cherry Hill.*

TELEPHONE-DIRECTORY LISTINGS

Telephone-directory listings present many opportunities to those interested in the cultural study of a region. A readily usable, if general, guideline to the ethnic-religious makeup of any part of the United States is the section of business-services-institutional listings in the telephone book (the "yellow pages").

Cultural geographer Wilbur Zelinsky has suggested a categorization of Christian religious denominations into three major types: British Colonial, Immigrant European, and Native American. British Colonial groups were present in large numbers, proportionally, before the Revolution; they include Protestant Episcopal, Presbyterian bodies, Methodist bodies, Congregational and Baptist bodies, and Friends (Quakers). Zelinsky's Immigrant European groups include Roman Catholic, Lutheran bodies, Evangelical and Reformed groups, Polish National Catholic, Armenian, Brethren, Mennonite, Reformed bodies, Eastern Orthodox, Uniate Catholics, and Moravian groups. Native American sects are those founded in America even though they may be based on earlier philosophical and theological concepts. These include Pentecostal, Disciples of Christ, Latter-Day Saints (known familiarly as Mormons), Adventist bodies, Churches of Christ, Jehovah's Witnesses, Unitarian and Universalist churches, Nazarene, Assemblies of God, Churches of God, Evangelical United, and Christian Science (Zelinsky 1961, 146).

The groupings were intended as general

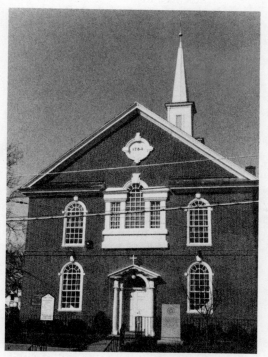

FIGURE 4.13. *Old Swedes Church, Swedesboro.* This 1784 brick church replaced a log church built by Swedish colonists three generations earlier. The Swedes were an early element in New Jersey's polyethnic heritage.

*Townships in New Jersey are the lowest order of local government, subsidiary to counties. They are almost always low-population-density rural areas.

FIGURE 4.14. *Holy Trinity Church, Vineland.* This Russian Orthodox church represents a migrational group two centuries removed from the early colonial Swedes. Eastern Europeans joined southern Europeans as the dominant groups among new arrivals a century ago.

categories for the entire United States and thus are not completely satisfactory for understanding New Jersey. Certainly, some later immigrants affiliated with "colonial" churches, and doubtless some descendants of colonial Americans joined "immigrant" churches. Also, many churches categorized as primarily immigrant were present before the Revolution. In New Jersey, colonial Dutch and French Reformed churches were both present before 1740 (Wacker 1975, 167), and so have been added to "colonial" for purposes of sampling New Jersey telephone-directory listings under "Churches" and "Synagogues and Temples." Five telephone directories were used: (1) *Jersey City–Bayonne–Hoboken and Vicinity,* to represent an aging core-city area; (2) *Bergen County,* to represent both inner- and outer-suburban rings; (3) *Hackettstown-Washington and Vicinity,* to represent the still primarily rural-exurban fringe of the northwestern Highlands (Warren County); (4)

Salem, to sample the relatively slow-growth agricultural landscapes of the southwest; and (5) *Cape May–Wildwood–Ocean City,* as a seashore area with both historic, early settlement and more recent growth through retirement and some immigration. With the transfer of Reformed churches to the colonial category, the number of listings for each category is shown in Table 4.1, and the number of different denominations and religious bodies in Table 4.2.

The cultural diversity of New Jersey is at once apparent. Even relatively lightly populated Warren and Cape May counties each have twenty different religious groups represented. Thirty-four percent of Jersey City–Bayonne–Hoboken's rich variety of religious groups were "colonial," while 55 percent of Warren County's were in that category. While no synagogues or temples were present in either Salem or Warren county (there are two Jewish community centers in Warren County), twenty-eight in

TABLE 4.1

Generalized Origin-Types of Religious Bodies as Represented
by Telephone-Directory Listings

County/ Area	Origin Categories of Christian Sects[a]			Jewish Congregations	Other
	Colonial	Immigrant	Native		
Jersey City, etc.	55	36	58	11	
Bergen County	100	46	58	28	
Warren County	22	5	13	--	
Salem	31	4	20	--	
Cape May, etc.	27	15	20	1	1[b]

Source: New Jersey Bell Telephone 1981 directories.

The numbers refer to congregations, churches, synagogues,
and temples. Church- or synagogue-related schools or
community centers are not separately tabulated or included
as religious bodies, even though they may offer religious
services. Obviously, there is no attempt to indicate size
of membership.

Listings that were not within a directory's geographic
area were not counted; some religious groups likely to
attract members over multiple-directory areas from
scattered minorities, like Jewish congregations in rural
areas, may list themselves in directories of adjacent
areas as a service.

[a]As modified from Wilbur Zelinsky, 1961.

[b]Masjic (Mosque) Muhammad.

TABLE 4.2

Number of Different Denominations and Religious Bodies
Present, According to Directory Listings

Jersey City	42	Salem County	20
Bergen County	48	Cape May County	23
Warren County	20		

Source: New Jersey Bell Telephone 1981 directories.

Bergen County indicates a large outflow from the former concentrations of Jews in New York City, so that Jewish congregations form 12 percent of that multiethnic county's total.

The statistics do not convey the full, rich variety of religious denominations; in the Hudson County (Jersey City) listings, Byzantine Catholic, Eastern Orthodox, Greek Orthodox, Polish National, and Russian Orthodox are all merged into "immigrant." In the same way, Native American churches have responded to the needs of many diverse groups of immigrants, as in Hudson County's two Latin American Pentecostal churches and Spanish-language Baptist and Church of Christ congregations

and Bergen County's Korean Methodists and Armenian Presbyterians.

The varying architectural styles, levels of affluence, size, and locations of religious bodies and their buildings form an interesting as well as informative part of the cultural landscape of any community. Since religious structures tend to be very solidly built, with dates of organization and/or construction prominently displayed, they help "date" the development of new neighborhoods in cities, give clues to both original settlement and later waves of immigrants, and even document "neighborhood succession" by different ethnic or racial groups through their sometimes apparent transfer to other religious groups. In urban neighborhoods populated largely by poor members of racial minorities, the use of former commercial buildings, such as banks or stores, as churches (see Figure 4.15) tells the observer something about both racial-ethnic succession and the decline of inner-city business districts due to suburbanization.

IS NEW JERSEY A POLITICAL BELLWETHER?

New Jersey's cross section of U.S. voters, reasonably typical of the nation even if skewed in favor of higher-than-average foreign stock, industrial-urban, and union-member proportions, has a somewhat uncertain record as a "bellwether," or truly representative sample of the mood of the national electorate. New Jersey voters, in presidential elections from 1840 to 1900, were almost as often out of step with the nation as they were supporters of winners (see Table 4.3). New Jersey voted against Abraham Lincoln, both times; consistently supported native-born Grover Cleveland, whether he won or lost; voted against Grant the first time, for him the second; and supported losing Democratic candidates in 1876 and 1880. From 1892 (Grover Cleveland) to 1912, New Jerseyans picked winners, two Democrats and four Republicans. New Jersey Governor Woodrow Wilson

FIGURE 4.15.   *Central City Abandonment and Recycling—A Converted Bank in Camden.*

TABLE 4.3
"So Goes New Jersey...?" New Jersey's Popular Vote Choices for President

Election	N.J. Vote[a]	Party of National Victor[b]	Election	N.J. Vote	Party of National Victor
1980	W	R	1908	W	R
1976	L	D	1904	W	R
1972	W	R	1900	W	R
1968	W	R	1896	W	R
1964	W	D	1892	W	D
1960	L	D	1888	L	R
1956	W	R	1884	W	D
1952	W	R	1880	L	R
1948	L	D	1876	L	R
1944	W	D	1872	W	R
1940	W	D	1868	L	R
1936	W	D	1864	L	R
1932	W	D	1860	L	R
1928	W	R	1856	W	D
1924	W	R	1852	W	D
1920	W	R	1848	W	(Whig)
1916[c]	L	D	1844	L	D
1912[c]	W	D	1840	W	(Whig)

Source: Compiled by the author from U.S. Bureau of the Census, Historical Statistics of the United States: Colonial Times to 1957 (Washington, D.C.: U.S. Bureau of the Census, 1961, pp. 686-689), and from contemporary voting records.

[a]W=Winner; L=Loser in national elections.

[b]D=Democratic; R=Republican.

[c]In these years, the only president who was an adult resident of New Jersey, Woodrow Wilson, ran, successfully, on the Democratic ticket. He won both elections.

won his state on his first try for the White House, but lost it in 1916. From 1920 to 1944, New Jersey again backed winners, voting three times Republican, four times Democratic. The state's voters rejected Harry Truman, but supported Eisenhower both times. All in all, Jersey ballots sup-

ported national winners more consistently in the twentieth century than in the nineteenth. Neither major party, clearly, can assume that New Jersey will be in its column. If there is a pattern in modern New Jersey's presidential politics, it is that New Jersey has been more consistently conservative than the nation as a whole. Starting with 1900, New Jerseyans have backed losing candidates in only four elections out of twenty-one; each of these "losing" votes was for a Republican (see Table 4.3).

The high degree of suburbanization may have a bearing on New Jersey's tendency to vote for Republicans, who in national elections are generally agreed to be the more conservative. In 1976, the closest of national elections among recent ones (1972 and 1980 amounted to Republican landslides), northern New Jersey showed a strong tendency to vote Republican outside the old urban-core counties of Hudson and Essex and the predominantly corridor counties of Middlesex and Mercer. Of the four shore counties, only Atlantic, with its aging and heavily Democratic core city of Atlantic City, voted for Carter, while the Philadelphia Metro and Southwest Farm regions* went Democratic.

*Philadelphia Metro, Southwest Farm, and New York Metro designate three of New Jersey's seven regions described in Chapter 10.

CHAPTER 5

POPULATION CHARACTERISTICS

After the effective reinforcement of their long-standing general claim to the area by the English in the late 1600s, the European population began to increase. By 1700, only a third of a century after New Jersey was officially named as an English colony, an estimated 20,000 Europeans (together with a few thousand Lenni Lenapes) lived in New Jersey (see Table 5.1). The first complete colonial census, in 1726, showed almost 30,000; the number climbed to 184,000 by 1790, the first U.S. census. This increase of over 500 percent in sixty-four years was New Jersey's first great population surge (Brush 1958, 17–19). It was fueled by emigration not only from England but also from the other colonies. Dissidents from the New England and Long Island communities quickly moved into New Jersey, together with Dutch from the Hudson Valley in search of cheap land. The basic outlines of New Jersey's settlement were filling in (this was shown in Figure 4.5). These early settlements showed the strong affinity for the Newark Basin Piedmont and inner coastal plain locales that still predominates in New Jersey's population distribution. The first permanent European settlements followed the banks of the Delaware Bay and Delaware River and the complex of waterways to the northeast— the Hudson River, Raritan Bay, Raritan River, Newark Bay, and the nearby areas. The Highlands were penetrated early, but settlement occurred only in accessible valleys; the outer coastal plain and seashore remained virtually empty.

POPULATION GROWTH PATTERNS

Slower-than-National-Average Growth

New Jersey, scene of many important revolutionary battles because it lay between the two most important cities in the colonies, was ravaged by war. It is said that only South Carolina suffered as much wartime destruction, proportionally. Then, too, large tracts of good farmland, available cheaply or for the taking, were more likely on the western frontier than in New Jersey. While the new state grew at rates that would be considered impressive now, the net growth rates from 1790 to 1840 were about half those of the nation as a whole (see Table 5.1). High natural-increase rates within New Jersey supplied a net out-migration during this early period (Brush 1958, 17–20).

After 1840 the industrialization of New Jersey, with its associated urbanization, began to attract large numbers of immigrants from overseas as well as some from neighboring states. Until the 1840s, however, the ethnic makeup of New Jersey changed relatively little. In 1807, U.S. geographer Jedidiah Morse could describe New Jerseyans as,

69

TABLE 5.1
New Jersey's Population, by Census Years, and Percent
Increase Between Census Years

Year	N.J. Population	Net Total Gain	% Increase Over Last Census N.J.	U.S.A.[a]
1700[b]	20,000[b]			
1726	29,861			
1790	184,139			
1800	211,149	27,010	14.7	35.1
1810	245,562	34,413	16.3	36.4
1820	277,575	32,013	13.0	33.1
1830	320,823	43,248	15.6	33.4
1840	373,306	52,483	16.4	32.6
1850	489,555	116,249	31.1	35.8
1860	672,035	182,480	37.3[c]	35.5
1870	906,096	234,061	34.8[c]	26.6
1880	1,131,116	225,020	24.8	26.0
1890	1,444,933	313,817	27.7[c]	25.5
1900	1,883,669	438,736	30.4[c]	20.7
1910	2,537,167	653,498	34.7[c]	21.0
1920	3,155,900	618,733	24.4[c]	15.0
1930	4,041,334	885,434	28.1[c]	16.1
1940	4,160,165	118,831	2.9	7.2
1950	4,835,329	675,164	16.2[c]	14.5
1960	6,066,782	1,231,453	25.5[c]	18.5
1970	7,171,112	1,104,330	18.2[c]	13.3
1980	7,364,158	193,046	2.7	11.4

Source: Compiled from U.S. census reports, years indicated
(1726 data from first complete colonial census).

[a]Percentage increases in U.S. population, 1790 to 1920
(and 1950 to 1960) include territorial acquisitions as
new states are added.

[b]Estimated.

[c]Intercensal gain exceeding national average.

. . . a collection of low Dutch [Hollanders], Germans, English, Scotch, Irish and New Englanders or their descendents. National attachment, and mutual convenience, have generally induced these several kinds of people to settle together in a body, and in this way, their peculiar national manners, customs and character are still preserved, especially among the poorer class of people. . . . There are in this state about fifty Presbyterian congregations . . . forty congregations of Friends, thirty of Baptists, twenty-five of Episcopalians, twenty-eight of Dutch Reformed, besides Methodists and a settlement of Moravians. (Morse 1807, 184)

Morse, a minister of the Congregational Church in Charlestown, Massachusetts, was least impressed by New Jersey's Dutch.

A great part of the inhabitants are Dutch, who although they are in general, neat and industrious farmers, have very little enterprise, and seldom adopt any new improvements in husbandry; because, through habit and want of education to expand and liberalize their minds, they think their old modes of tilling the best. Indeed this is the case with the great body of the common people, and proves an almost insurmountable obstacle to agricultural improvements. (Morse 1807, 184–185)

Industrial-Immigrant Boom, 1840 to 1930

The percentage increase in New Jersey's population, between censuses, almost doubled from 1840 to 1850 in comparison with the preceding series of census years (see Table 5.1). In 1860, New Jersey's rate of population growth exceeded the national average for the first time; it remained above the national average until 1940 with only one exception, the 1870–1880 period.

The series of computer-generated maps, Figures 5.1 through 5.5, shows changes in *relative* density of population within the state, not growth of density overall. The maps are based on quintiles (fifths), such as the highest 20 percent of the state's range of population density within that census year. The map series indicates a population-density distribution that has moved from a fairly dispersed rural farm population with industrial-commercial cities rising in the northeast (see Figure 5.1) to an increasingly sharply defined urban-rural forking, then a suburbanizing population expanding the area of the medium-density zone. Interestingly the urban northeast (Hudson and Essex counties in particular) has been the most densely populated portion of the state for a century.

For forty years after 1840, the majority of European immigrants to New Jersey were Irish, fleeing the deadly combination of potato blight, mismanagement of charitable relief, and the long persistence of absentee-landlord feudalism at home. Germans and English supplemented the Irish, and the ethnic makeup remained strongly northwest European in origin until 1900. Then the tide shifted in origins toward southern and eastern Europe: Italy and Poland joined Germany and the United Kingdom as major sources. As late as 1970, 30 percent of all Jerseyans were listed by the census as being of "foreign stock"— persons who either were born overseas or had at least one foreign-born parent. Italy alone supplied almost one-quarter of New Jersey's "foreign stock."

After 1860, of course, New Jersey's beckoning frontier was one of cities and industrial jobs rather than one of cheap farmland, although a minor invasion of the Pinelands in southern New Jersey continued (see Figure 5.2). There, an agricultural frontier was created by new, cheaper fertilization techniques, and both Italians and eastern European Jews were attracted to new farming communities.

The definite slowing of overseas immigration after World War I had little overall effect on New Jersey's growth rates. Indeed, the 1920–1930 expansion of 28 percent was nearly double that of the U.S. average. The suburbanization of both New York Metro and Philadelphia Metro was well under way, adding much of the 885,000 gain (see Figure 5.3). The 1930s, however, produced the second-lowest intercensal

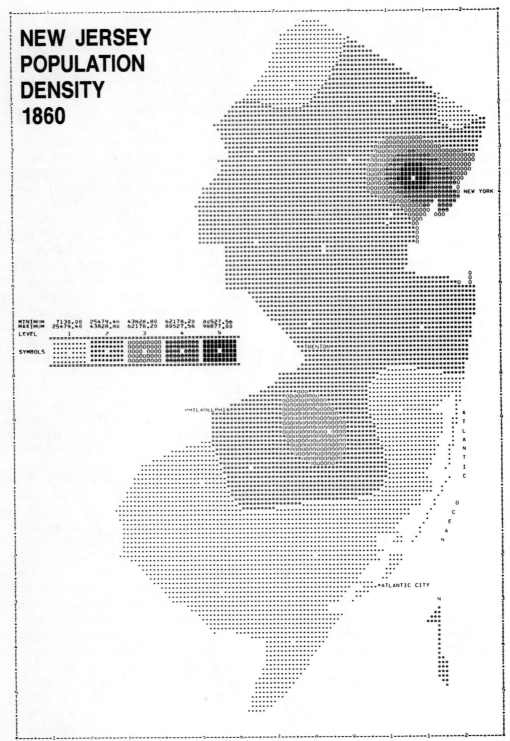

FIGURE 5.1. In 1860, the farming populations of the inner coastal plain and Newark Basin provided a broad area of low-medium relative density, with an extension into the iron- and glass-producing Pinelands and a center at Newark. Figures 5.1 through 5.5, computer-generated maps based on U.S. census data, were programmed by Emilio Cruz.

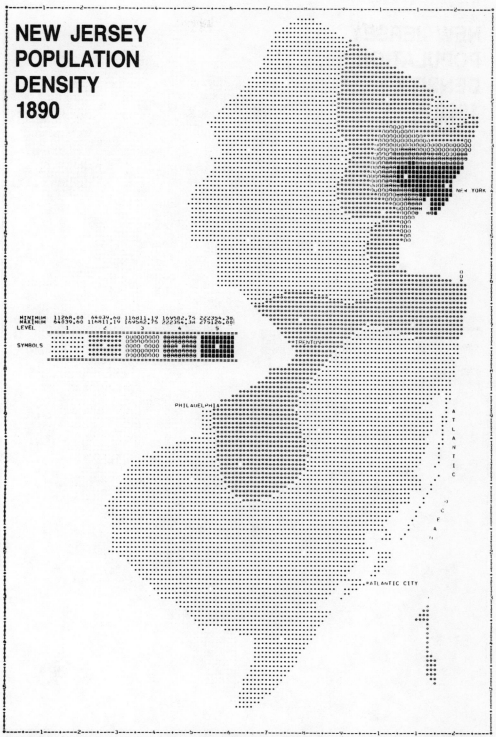

FIGURE 5.2. The urbanization of an industrial population is evident on this map, with the Pinelands, northwestern mountains, and southwestern farm belt all much lower in relative density.

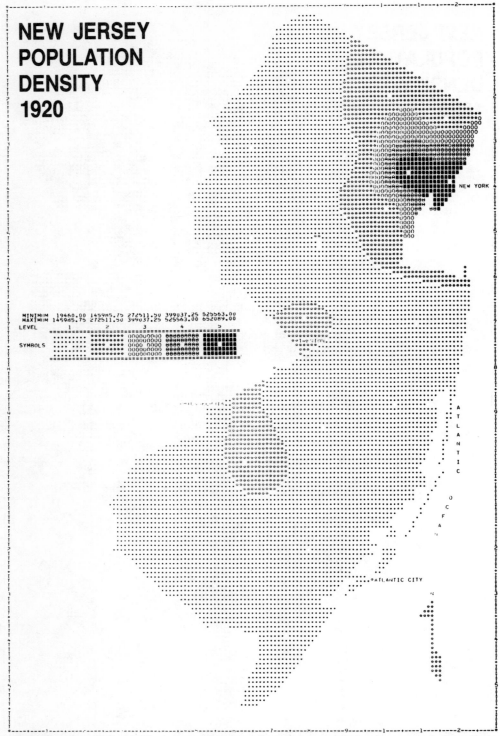

FIGURE 5.3. The 1920 census shows a highly concentrated urban population, little different in pattern than in 1890, but on the threshold of suburbanization.

growth rate ever recorded for New Jersey, 2.9 percent (see Table 5.1). In the economic chaos of the Great Depression, natural-increase rates plummeted. In addition, the birthrate normally is lower among urban-ites than rural populations, so that New Jersey's birthrate fell to about thirteen per thousand people in 1940 compared to about twenty-eight per thousand in 1920 (Brush 1958, 19–21). The 1920s had been the last of a long series of years in which increase by net in-migration exceeded increase through births. In the decade of the 1920s, net increase by immigration to New Jersey was over half a million. In the 1930s, two effects of the depression led to a net loss through migration for the first time in almost a century. With few prospects for jobs and an overall uncertainty about the economy, fewer people migrated into heav-ily urbanized New Jersey. In fact, in the face of near starvation, many recent immi-grants from other states went "back home" to weather the depression by moving back in with relatives and perhaps doing a little farming on the old homestead.

The Postwar Years

World War II was the beginning of a recovery, in terms of the economy and associated population growth. The growth rate was over 16 percent between 1940 and 1950, the second-lowest rate in a century, but still a strong comeback. Industries pow-ered by war orders provided the jobs that lured workers to New Jersey, with huge shipyards in Newark and Camden, aircraft-engine plants in Paterson, and hundreds of other industrial plants around the state producing for the war effort.

The acceleration of suburban develop-ment after the war built on the base already established (see Figure 5.4). During the 1950s, the intercensal growth rate climbed to over 25 percent, the highest since the 1920s; 1,231,000 people were added, the greatest numerical gain ever achieved in New Jersey. The decade of the 1960s saw a decline in the rate to 18 percent, but that, on top of the larger population base

of 1960, still added well over a million people to the state. Suburban growth seemed everywhere—around the two metropolitan centers, in the central corridor, and along the seashore. The powerful growth dy-namics of megalopolis propelled the move-ment of plants, warehouses, and retail fa-cilities, along with people, from the two neighboring metropolitan centers. It seemed that New Jersey was to become the "sub-urban state" with constantly proliferating shopping malls, industrial parks, and sub-urbs—suburbs that ranged from among the fanciest in the world ("champagne" or "martini" subdivisions) to frankly working-class refuges from cities ("sixpack" sub-urbs).

The decade of the 1970s saw an abrupt return to the slow growth characteristic of the 1930s. The 1970–1980 growth rate of 2.7 percent was the lowest in the history of the state. The actual numerical increase was the lowest, except for the Great Depres-sion, since the Civil War. The dynamics of suburban growth—which, after all, are related to slower growth, then stagnation, then decline in the central cities—had fi-nally caught up with New Jersey (see Figure 5.5). The aging industrial satellites and smaller metropolitan centers of New Jersey were in decline for the same reasons as the "central stars" of their constellations. All five northeastern New York Metro counties of New Jersey—Bergen, Essex, Hudson, Passaic, and Union—experienced an overall decline in population (see Table 5.2). In Hudson County, only three small municipalities (each under 15,000 popu-lation) showed a gain, East Newark Bor-ough remained precisely the same, and the rest of the county declined. Population loss was confined to these five counties (see Figure 5.6), but those net losses were so heavy that, despite significant gains in most other counties, New Jersey barely gained between 1970 and 1980. At that, New Jersey's showing was far better than New York's −3.8 percent change and Pennsyl-vania's bare 0.6 percent gain. (Delaware, however, had an 8.6 percent gain.) Bergen,

76

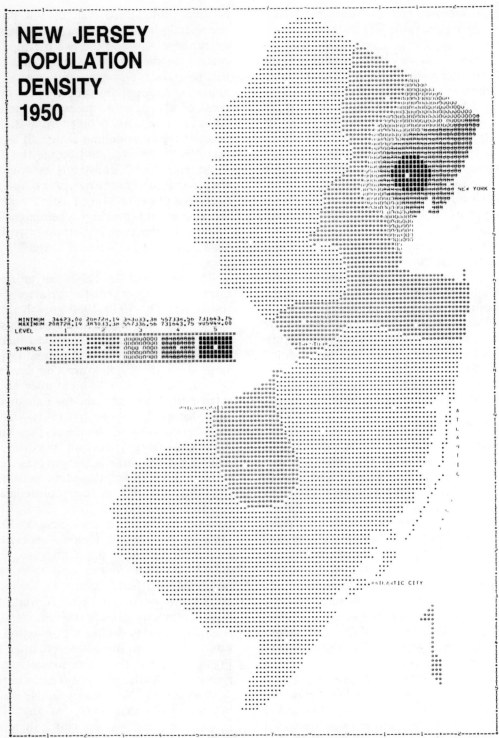

FIGURE 5.4. The effects of suburbanization are becoming apparent, along with the future population outflow from big cities heralded here by Hudson County's decline to the second-highest relative-density category.

**NEW JERSEY
POPULATION
DENSITY
1980**

FIGURE 5.5. The long-standing sharp differentation of relative densities between rural and urban counties is beginning to blur, even on these generalized maps. The exurban frontier is advancing further from the cities, which themselves are losing population.

TABLE 5.2
Recent Changes in County Population

	Population 1960	Population 1970	Population 1980	% Change 1960-1970	% Change 1970-1980
New Jersey	6,066,782	7,171,112	7,364,158	18.2	2.7
Atlantic	160,880	175,043	194,119	8.8	10.9
Bergen	780,255	898,012	845,385	15.0	- 5.8
Burlington	224,499	323,132	362,542	43.9	12.2
Camden	392,035	456,291	471,650	16.4	3.4
Cape May	48,555	59,544	82,266	22.7	38.2
Cumberland	106,850	121,374	132,866	13.6	9.5
Essex	923,545	929,986	850,451	1.0	- 8.5
Gloucester	134,840	172,681	199,917	28.1	15.8
Hudson	610,734	609,266	556,972	- 0.5	- 8.6
Hunterdon	54,107	69,718	87,361	28.9	25.3
Mercer	266,392	303,968	307,863	14.2	1.2
Middlesex	433,856	583,813	595,893	34.6	2.0
Monmouth	334,401	459,379	503,173	38.1	9.5
Morris	261,620	383,454	407,630	46.6	6.3
Ocean	108,241	208,470	346,038	92.6	65.9
Passaic	406,618	460,782	447,585	13.3	- 2.9
Salem	58,711	60,346	64,676	2.8	7.2
Somerset	143,913	198,372	203,129	37.8	2.4
Sussex	49,255	77,528	116,119	57.4	49.8
Union	504,255	543,116	504,094	7.7	- 7.2
Warren	63,220	73,879	84,429	17.0	14.3

Source: U.S. Bureau of the Census, 1960, 1970, 1980.

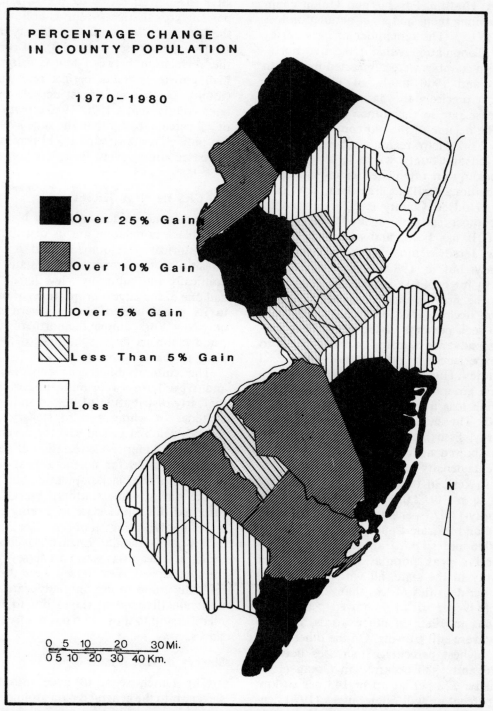

PERCENTAGE CHANGE IN COUNTY POPULATION

1970–1980

Over 25% Gain

Over 10% Gain

Over 5% Gain

Less Than 5% Gain

Loss

0 5 10 20 30 Mi.
0 5 10 20 30 40 Km.

N

FIGURE 5.6. U.S. census data indicate that those counties peripheral to the main axis of the megalopolis are the ones with the faster rates of growth. The long decline of Hudson, later joined by Essex, has now spread to other northeastern counties.

Essex, Hudson, Passaic, and Union counties among them had a net population loss of 236,675. The remainder of New Jersey had a population *gain,* if the five northeastern counties were subtracted from both 1970 and 1980 totals, of 11.5 percent, almost precisely the national population-increase rate in that time.

The decline of the old core cities in the New York Metro region was foreshadowed by Hudson County, where Jersey City and Hoboken were often cited as having denser populations per land area than New York City. Hudson County is distinguished by two, most certainly related phenomena. First, it has been, and continues to be, New Jersey's most densely populated county; but its 1980 density was 12,004 per sq mi or 4,633 per sq km. Second, it was the first to experience overall population decline. Hudson County, for those who seek portents of the future, has provided advance warning of the declines to be experienced by other, heavily urbanized counties. Hudson reached its peak population around 1930 and first showed population loss from the preceding census in 1940. The next most densely populated county, Essex, had its peak year in 1960 and showed a decline by 1970, at which time its density was 7,317 per sq mi (2,824 per sq km). In 1970, Union County (5,277 per sq mi or 2,036 per sq km), Bergen County (3,825 per sq mi or 1,476 per sq km), and Passaic County (2,400 per sq mi or 926 per sq km) all reached their respective peak populations. Every other county in the state, all with overall population densities of less than 2,200 per sq mi (849 per sq km), showed peak populations in 1980; in other words, in 1980 they were still growing. On the other hand, the highest percentage increases between 1970 and 1980 occurred in Ocean (1970 density: 372 per sq mi or 143 per sq km; 66 percent growth rate), Sussex (1970 density: 147 per sq mi or 56 per sq km; 50 percent growth rate), Cape May (1970 density: 226 per sq mi or 87 per sq km; 38 percent growth), and Hunterdon (1970 density: 162 per sq mi or 62 per sq km; 25 percent growth rate)—four counties near the bottom of the population-density range for New Jersey (see Table 5.3). Of course, the correlation between low density and high growth is not a perfect one. Salem County, New Jersey's least densely populated county, had a 1970–1980 growth rate of 7.2 percent, better than the state average, but only eleventh (midpoint) in percentage increases among New Jersey's counties.

BLACKS IN NEW JERSEY

Among the unique aspects of New Jersey's black population are its distribution, its historical development, and its relationship to the growth of the state, economically and culturally. New Jersey long had one of the largest proportions of blacks in its population of any northern state; only New York, among the northern states, could claim as large a number of blacks prior to the Civil War.

The cultural differences between East and West Jersey were quite important in the early distribution of blacks and in the attitudes of whites toward slavery. New Jersey's colonial period saw the reverse of the overall American association of slavery with the South, for northern East Jersey had most of the black population and most of the slaves, while southern West Jersey early led the future state in freeing slaves and in advocating abolition (see Figure 5.7). Both Dutch and English slaveholders brought African slaves to East Jersey, while the Quakers of West Jersey were the first religious group to not only advocate manumission (freeing) of slaves but to refuse membership to those who did not free their slaves.

Slavery in East Jersey

The Dutch seem to have introduced slavery into the general region around 1625, probably with blacks captured from the Spanish or Portuguese (Wacker 1975, 189). The early Dutch settlement in northeastern New Jersey certainly had slaves, and the

TABLE 5.3
Changes in Population Density Per Square Mile (Square
Kilometer) for New Jersey Counties

County	1960 Density		1970 Density		1980 Density	
Atlantic	284	(109)	309	(119)	342	(132)
Bergen	3,326	(1,283)	3,825	(1,476)	3,605	(1,391)
Burlington	275	(106)	395	(152)	443	(170)
Camden	1,766	(681)	2,055	(793)	2,125	(820)
Cape May	184	(71)	226	(87)	312	(120)
Cumberland	213	(82)	242	(93)	265	(102)
Essex	7,247	(2,797)	7,317	(2,824)	6,675	(2,576)
Gloucester	411	(158)	526	(203)	609	(235)
Hudson	13,157	(5,078)	13,094	(5,054	12,004	(4,633)
Hunterdon	126	(48)	162	(62)	203	(78)
Mercer	1,179	(455)	1,346	(519)	1,362	(525)
Middlesex	1,395	(538)	1,877	(724)	1,916	(739)
Monmouth	709	(273)	979	(377)	1,067	(411)
Morris	556	(214)	815	(314)	867	(334)
Ocean	170	(65)	372	(143)	543	(209)
Passaic	2,118	(817)	2,400	(926)	2,331	(899)
Salem	169	(65)	174	(67)	187	(72)
Somerset	471	(181)	649	(250)	665	(256)
Sussex	93	(35)	147	(56)	220	(84)
Union	4,899	(1,891)	5,277	(2,036)	4,899	(1,891)
Warren	175	(67)	205	(79)	234	(90)

Source: U.S. Bureau of the Census.

Counties with more than 2,200/square mile (849/square
kilometer) lose, those with less, gain. 2,200/square mile
seems to be about the breaking point between gain and loss,
1970 to 1980.

English takeover of the Dutch colonies had little effect on the strong association of the Dutch with the institution of slavery. The Dutch acceptance of slavery, particularly the enslavement of Africans, has had far-reaching consequences elsewhere, as in South Africa. Even after the political defeat of the Dutch in the New World, the Dutch population of East Jersey continued to climb as many Dutch people took advantage of readily available land in the Jersey colonies. Why should ambitious Dutch farmers remain tenants on the great patroonships of the Hudson Valley when they could work for themselves in East Jersey?

After the American Revolution the English became one of the first nations to forbid slavery. At the time of colonial control, however, the English felt that New Jersey's economic development required slave labor. In Queen Anne's government's instructions to the first royal governor of

82

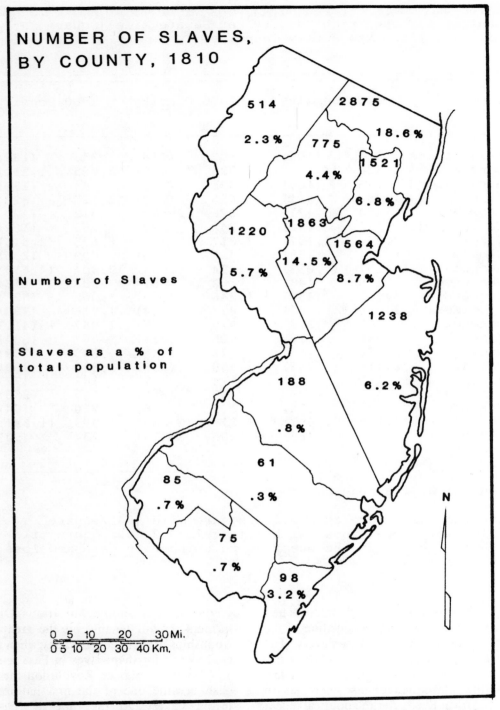

FIGURE 5.7. New Jersey slaves were frequently in industrial settings rather than agricultural, and many slaves were skilled in building and industrial trades. (County boundaries are as of 1810.) (Based on information in Peter Wacker, *Land and People: A Cultural Geography of Preindustrial New Jersey: Origins and Settlement Patterns.* New Brunswick, N.J.: Rutgers University Press, 1975, pp. 190–194)

New York and New Jersey, Lord Cornbury, he was told to

> . . . give all due encouragement and invitations to merchants and others who shall bring trade into our said province, or any way contribute to the advantage thereof, and in particular the Royal African Company of England . . . that this said province may have a constant and sufficient supply of merchantable negroes at moderate rates. . . . (Pomfret 1964, 47)

In addition to the Dutch, English planters from the Caribbean "sugar island" of Barbados acquired land in East Jersey; this introduced more wealthy and influential people who were familiar with the use of slave labor in plantation agriculture. In 1680, there were about 120 black slaves in New Jersey, about 60 to 70 of them on one plantation at Shrewsbury. Most of the remaining slaves at the time were employed at an iron "plantation" at Tinton Falls. It is not unusual that industrial and craft employment was so important, early and consequently, for New Jersey's blacks. Slaves were often advertised for sale as having skills in iron working, carpentry, stonemasonry, brewing, and bricklaying. By 1726, Bergen County (which included Hudson County's territory at the time) had a black population of 18 percent of the total; Somerset, 17 percent; Middlesex and Essex each had over 7 percent. In contrast South (West) Jersey's counties each had less than 4 percent. East Jersey then had about half the total New Jersey population but three-quarters of the black population (Wacker 1975, 189–191).

Although the colonial government of New Jersey took some official interest in the welfare of black slaves, it also continued to act to retard any large-scale manumission. Lord Cornbury's instructions included a charge that he

> shall endeavor to get a law passed for the restraining of any inhuman severity, which by ill masters or overseers, may be used toward their Christian servants and their slaves and that provision be made therein that the willful killing of Indians and Negroes may be punished with death and that a fit penalty be imposed for the maiming of them. You are also with the assistance of the Council and Assembly to find out the best means to facilitate and encourage the conversion of Negroes and Indians to the Christian religion. (Whitehead et al. 1810, p. 532)

"Christian servants" usually referred to Europeans who were bonded (indentured) servants. These were people who, in theory at least, had voluntarily entered servitude for a definite term, usually seven years, to clear their debts at home and pay for their transportation across the Atlantic. Not all of these indentured servants were really volunteers—many were simply shipped across the Atlantic as such to help solve two problems simultaneously, the reduction of the "welfare burden" in England and the labor shortage in the American colonies. The very poor, landless, and indebted people in England, some of whom were in prison simply because they could not pay their debts, were thus exported to the New World. When their period of service was up, the "Christian servants" were to be given 60 acres (24 ha) of land, farm implements, and clothing. Non-Christian servants (Africans and Indians) were not owed anything when freed. The law specifically stated that baptism did not alter the status of black or Indian slaves. Thus, *Christian* in that context referred to race rather than religious belief.

Antislavery Activities

The colonial government also passed a law in 1713 that discouraged manumission by requiring the former owners to post a large bond for each freed slave. This may have been in response to widespread manumission by Quakers in West Jersey. These Quakers, mostly members of the Philadelphia Yearly Meeting of Friends, had opposed the importation of slaves as early as 1696 and by 1776 had refused membership to any slaveholders. Joseph Woolman, a Quaker of Mount Holly, was among the first to publicly call for abolition of slavery. Around the middle of the eighteenth century he published a powerful tract opposing slavery. The cover featured a black man, kneeling, in chains, with the poignant question, "Am I not a man and a brother?"

Slave ships anchored off Camden and Perth Amboy in the 1740s and 1750s despite the growing abolition movement, which did succeed in moderating some of the harsher laws governing Negroes. In 1768, the special courts dealing with blacks were abolished, and in 1769 a special tax was levied on each slave imported into the state. By 1778, special laws on criminal acts by blacks were abolished. In 1775, the first antislavery organization in America was organized in New Jersey to free blacks who had been free and then kidnapped back into slavery. By 1794, there were at least three antislavery societies in New Jersey—at Trenton, Burlington, and Salem, all in "west" Jersey. Sometimes these societies purchased the freedom of slaves if they could not convince the owners to give it voluntarily. The actions of the Quakers and abolitionists meant that former West Jersey had a higher proportion of free blacks than did the former East Jersey.

In 1804, New Jersey passed its "gradual abolition" act that required that all children born of slaves be free. These children were, however, to remain servants of their mother's master until age twenty-five for males or twenty-one for females. The importation of foreign-born slaves had already ended, but the slave trade continued as a domestic industry.

The Underground Railroad

Many New Jerseyans, whether freed blacks or whites, did more to fight slavery than join abolition societies, buy freedom for some, and organize political campaigns—they actively aided in the successful escape of runaway slaves (New Jersey Writers' Project 1939). In 1786, George Washington (a slaveholder who advocated

gradual abolition) noted that it was not easy to recapture runaway slaves in Pennsylvania and West Jersey as there were more people aiding the runaways than there were trying to capture them. By 1810, there were established routes for aiding runaways, with safe places to stay, guidance on to other safe places, and regular "shipments" to freedom. The "underground railroad," as it came to be called, had secret shelters as its "stations," with an "agent" in charge of each station and "conductors" as guides. Being active in the underground railroad was serious business, as Congress had passed a Fugitive Slave Act in 1793 that punished anyone aiding runaway slaves. New Jerseyans in the underground railroad were active in helping slaves escaping up Chesapeake Bay and across the Delaware, heading for the Hudson Valley and, eventually, the freedom of Canada.

Three principal routes through New Jersey were developed (see Figure 5.8). The most important followed the Delaware River from Camden to Burlington, then through Bordentown, Princeton, and New Brunswick. Another route ran from Salem through Woodbury and Mount Laurel, joining the first route at Bordentown. A third line ran from Greenwich to Swedesboro to Mount Holly, joining the "main line" at Burlington. Some less frequently used routes lay through Pennsylvania to Phillipsburg or Trenton, then either across to Jersey City or up the Delaware Valley into New York State. When "spies" were spotted, the "trains" would be switched to another route. Perth Amboy was a major station at which the runaways were placed aboard boats bound for Canada. Jersey City was the ferry station for New York City or up the Hudson via Albany. The Jersey City station was so busy that as much as $100 might be spent on ship or ferry tickets in one night.

Antiabolitionist mobs sometimes broke up abolition meetings and harassed suspected underground-railroad members, but the abolitionists were good at retaliation. In Salem, citizens were awakened by the

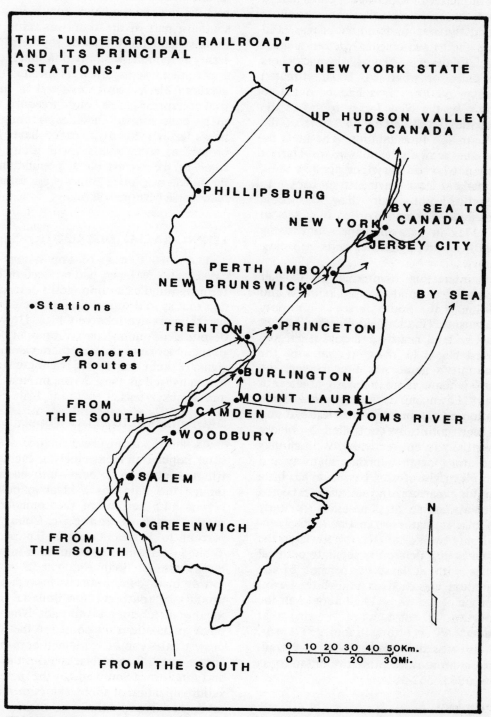

FIGURE 5.8.

cries of chained blacks being carried in a wagon back to slavery. Townspeople stopped the wagon, freed the slaves, and hauled the "slave catcher" before a magistrate! In other instances, slave catchers were killed or wounded. It is estimated that over 50,000 slaves had been led to freedom by the New Jersey routes of the underground railroad by the time of the Emancipation Proclamation. The most famous conductor on the railroad was Harriet Tubman, who had herself escaped in 1849. She made at least nineteen trips back into the South, leading more than 300 people to freedom. Tubman worked in hotels in Cape May in between trips south, using her earnings to pay for her raids into slave territories.

An interesting by-product of Quaker support for the underground railroad and abolition is the South Jersey community of Lawnside. Haddonfield Quakers bought a tract of land nearby and sold it cheaply to freed blacks in 1840. At that time the community's name was Free Haven; the Lawnside name came in the late nineteenth century. Lawnside, or Free Haven, became a station on the underground railroad and has been politically controlled by blacks for virtually its entire history. With chunks sliced away for an interstate highway and a turnpike right-of-way, Lawnside has little room for expansion and so can be expected to remain stable in population. A study by a black geographer in the 1960s identified only twelve "all-Negro" towns in the United States, defined as separate political entities with at least 95 percent of the population classified as nonwhite. Lawnside (one of the twelve) had about half the proportion of substandard housing that Camden had, according to the 1960 census, and also was the most affluent of the all-Negro communities in metropolitan areas (Rose 1965, 362-381).

Conclusions

Thus the black population of New Jersey is distinctive among the states for several reasons. The northern part of the state, for historical and cultural reasons, has always had the bulk of the black population. The southern part of the state was more abolitionist, and the blacks of southern New Jersey are commonly located in small towns and rural areas as much as in cities. The northern blacks, early involved in industrial enterprises, even before freedom, tend to be concentrated in cities. Throughout New Jersey's history, blacks have been prominent as an ethnic-racial group, and some of the largest black populations of the northern United States were found in New Jersey before 1900.

ETHNIC-RACIAL DISTRIBUTIONS

The 1980 Census of Population indicated that New Jersey had retained its long-term tradition as an immigrant destination and that spatial segregation, particularly of blacks, remained relatively high. However, despite a continuing concentration of blacks in the older central cities, there were some signs of suburbanization of New Jersey blacks as well as those living in New York and Pennsylvania.

Distribution of the Black Population

As shown on Figure 5.9, New Jersey's black population is extremely unevenly distributed, even on a county-unit basis. Although the state has a black population that is 12.5 percent of the total, county proportions range from Essex County's 37 percent to Sussex County's 0.6 percent. Table 5.4 lists nine communities in which blacks are the majority. The most uniformly black community is Lawnside, the product of southern New Jersey's efforts in the underground railroad. The large black populations in some of the state's biggest cities can be explained both by the continuing inflow of blacks from the rural and small-town South and by the increasing suburbanization of nonblacks. New Jersey's other racial and ethnic minorities have somehow more successfully suburbanized than have blacks. Six of New Jersey's large cities that lost population between 1960

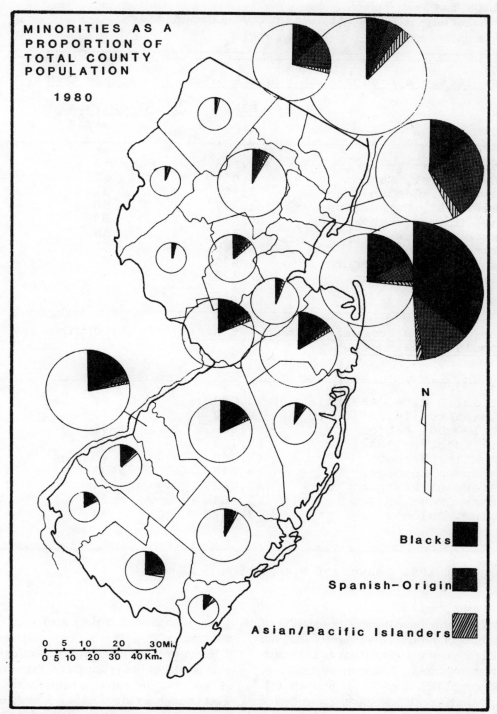

FIGURE 5.9. Officially designated census minorities are shown as a proportion of total population. The more urban-dominated counties have the higher proportions of minorities, as a general rule.

TABLE 5.4
New Jersey's "Minority-Majority" Communities

New Jersey's Predominantly Black Communities (and County)

	# Black	% of Total
Camden, Camden	45,008	53
Chesilhurst, Camden	1,058	66
Lawnside, Camden	2,967	97
Fairfield, Cumberland	2,867	50
East Orange, Essex	64,354	83
Newark, Essex	191,743	58
Orange, Essex	17,840	57
Asbury Park, Monmouth	8,535	50
Plainfield, Union	27,420	60

New Jersey's Communities with at Least One-third Black Population (and County)

	# Black	% of Total
Atlantic City, Atlantic	20,029	49
Pleasantville, Atlantic	6,712	49
Englewood, Bergen	9,629	41
Willingboro, Burlington	15,102	38
Trenton, Mercer	41,860	45
Neptune, Monmouth	9,242	33
Paterson, Passaic	47,091	34
Penns Grove, Salem	1,908	33
Salem, Salem	3,057	44

Source: 1980 Census of Population.

and 1980 now have a black population of one-third or more. This suggests that the nonblack outward movement is as important as continuing black in-migration in producing black-majority or at least disproportionately black cities (considering the state's overall black-population proportion). Simply put, fewer blacks than nonblacks have been able to leave the decaying central cities for the improved living standards generally associated with suburbia.

Even in those cases where suburbanization of blacks has taken place, many times it has been to older, inner suburbs like East Orange. In some cases this has created non-central-city ghettos, if "ghettos" can be used to describe some quite attractive suburbs as compared to the grim decay of portions of Newark and Camden. Chesil-

TABLE 5.5
New Jersey Communities with Spanish-Origin Population of
15 Percent or More

Community, County	# Spanish Origin[a]	% of Total
Camden, Camden	16,308	19
Woodbine, Cape May	462	16
Vineland, Cumberland	9,804	18
Newark, Essex	61,254	19
Hoboken, Hudson	17,074	40
Jersey City, Hudson	41,672	19
Union City, Hudson	35,525	64
West New York, Hudson	24,735	63
Perth Amboy, Middlesex	15,841	41
Dover, Morris	3,917	27
Passaic, Passaic	17,933	34
Paterson, Passaic	39,650	29
Elizabeth, Union	28,305	27

Source: 1980 Census of Population.

[a]Spanish origin is an ethnic, not a racial designation.
Persons of Spanish origin may be of any race.

hurst in Camden County, Plainfield and Englewood in northern New Jersey, and Pleasantville outside Atlantic City are examples of these older suburbs now with large black populations. Willingboro, in the Burlington County sector of Philadelphia Metro, is a rare example of a relatively new suburb now experiencing significant inflows of black residents.

Spanish-Origin Population Patterns

The statewide pattern of Spanish-origin New Jerseyans shows an orientation to the older central cities that are the traditional reception centers for incoming migrants, but also a somewhat surprising tendency to have "colonized" the rural-suburban counties of the northwest (see Table 5.5). This group is now the largest census-recognized minority in the latter area. The Spanish-origin (an ethnic, not a racial, designation) population is 6.7 percent of New Jersey as a whole, but every county has at least 1 percent Spanish. The same degree of dispersal for blacks would require an approximate minimum of 2 percent blacks in each county, a minimum not attained in three northwestern counties—Sussex, Warren, and Hunterdon.

Spanish-origin population does concentrate in the old central cities—in many cases, cities that are experiencing overall population decline. Hudson County is 26 percent Spanish, and Passaic County, 14 percent. Union City, at 64 percent Spanish, is said to have the largest concentration of Cuban Americans north of Florida, and West New York registers 63 percent Spanish. Hoboken, Perth Amboy, and Passaic each are over one-third Spanish, while

FIGURE 5.10. *A Spanish-Language Church Facility, Passaic.* Spanish-speaking Americans now form the largest minority present in Passaic County and in many communities throughout the state. This group appears to have been more successful at "pioneering" new minority settlements than have blacks.

Spanish-origin New Jerseyans make up more than a quarter each of Paterson, Elizabeth, and Dover. The Southwest Farm region has a sizable minority of Spanish, especially in Vineland (18 percent); many of these first arrived as seasonal farm laborers and returned to stay.

The Asian–Pacific Islanders Group

The distribution of the Asian and Pacific Islanders group shows a very high degree of suburbanization. The affinity of Asian–Pacific Islanders for the suburbs—in many cases, the more affluent suburbs—may reflect three social factors. For one thing, Asians and Pacific Islanders make up only 1.4 percent of the state's population. Because their educational and income levels surpass those of other minorities, their relatively small number may induce less concern over potential "outnumbering" among suburban whites and a resultant lower rate of discrimination.

Also, the ability of the Asian–Pacific Islanders to move into upper-middle-income municipalities rather than "six-pack suburbs" may well produce less of a threat in racially sensitive areas. In addition, some Asians are present in the suburbs as a result of sponsorship of Southeast Asian refugees by suburban church congregations and similar groups.

A result is that Asian–Pacific Islanders do not concentrate in the traditional immigrant reception areas, but rather head for the suburbs, there to form the largest minority present in many communities, primarily in New York Metro (see Table 5.6). Almost one in ten residents of Fort Lee is Asian, and Asian–Pacific Islanders form the largest local minority in half a dozen other Bergen County communities. Cherry Hill, in Camden County, is the only South Jersey community in which Asian–Pacific Islanders are the largest minority, at 3 percent.

TABLE 5.6

New Jersey Communities with Asian-Pacific Islanders as the
Largest Minority Present

Community, County	# Asian-Pacific Islander	% of Total
Fort Lee, Bergen	2,959	9
Palisades Park, Bergen	779	6
Paramus, Bergen	856	3
Tenafly, Bergen	618	4
Upper Saddle River, Bergen	139	2
Washington, Bergen	190	2
Wyckoff, Bergen	206	1
Cherry Hill, Camden	2,248	3
East Windsor, Mercer	383	4
Edison, Middlesex	2,245	3
Old Bridge, Middlesex	1,159	2
South Brunswick, Middlesex	906	5
Haslet, Monmouth	490	2
Howell, Monmouth	256	3
Parsippany-Troy Hills, Morris	1,845	4
Randolph, Morris	439	2
Rockaway, Morris	358	2
Roxbury, Morris	313	2
Dover, Ocean	420	0.6
Warren, Somerset	203	2

Source: 1980 Census of Population.

The surprisingly long list of communities in which Asian–Pacific Islanders are the largest minority present is, of course, a reflection of negatives for other minority groups as well as positives (higher education and income) for Asians. Black and Spanish-origin New Jerseyans may lack both the requisite income levels and non-threatening "low profile" of Asians that combine to counter the more blatant, if illegal, forms of housing discrimination.

CASE STUDY: ESSEX COUNTY

Essex County, with its overall decline in population and its communities that range in size from Newark (still the largest municipality in New Jersey despite a sharp decline in population from 405,220 in 1960 to 329,248 in 1980) to Essex Falls (population 2,363), is reasonably typical of the urban-suburban counties in northern New Jersey (see Figure 5.11). Its long-established

92

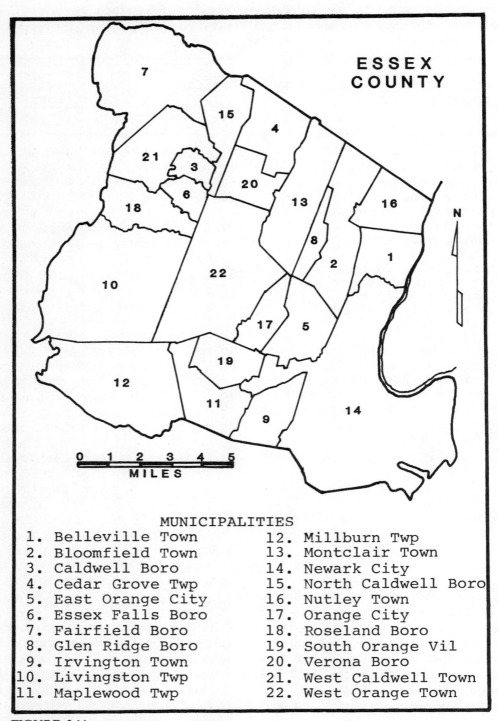

ESSEX COUNTY

N

0 1 2 3 4 5
MILES

MUNICIPALITIES

1. Belleville Town
2. Bloomfield Town
3. Caldwell Boro
4. Cedar Grove Twp
5. East Orange City
6. Essex Falls Boro
7. Fairfield Boro
8. Glen Ridge Boro
9. Irvington Town
10. Livingston Twp
11. Maplewood Twp
12. Millburn Twp
13. Montclair Town
14. Newark City
15. North Caldwell Boro
16. Nutley Town
17. Orange City
18. Roseland Boro
19. South Orange Vil
20. Verona Boro
21. West Caldwell Town
22. West Orange Town

FIGURE 5.11.

and expanding black population makes it an excellent case study in examining the "suburbanization" pattern of blacks compared to those of whites and "other races." Municipal population data from the 1960, 1970, and 1980 censuses are used to show both the overall population change and the racial makeup of those populations.

The black population of Newark had been expanding, even if at rates that did not significantly alter its proportion of the total population, from the post–Civil War period to World War I. The number of blacks in 1880, for example—3,310—was 2.4 percent of the total; although the number by 1910 was 9,475, that was still only 2.7 percent of the overall population. At such low numbers and proportions, notes Clement Price, there was a superficial racial tolerance. At a time when Jim Crow racial segregation laws were proliferating through many parts of the country, the Newark Board of Education closed the segregated black school in 1909, ending eighty-one years of education segregation at the elementary level. Newark's industrial and civic leaders (who were white) liked to term their city "the city of opportunity," and doubtless it was for many of the Irish, Italians, Germans, Poles, and Russians who got jobs there, established homes, and often saw their children and grandchildren move—move up economically and socially and move out of the city to the suburbs. For most black Newarkers, however, the move to the suburbs was a distant dream.

Clement Price's study of the plight of blacks in Newark showed that for most of them, low paying occupations with little chance of better opportunity were the facts of life. In 1890, for example, 88 percent of employed black women were servants or laundresses, while 64 percent of black men were unskilled laborers, servants, teamsters, or stable workers (Price 1975, 10–45). On the other hand, there were some highly visible success stories among Newark's blacks at the time—restaurateurs, caterers, hoteliers, and proprietors of moving and storage businesses, as well as a cadre of professionals serving the needs of the black population—lawyers, physicians, dentists, and undertakers. Interestingly, catering and operating restaurants was an old black urban specialty, for blacks had been prominent at one time in these businesses in Washington, D.C., Philadelphia, and New York. Fraunce's Tavern in New York, where George Washington had held a farewell party with his officers, was then operated by a black, for example. It was a logical specialization for those who had more family labor available to them than they had capital. It is said that blacks did so well in food businesses that jealous whites manipulated licensing laws to exclude them. At any rate, the average black Newarker was making little economic progress even if discrimination was both less obvious and less violent than in some other parts of the country.

As Newark's total black population was increasing from 6,977 in 1920 (4 percent of the total) to 45,760 in 1940 (10.7 percent), the pattern of discrimination in housing was becoming more obvious. Price showed that the distribution of blacks among Newark's sixteen wards indicated strong and continuing patterns of segregation. Wards 12 and 13, for example, had less than 1 percent of their numbers blacks in 1910, and this was still true in 1940, roughly a generation later. The third ward, in contrast, held 23 percent of Newark's blacks in 1910 and 36 percent in 1940; the third ward had been described in 1916 as an unsightly slum, where growth had been "unrestricted, haphazard, muddled, ignorant and irresponsible" (Price 1975, 25–31). One can assume that the city did little to improve these planning errors as the ward's total population decreased and its black population increased (from 1,356 in 1910 to 16,352 in 1940).

The black population of Essex County has been slow to suburbanize, as indicated in the maps showing the total population and the proportions of that population classified as "white," "black" ("Negro" on earlier censuses), and "other" for the years 1960, 1970, and 1980 (Figures 5.12, 5.13,

94

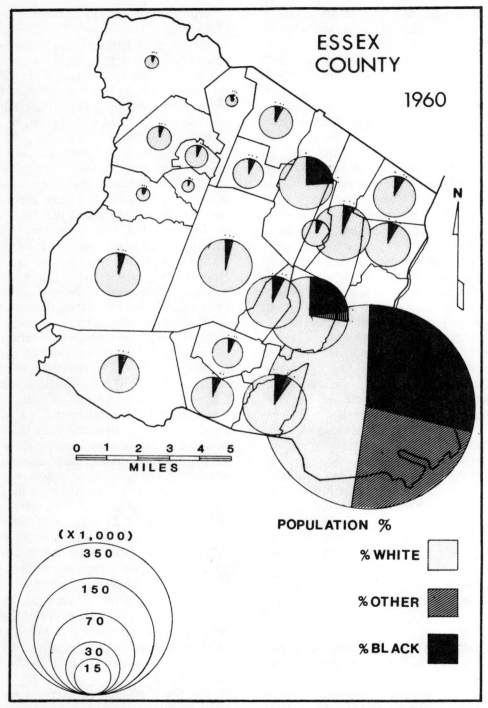

FIGURE 5.12. *Essex County, 1960: Suburbanization and Ethnicity.* This map series shows total population size and racial makeup as reported by the Bureau of the Census. In 1960, there was an obvious segregation pattern in which only Newark, East Orange, and Upper Montclair had significant proportions of black and "other" (mostly Spanish-speaking—an ethnic rather than racial category) groups.

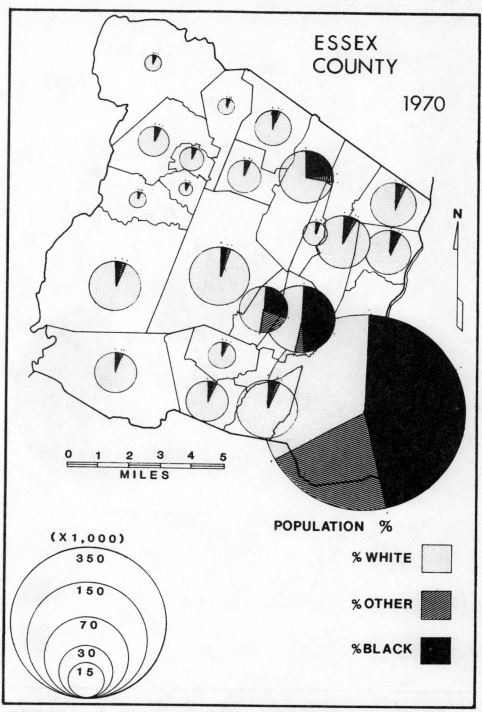

FIGURE 5.13. Essex County, 1970: Suburbanization and Ethnicity. By 1970 "non-white" populations had expanded considerably in Newark and its immediately adjacent suburbs but made little progress in moving into other suburban municipalities.

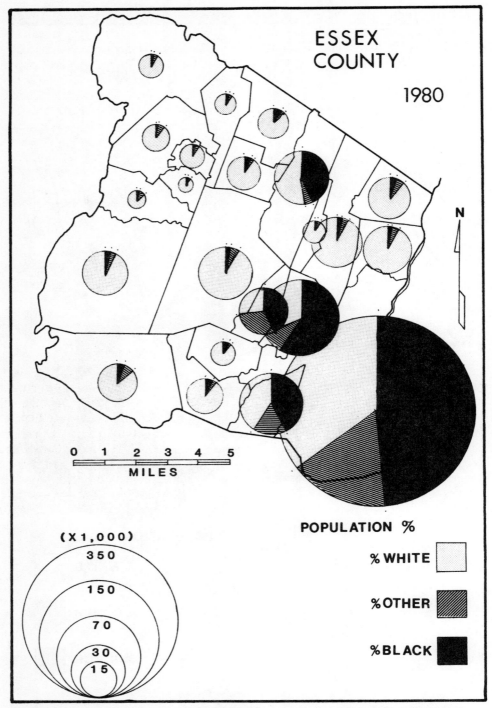

FIGURE 5.14. *Essex County, 1980: Suburbanization and Ethnicity.* The suburban-ization of blacks appears to concentrate in those municipalities that already had a sizable number of blacks, with the exception of older, inner suburbs such as Irvington (on Newark's southwest boundary), which experienced a very rapid racial transition from 1970 to 1980.

and 5.14). In 1960, after New Jersey's postwar suburban boom, blacks were still heavily concentrated in Newark. The only suburbs in which blacks appeared in numbers proportionate to, or surplus to, their overall ratio in the state's population were adjacent East Orange and nearby Montclair. Between 1960 and 1970, a decade of continuing suburbanization overall, there was little real change in the concentration of the black population. In fact, there was significant growth in the already large black population of Newark and East Orange, with a significant increase in the black population of Orange, just to the west of East Orange.

The changes from 1970 to 1980 show both a continuing, wavelike spread of blacks into municipalities immediately adjacent to established black concentrations and a tendency for "other races" to more successfully "pioneer" the further suburbs. While the black proportion of Newark's declining population (1970 to 1980 saw a 14 percent drop in total numbers of people) remained roughly the same, during the decade of the 1970s East Orange became a predominantly black community, the already sizable black populations of Orange and Montclair approached half of the total, and Irvington, a municipality more than half surrounded by Newark, witnessed an abrupt upward surge in its black population. East Orange and Irvington were among

the few Essex County communities to have an expanding population from 1970 to 1980, and probably not coincidentally, they also have the highest overall population densities in the county. Of the large concentrations of blacks, only Montclair has a lower-than-county-average density.

The crowded, older suburbs are thus the most likely to absorb a "spill-over" from Newark's (and elsewhere's) suburbanizing black population. The lower-density suburbs more distant from long-established black concentrations, Millburn and Nutley, for example, consistently show very small black population ratios. By 1980, "other races" there were the largest minorities (Spanish is an ethnic rather than racial designation and is not an identifiable part of any racial category).

The experience of Essex County's blacks would indicate that the suburbanization of blacks is more often a traditional "trickle down" of obsolescent housing from the majority group that has perceived the lessened desirability and moved on, leaving the housing to the generally less-affluent blacks. Additionally, few would argue that de facto residential segregation persists long after being outlawed and that differences in economic opportunity and apparently lower levels of discrimination have allowed other racial minorities to penetrate the farther-out, lower-density suburbs more effectively than blacks.

CHAPTER 6

TRANSPORTATION

New Jersey's evolving patterns of land use, population density, and industrialization have always been intimately related to transportation efficiency and accessibility. This highest-density state in population is also the highest density in rail mileage, highway traffic, and general intensity of transportation networks. The volume of vehicular traffic across the New Jersey–Pennsylvania border is the highest interstate volume in the United States; the volume crossing the New Jersey–New York border is second. New Jersey and its neighboring states in the northeastern megalopolis have long been in the forefront of transportation development.

New Jersey has been the scene of some early, novel experiments in transportation. The state was once part-owner of one of the most lucrative railroads ever built, and each of the state's major industries—chemicals, agriculture, and tourism—owes much to New Jersey's combination of location and transport development. The first air voyage in the United States, and an interstate one at that, took pioneering French balloonist Jean Blanchard from Philadelphia southeast over the Delaware to land in Deptford, New Jersey, in January 1793. A wagon and ferry carried Blanchard and his balloon back to be congratulated by President Washington. Pioneer inventor John Stevens of Hoboken built a steamboat as early as 1798; in 1808, he launched a 100-foot (30.5-meter)-long steamboat; and, in 1815, he built a working steam locomotive to demonstrate his idea that rail-

roads were the wave of the future. Stevens had published a booklet in 1812 advocating a nationwide network of steam railroads. He was about twenty years ahead of his time, for the canal age delayed interest in his railroad concept until the 1830s.

CANALS AND ECONOMIC GROWTH

Canals had long been advocated, mostly to develop the growing western trade by overcoming the nonnavigability of the natural rivers to the west of the fall-line cities. The eminently practical Benjamin Franklin, then representing Pennsylvania at London, wrote home advocating canal building. He believed that England's prosperity and industrialization were based on its extensive internal waterways system. George Washington had advocated canalizing the Potomac even before the Revolution.

With such prestigious leadership and advocacy, Americans came to be caught up in a canal fever. Some ludicrously impractical canal plans were envisioned, some of which were carried out. George Washington's Potomac Canal has been judged the engineering masterpiece of the late eighteenth century, while New Jersey's neighbors built canals of contrasting utility and engineering challenge. New York's Erie Canal, taking advantage of the Mohawk Valley and Lake Ontario Plain, was an immediate success; its modern successor, the New York State Barge Canal, is still in operation. The Pennsylvania Canal, an ingenious—if awkward—display of engi-

FIGURE 6.1. *Woodbridge.* An interchange of the New Jersey Turnpike with the Garden State Parkway (*right*) in the heavily traveled main axis of megalopolis. Note the twelve-lane width of the turnpike in this section. (Courtesy of New Jersey Turnpike Authority)

neering talent, had to surmount the edge of the Allegheny Plateau with inclined planes hauling the canal boats over hills on giant wheeled cradles.

The Morris Canal

New Jersey built a similarly cumbersome, and likewise ultimately unsuccessful, canal across its mountains—the Morris Canal. It was completed in 1831 between Phillipsburg and Newark, and in 1836 a link between Newark and Jersey City was completed. The 106-mile (170-kilometer)-long Morris Canal crossed some of the most-difficult terrain available in New Jersey, cutting across the topographic "grain" to link the upper Delaware with the growing industrial cities of the Piedmont, in particular Paterson and Newark, and ultimately with the Hudson.

Unlike the other famous canals contemporary with it, the Morris Canal was not intended to "open the west" and channel its trade through a specific East Coast port. The Morris Canal was motivated by energy—it was the early-nineteenth-century equivalent of today's oil and gas pipelines from the Gulf Coast to the northeastern seaboard. Pennsylvania anthracite or hard coal—nearly smokeless and with a high energy content—was the obvious replacement, or supplement, for waterpower for the industrial centers of north Jersey. As lunatic as it may seem now, the Morris Canal was an essential route, even though it had to overcome vertical differences of from sea level at Newark to 914 ft (278 m) at Lake Hopatcong, then back to 155 ft (47 m) above sea level at Phillipsburg on the Delaware (see Figure 6.2). The twenty-three locks and twenty-three inclined planes proved too slow and expensive, but a later railroad (via a somewhat different route) proved the necessity of

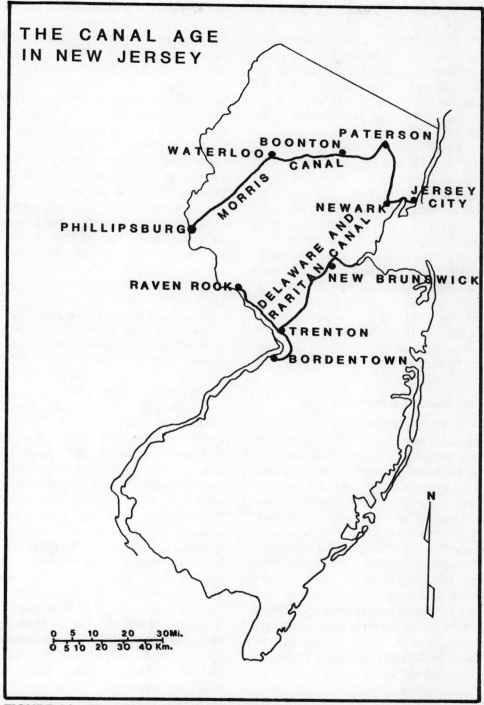

FIGURE 6.2. The major functions of the two canals were to move Pennsylvania hard coal to the industrial and urban markets of New Jersey and New York City. Both the Morris and Delaware and Raritan canals contributed much to the economic development of New Jersey and, in both cases, their real utility was foreshortened by their purchase by competing railroads.

linking the anthracite fields with the burgeoning cities, and the routeway was vindicated. The Morris Canal never generated big dividends owing to its cost of construction and operation, but it did generate regional economic growth for New Jersey. By 1832, between 90 and 100 barges were going through Newark every week, and Newark was entering a century-long industrial boom.

Freight on the Morris Canal hit an all-time high in 1866, when it carried 889,220 tn (806,522 t), 51 percent of which was coal. Other main items were charcoal, iron ore, pig iron, scrap, and building materials. A railroad paralleled the canal by 1875, a few years after the Lehigh Valley Railroad had leased the canal to control competition. By 1902, freight tonnage had dropped to 27,000 tn (24,489 t), most of which was coal, and in 1912 a state commission described the Morris as "little more than an open sewer" (Veit 1963, 30). The state bought the rights to the canal and drained it in 1924.

The Delaware and Raritan Canal

New Jersey's other canal, the Delaware and Raritan, was completed in 1834, but this was a year after the Camden and Amboy Railroad inaugurated steam travel across the already heavily traveled corridor (see Figure 6.2). The Delaware and Raritan was much easier to build and operate than was the Morris Canal. The Delaware and Raritan only had to cope with a vertical rise of some 57 ft (17 m), overcome with fourteen locks. This canal, 70 ft (21 m) wide and stretching only 43 mi (69 km) through a very busy, densely populated corridor, remained important for a century. Peak traffic was in 1871, the year it was purchased by the Pennsylvania Railroad. It was abandoned in 1931.

RAILROADS' EFFECTS ON DEVELOPMENT

New Jersey has long capitalized on its position astride the transport backbone of the evolving megalopolis. New Jersey's "corridor" function between two great cities presented economic opportunities that New Jerseyans were quick to understand, and the significance of the corridor route long eclipsed the attention of railroaders to those sections of New Jersey peripheral to the northeast-southwest megalopolitan corridor. When railroads were developed to the northwest of the corridor, it was for the following reasons: commuting, bringing the coal of Pennsylvania's northeastern anthracite regions to the industrial cities of northeastern New Jersey, and, later, taking urbanites to the recreation amenities of the mountains and lakes of New Jersey's Appalachian Highlands and Valley and Ridge regions. Except in the form of a slow, discontinuous journey, the railroads of northwestern New Jersey were not significant as links in any major east-west transportation system; major routes to the west were from either New York City through Philadelphia to Harrisburg and Pittsburgh or New York City through the Hudson Valley to the Mohawk Valley.

Similarly, the railroads of the section of New Jersey south and west of the corridor (with the exception of the Raritan and Delaware Bay) were not intended to be links in any interregional system. Their major functions were commuting, developing the truck-farming areas of southwestern New Jersey, and very deliberately creating seashore resorts.

Although the first really practical steam locomotive generally is recognized to have been George Stephenson's 1829 Rocket, experimentation with the idea had been going forward for more than a quarter of a century. John Stevens of Hoboken, an early developer of steamboats, foresaw the economic value of railroads and petitioned the New Jersey legislature in 1811 for a charter to build a railroad across the state. As it was obvious that the heavy traffic was concentrated in the New York–Philadelphia corridor, his proposed route connected existing steamboat lines on the Delaware and Raritan rivers; early conceptions of railroads as short links between navigable waterways were common.

The C and A Monopoly

Although Stevens was not able to demonstrate a reasonably powerful and dependable locomotive until 1825, he was granted the first railroad charter in the United States by the New Jersey legislature in 1815. When the Delaware and Raritan Canal, in the same corridor, was completed a year after the railroad, few people would buy stock in a rail-competing canal proposed at the dawn of railroading; so the New Jersey legislature agreed to a merger of the Delaware and Raritan Canal Company with the Camden and Amboy (C and A) Railroad. The legislature also "declares it lawful for the new company to give 1000 shares of stock outright to the state" (Lane 1939, 325). A monopoly was guaranteed to the Camden and Amboy/Delaware and Raritan Canal, the "joint companies." No public highway could be built within 5 mi (8 km) of the canal; no other railroad could

carry *anyone* or *anything* across the state. The Camden and Amboy pioneered *containerization* in 1833 (passengers' baggage was placed in large crates that were lifted from ferry to rail car and vice versa by cranes) and monopolized passenger traffic and first-class freight from New York to Philadelphia, while its canal partner monopolized bulk freight. At a time (before the Civil War) when the average rail fare in the northeast was $0.0285 per mile, the C and A charged $0.0454. The service was of the arrogant level predictable of monopolies—a contemporary journalist asserted that the C and A treated passengers as "live lumber."

Several attempts were made to break the monopoly, which was to end legally in 1869. One proposal, the Raritan and Delaware Bay, planned to link New York with the south by paralleling the Jersey shore to Cape May; ferries were to connect the rail lines from New York to Norfolk. The Camden and Amboy did not bother to oppose this route among its friends in the

FIGURE 6.3.   *A section of the Camden and Amboy Railroad in Bordentown* is depicted here. The density of traffic within the New York-Philadelphia corridor gave the "joint companies"—the combined railroad and Delaware and Raritan Canal—impressive profits but led the federal government to complain about the monopoly's inability to handle the great volume during the Civil War. (*Early Woodcut Views of New York and New Jersey.* New York: Dover Publication, 1975, p. 79)

legislature, on the grounds that it would not be a profitable one. (The C and A people were right—the Raritan and Delaware Bay went bankrupt in 1867.) The line down the coast never was completed as planned but instead angled away from the coast through the Pine Barrens and headed for Delaware Bay opposite Bombay Hook, Delaware, where a ferry was to connect it through toward the south. In the process, it formed a bypass alternative to the C and A by forming a junction with the newly built Camden and Atlantic Railroad into Camden. The Raritan and Delaware Bay line also tapped the rich oyster beds of Delaware Bay for New York's delectation. Although the proposed "air line" (direct route) railroad from New York to the south could not overcome the cost and congestion handicaps of the cumbersome system of multiple ferry and rail segments, the Raritan and Delaware became the Jersey Central, a major north-south rail route in the state.

The Camden and Atlantic Develops South Jersey

Aside from the Camden and Amboy (absorbed by the Pennsylvania Railroad in 1873), the major single influence on the railroads of South Jersey was the Camden and Atlantic, chartered in 1852 and built by 1854, twenty years after the Camden and Amboy was completed. "No great demand existed at the time for seaside resorts in [north shore] Monmouth County to attract New York City dwellers, who have ocean beaches on nearby Long Island, while Philadelphia's thousands had no ocean beach nearer than the Jersey shore" (Wilson 1964, 44).

The Camden and Atlantic preceded north-shore railroads by a decade. Like many other seaside lines, its real success was as a real estate developer. The shoal waters of the gently shelving sandbars and the treacherously shifting tidal inlets between these barrier beaches were backed by a virtually empty hinterland—the famous Pine Barrens. Very little in the way

of economic development took place until the recreation demand of urban populations, in particular Philadelphians, could be connected cheaply and quickly with the recreation resources of the virtually empty, gleaming sands (see the case study on Atlantic City in Chapter 9). When the Camden and Atlantic Railroad bought up land in such quantities that the state legislature prohibited its buying more, the stockholders simply organized the Camden and Atlantic Land Company, which continued to acquire much of Absecon Island, the seashore terminus of the railroad. Because freight revenues were disappointing and passenger service heavy but highly seasonal, the Camden and Atlantic Railroad went bankrupt in 1857. It was reorganized by the stockholders of the Camden and Atlantic Land Company with knowledge that their real estate holdings were useless without the rail service. They were onto a good thing: Absecon Island, the site of Atlantic City, had been almost worthless before the rails came; by 1900, land that was selling at $10 per acre ($25 per ha) in 1854 was selling at $500 to $800 a front ft ($1,645 to $2,632 per m). Atlantic City real estate was valued at $50 million that year (Wilson 1964, 531).

Development of the Seashore

Atlantic City had quickly captured an enormous tourist hinterland, thanks to the speed and convenience of the trains. Its success inspired frantic endeavors to initiate reasonable facsimiles of Atlantic City on every beach along the coast. A railroad map of 1861 showed only the Camden and Atlantic in the south and a shore connector of Long Branch with a lower-bay ferry terminus in the north; a similar map in 1880 reflected the great flurry of railroad building along or to the shore that took place from the mid-1870s to the late 1880s (see Figure 6.4). The New York and Long Branch Railroad did not arrive at Seaside Park (only 25 mi or 40 km south of Long Branch) until 1885, even though the railroad had already reached Cape May (85

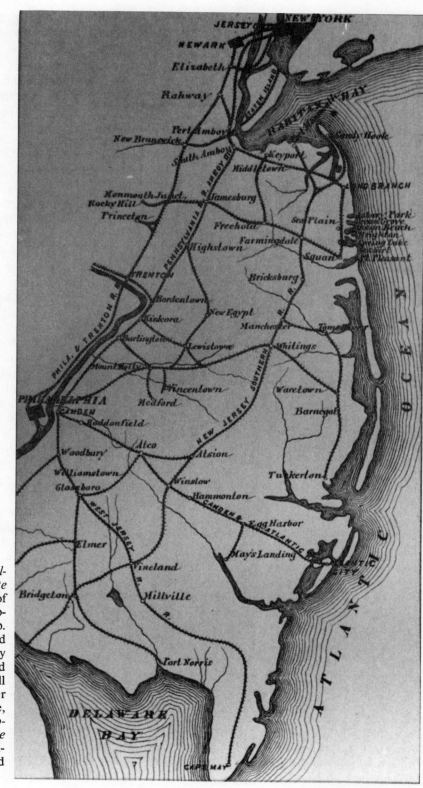

FIGURE 6.4 *Railroads to the Shore, Late 1870s.* The skeleton of the future rail net is apparent in this old map. By 1910, railroads had reached virtually every point on the beaches and often laid tracks the full length of the barrier beaches. (T. F. Rose, *Historical and Biographical Atlas of the New Jersey Coast.* Philadelphia: Woolman and Rose, 1878, p. 213)

mi or 136 km from Camden), the only south-shore resort established before the railroad era, in 1863.

The presence of the railroad spawned resorts between Cape May and Atlantic City during the 1880s, and the effect on the seashore was dramatic. In the 1850 census, the population of the four coastal counties was 55,700. By 1885 it was 111,000, having doubled in thirty-five years. Atlantic City in 1865 had 700 permanent residents; in 1900, 28,000. Its population growth rate from 1870 to 1880 alone was 425 percent. "The area [the shore] passed through its period of greatest growth between 1850 and 1900. After 1900 new growth was mostly in the form of increasing population and not in the foundation of new resorts" (Wilson 1964, 49).

Traffic increased rapidly. By 1873, the Camden and Atlantic ran six round-trip trains daily with two extras on Sunday. In 1877, the Philadelphia and Atlantic Railroad was built to compete with the Camden and Atlantic. Competition dropped the price of a round-trip ticket from three dollars to as low as one dollar. New crowds were attracted, and new investment flooded in. The Pennsylvania Railroad added a third line to Atlantic City in 1880. The broader back bays between the barrier beaches and the mainland were bridged last. A trestle to Long Beach Island was completed in 1885, four years after a similar trestle to Seaside Park. The last rail connection directly to the beach was at Brigantine, just north of Atlantic City, in 1897 (the trestle was destroyed in a storm in 1903 and never rebuilt).

The separation of New York's and Philadelphia's day-trip vacation hinterlands along the Jersey shore is quite clear on a railroad map. The southward advance of the rails from Long Branch and Toms River halted on the bay near Tuckerton (just 16 mi or 25 km north of Atlantic City); although rail service between New York and Atlantic City was possible, it was hardly the most direct route. An 1889 excursion book listed fares from New York as follows:

Long Branch, $1.50; Manasquan, $2.25; but Atlantic City, $4.50 (Kobbe 1970, 9).

Service was superb; Amtrak should aspire to the standards of the turn of the century (if they could count on the volume of business enjoyed then). In 1920, of the sixteen fastest trains in the world, thirteen were in the Atlantic City service.

Automobiles Cause Rail Decline

Alas, by 1923 more vacationers were arriving at Atlantic City by car than by rail. Having played their critical role in fostering the seashore resorts—actually creating most of them—the rails began their long decline (see Table 6.1). In 1920, the revenue-passenger-miles of U.S. railroads reached an all-time high of 47 billion. Passenger traffic generally has fallen dismally across the country; in New Jersey the railroads' special situation has given rise to special problems. Aside from the still relatively well used corridor with its metroliner service and commuting functions, the Jersey rails tend to dead-end either in the New York exurbs of northern New Jersey or on the Jersey shore. Since the seashore railroads had always relied unusually heavily on passenger traffic, they are the hardest hit in an increasingly highway-oriented state. The north shore has even less passenger service remaining, in route miles, than the southern part of the state. However, in passenger volume, the north shore far exceeds the southern area. This reflects the long-established commuting function of the north-shore railroads. Total annual rail-passenger trips for the north Jersey coast for 1978 were 4,998,000, while the south's Seashore Division carried but 115,000 (the northeast corridor was highest at 9,940,000) (*Statistical Almanac–New Jersey* 1981).

The use of southern New Jersey's railroads by commuters has always been hampered by the lack of a through rail connection from downtown Philadelphia to the Jersey suburbs. Whereas the South Jersey commuter lines have always radiated out from Camden, no rail bridge has ever

TABLE 6.1
Railroad Mileage in New Jersey

Year	Miles
1834	61
1840	194
1850	254
1860	560
1870	1,125
1880	1,684
1890	2,047
1900	2,257
1910	2,260
1920[a]	2,352
1930	2,299
1940	2,123
1978[b]	1,619

Source: Compiled from Cranmer, H. Jerome, New Jersey in the Automobile Age: A History of Transportation (Princeton: Van Nostrand, 1964) and Statistical Almanac-New Jersey: A Compilation of Key New Jersey Facts and Figures (Union City: William H. Wise and Company, Inc., 1981).

[a]The decline in mileage after 1920 indicates the consequences of automobile competition.

[b]The collapse of passenger rail service accelerated after the 1950s; only a skeletal shadow of the former system persists.

crossed between Philadephia and Camden; the nearest rail bridge is at Delair, about four miles north of the Benjamin Franklin (Philadelphia-Camden) Bridge. Thus, commuting from Camden to Philadelphia involved transferring to the bridge line (now part of the Lindenwold High Speed Line) or using the Market Street ferries, in operation until the early 1950s. The main line from New York to Philadelphia has long crossed the Delaware at Trenton, so that there never has been a through train from Philadelphia to South Jersey *via* Cam-

den. The present rail service from Atlantic City terminates at Lindenwold, where passengers must transfer to the High Speed Line, which delivers them to downtown Philadelphia.

Railroads may once again figure in resort growth, this time a revitalization, if proposed Philadelphia to Atlantic City and New York to Atlantic City lines are built. New railroads, built to modern standards of high-speed service, may be a feasible solution to Atlantic City's infamous traffic jams and virtually nonexistent parking. It

FIGURE 6.5. *PATH (Port Authority–Trans Hudson) Train at Newark.* Newark is nineteen minutes from the World Trade Center in Manhattan via these air-conditioned electric trains. 160,000 passengers are carried during a typical weekday. (Courtesy of Port Authority of New York–New Jersey)

is not inconceivable that the long cycle of decline of passenger service to the seashore could be reversed, at least for the resurrected "Queen of the Jersey Shore."

Rail Development in North Jersey

North of the New York–Philadelphia corridor, railroads profited by the two *c*'s—coal and commuters. If the heaviest volume of rail traffic followed the corridor for over a century, coal carrying meant prosperity for the north Jersey railroads until after World War II. The routes west to the coalfields had a difficult time, unlike the Camden and Amboy. The C and A, like the Delaware and Raritan Canal, followed an already high-traffic-demand corridor (it was carrying one and one-third million passengers a year before the Civil War and incidentally paying such dividends and taxes to its part-owner, the state of New Jersey,

that it carried almost 70 percent of *total* state expenditures from 1834 to 1850) and had no significant topographic barriers to overcome. The routes north of the New York–Philadelphia corridor were considerably more expensive to construct than were such near-level routes as the Camden and Atlantic. Fortunately, the much more difficult terrain of the northern New Jersey east-west routes attracted abundant capital, lured by the riches of the coalfields. The Morris and Essex Railroad (now the Lackawanna) ran its first train from Newark to Morristown in 1838, but did not reach Dover, a dozen miles away, until 1848 and finally reached Phillipsburg in 1865. In the meantime, the Elizabethtown and Somerville Railroad—later called the Jersey Central—had reached Phillipsburg by 1852 via a more southern route, bypassing the worst of the Appalachian Highlands. The Lackawanna and the Jersey Central were later generally paralleled by the Lehigh Valley Railroad, running west from Bayonne to the Jersey border at Phillipsburg.

The rise of commuter traffic occurred early in the north, with some commuters using the railroad from Morristown into Newark as early as the 1840s. The Lackawanna became a major commuter railroad, famous for the splendid stations it built in the suburbs it served. The Lackawanna knew the value of intermediate-haul traffic on its lines to supplement the coal shipments. Lake Hopatcong became a popular resort area when both the Jersey Central and Lackawanna served it. The Lackawanna also developed Cranberry Lake to the west of Hopatcong as a summer resort to boost ticket sales. By 1890, Lake Hopatcong drew 50,000 visitors a year.

The northern rail companies, like their southern counterparts, formed real estate development companies to sell lots to prospective suburbanites, conveniently close to train stations, of course. Whole strings of towns were, more or less, the creation of the various railroads trying to increase passenger revenues. The Erie Railroad lured new residents to such towns as Englewood, Tenafly, and Montclair; the Central of New Jersey boosted Plainfield and Bound Brook; while the Lackawanna favored real estate promotions in Millburn, Short Hills, Chatham, Madison, and Morristown. The rapid increase in rail mileage within the state (Table 6.1) demonstrates the enthusiasm of railroad builders.

OCEAN PORTS

New Jersey is situated superbly in terms of accessibility to ocean ports. The Port of New York–New Jersey (New York Bay, Hudson River, Raritan Bay, East River, Newark Bay, the Kill Van Kull, Arthur Kill, and associated channels) is, by any measure, one of the greatest ports in the world. The Delaware River ports southward from Trenton, including Philadelphia, Camden, Wilmington, and the specialized

petroleum ports—Marcus Hook, Paulsboro, and Delaware City—constitute another major port complex of 50 mi (80 km) of active waterfront. New York–New Jersey ports handle almost 200 million tn (181.4 million t) of cargo a year, and Philadelphia Harbor handles about 50 million tn (45.3 million t) a year. Neighboring oil ports, including Marcus Hook at 30 million tn (27.2 million t) and Paulsboro at 27 million tn (24.5 million t), when combined with Wilmington (3 million tn or 2.7 million t), Trenton (1 million tn or 0.9 million t), Camden-Gloucester (7 million tn or 6.3 million t), New Castle, Delaware (11 million tn or 9.9 million t), and Penn Manor (United States Steel's facility, importing iron ore), approach two-thirds or so of New York–New Jersey's volume (*Statistical Almanac—New Jersey* 1981). These ports along the Delaware are called "Ameriport" by the port authorities.

There are a number of statistical methods of ranking ports, which is why several different ports (New Orleans and Ameriport among them) can assert that they are ranked above New York–New Jersey. Tonnage imported, tonnage exported, bulk-cargo tonnage, and general-cargo volume and value are all used in ranking ports, along with total tonnage of ships clearing the port. Number of passengers handled would give still other rankings (Miami would top New York, owing to Caribbean cruises).

A key question for New Jersey is the relative significance of the two huge port complexes in which the state participates and the prospects for those ports. Both port complexes are more important to the economy of the state as import facilities than as export centers. It is estimated that, although New Jersey ranks ninth among the states in exports, it exports less than 5 percent of its total manufactured goods. The sheer volume of trade handled through the ports benefits New Jersey to some degree, of course, even if the inbound or outbound cargoes are transient through the state. The petroleum refining industry and the interrelated "chemicals and allied products" group are the most important industries in the state; their relationship to petroleum imports is an obviously vital one. (Because the petroleum refining industry in New Jersey is dominated by a relatively few giants, the Bureau of the Census will not reveal any statistics at the state level to avoid disclosing confidential data, but no one familiar with the state can doubt the importance of oil refining here.)

The Ports' Basic-Nonbasic Functions

Important to an understanding of the ports' functions and relationships to New Jersey's manufacturing is the *basic-nonbasic* concept. It is assumed that cities, regions, and states must do something or provide something, surplus to their own local consumption, to trade with the larger economies of which they are part—national and international. To the extent that goods or services are exported or performed for

TABLE 6.2
The Port of New York-New Jersey

Major Oceanborne Imports, by Rank-Order in Tons, 1980

    petroleum
    non-metallic minerals and slag
    sugar
    alcoholic beverages
    bananas
    coffee
    motor vehicles
    lumber
    salt
    vegetable oils

Major Oceanborne Exports, by Rank-Order in Tons, 1980

    iron and steel scrap
    plastics
    machinery
    motor vehicles
    waste paper
    paper and cardboard
    inedible tallow
    textile waste
    organic products
    steel plates and sheets

Source: Port Authority of New York-New Jersey, 1981.

customers beyond the local area, these are basic to the area's economy and thus build it by generating jobs and bringing in money from the "outside." On the other hand, those enterprises that exist solely to produce for, or serve, the local population are not basic to the economy; they exist because people are there; people are not there because of the economic opportunity thus provided. In Princeton, the university would be basic to that community's economy: the university has a large payroll, the students there (most of whom did not previously live in Princeton) spend money on goods and services provided in the town, and government and corporate grants and research contracts help support the university. Clearly, the town thrives largely because the university is there, not the other way around. A public elementary school in Princeton, on the other hand, would be a nonbasic function, its existence due purely to the local market for its educational services. Similarly, a huge brewery in Newark would be basic to Newark's economy; most of its production would be "exported" beyond Newark, but its taxes, payroll, and need for services would benefit Newark's economy. A small neighborhood tavern across the street would be nonbasic, serving almost entirely a local clientele.

Table 6.2, listing the major imports of the Port of New York–New Jersey, indicates a rather heavy market-orientation of the port. Sugar, alcoholic beverages, bananas, and coffee are clearly consumer items; they will be processed, packed, and distributed throughout the region. The basic-nonbasic concept, of course, depends on a boundary, across which goods or services are "exported" and within which nonbasic goods and services are consumed. Choosing the boundary is critical. If the basic-nonbasic boundary is the state of New Jersey, then many of the ocean-borne imports unloaded and processed within the state are classifiable as basic; if the boundary is expanded to at least the Middle Atlantic states or the central megalopolis, then a

FIGURE 6.6.   The signboard lists the shipping lines serving the South Jersey Port and the Rent This Building sign tells the economic problems of this port facility in an abandoned shipyard. High costs of channel maintenance combined with a relatively cramped site are obstacles to success here.

larger proportion becomes nonbasic.

The Port of New York–New Jersey's list of major exports, by volume (Table 6.2), features an interesting mix of manufactured goods and scrap and waste items. Metal scrap is largest in volume and three other waste or scrap categories place in the top ten volume exports.

The international connections of any port can be divided into its *hinterlands,* the areas that supply the port's imports, and the *forelands,* areas receiving that port's exports. Of course, the rest of New Jersey and the northeastern megalopolis form landward hinterlands and forelands for New Jersey's ports; international hinterlands and forelands, generally considered more important and statistically easier to identify, are indicated in Table 6.3. Both imports and exports primarily are interchanged be-

TABLE 6.3
Trade Relationships of General Ocean-Borne Cargo of The
Port of New York-New Jersey, 1980

Leading International Hinterlands for Imports, Ranked by
Tonnage

Bahamas
Japan
West Germany
Brazil
Italy
United Kingdom
France
Canada
Netherlands
Taiwan

Leading International Forelands for Exports, Ranked by
Tonnage

Japan
Italy
Spain
West Germany
Venezuela
United Kingdom
Saudi Arabia
Taiwan
Greece
France

Source: Port Authority of New York-New Jersey, 1981.

tween New Jersey ports and those of other industrial nations and regions, mostly western Europe and Japan, along with rapidly industrializing Taiwan, Venezuela, and Saudi Arabia. The Bahamas ranks first as a source of imports by volume due to its supplying the port with large quantities of low-value minerals, such as lime, salt, and slag.

**Containerization Favors
New York-New Jersey**

The New Jersey portion of the Port of New York–New Jersey may well not only retain its sizable lead over the New Jersey bank of the ports along the Delaware but even increase its traffic while the southern New Jersey ports stagnate or actually de-

FIGURE 6.7. *Decaying Hudson River Piers.* Much of the business of the whole port has shifted from old-fashioned finger piers to the more spacious handling and storage facilities on Newark Bay. The Hudson waterfront of New Jersey, from Bayonne to Weehawken, is characterized by similar abandonment and decay, although some modernized facilities remain in operation.

cline. A major advance in general cargo-handling technology favors the continued shift of port traffic from the Hudson and East rivers to Newark Bay. The "finger piers" (piers jutting out from shore like fingers from a palm) that once lined both banks of the Hudson are obsolescent for two reasons. First, maneuvering ships into and out from these narrow slips is difficult, often requiring the expensive services of tugboats. Second, the piers themselves, mostly dating back half a century and more, were designed for the unloading of cargo by means of shipboard cranes and a great deal of human muscle, and storage space, though under cover, typically was limited.

Labor efficiency is greatly increased by the trend toward *containerization*—the packing of general-cargo merchandise (machinery and parts, photographic and communications equipment, clothing, and so

on) into steel containers, generally 8 ft (2.4 m) by 8 ft by 30 or 40 ft (9 or 12 m). Huge dockside cranes transfer the containers between ship and shore, loading them into ship's holds or onto flatbed trucks or stacking them for storage. The containers can be stored safely out of doors, and pilferage, a major cost in cargoes handled the older way, is virtually eliminated (although entire containers have been known to disappear at Port Elizabeth and Port Newark). A great deal of space is necessary for containers, and the old-fashioned finger piers were far too congested and had no expansion room. Additionally, modern container-ship captains prefer to be able to draw alongside a dock parallel to the shoreline, not at an awkward right angle to it. New Jersey's portion of the great port has the space to accommodate the container ships and the handling and storage

FIGURE 6.8. *Port Newark.* The large amount of space necessary for efficient cargo handling and storage is the major reason for the shift in port activity from the old Hudson River finger piers to the spacious facilities of Port Newark and neighboring Port Elizabeth. Together, these are the largest container ports in the United States. (Courtesy of Port Authority of New York–New Jersey)

facilities. The Ameriport's two large container facilities are both on the Pennsylvania side.

Other Handicaps to Ameriport's Future

The Delaware River ports have several handicaps compared to the New York–New Jersey port. The largest port in a region usually has the fact of its sheer size as an advantage. The largest port tends to remain the largest port and even to increase its dominance in a snowball effect known as *frequency of sailing.* Import-export agents need to serve their customers as efficiently as possible or lose their business. If there is a choice among ports through which to

direct their customers' merchandise, the agents will compare not only port costs but also the costs of collecting or forwarding merchandise by land connections to and from the port and the speed with which the ocean-borne connections will be made. If a shipment of machine parts with some time value is to move from, say, Trenton to Genoa, the fact that Philadelphia-Camden is the closest international port may not lead to the shipment leaving via the Delaware. If regularly scheduled general-cargo ships sail between, say, Port Elizabeth and Genoa more frequently than from Delaware River ports to Genoa, the frequency-of-sailing factor will attract the cargo to

Port Elizabeth. The ports that attract more cargo attract more ships that attract more cargo, and the snowball thus gets bigger faster.

Another factor in attracting ships is known as *turnaround time*. A ship is earning money when it is moving; time in port should be as brief as possible. The most modern and efficient cargo-handling and ship-servicing facilities (for refueling, reprovisioning, and perhaps minor repairs) shorten this unproductive time in port and boost profits all around. Once a port stops continual modernization, it may be doomed to decline.

Over time, ships tend to be built larger, as in that way more cargo can be moved without proportional increases in labor and fuel costs. Deep channels and wide turning basins are thus desirable. The Delaware River Ameriport has some problems of channel depth, and the narrowing width by Philadelphia is another handicap. New York is 200 mi (322 km) closer to European ports than is Philadelphia, and as noted, Europe is an important hinterland/foreland for both Ameriport and New York–New Jersey.

Land connections from the port toward the interior of the continent have always been important considerations in the economic health of ports. Baltimore, always a prime competitor to the Delaware Valley, surpassed Philadelphia in value of exports around 1800; Philadelphia's answer was to build the nation's first paved turnpike from Lancaster to Philadelphia (Currier 1979, 202). The competition among the major ports of the future megalopolis continued through the canal and railroad eras into the present. The contemporary highway system connecting the midwestern and northern Appalachian hinterlands with East Coast ports would seem to favor New York over Philadelphia. The major east-west superhighway channeling cargo to and from the ports of Philadelphia, the Pennsylvania Turnpike (Interstate 76), is a toll road,

FIGURE 6.9. *A Container Ship Heading Up the Kill Van Kull for Port Newark–Elizabeth.* The speedy turnaround time resulting from mechanized operations helps attract container ships to the New Jersey portion of the Port of New York–New Jersey. The very little dredging required in this port, meaning low-cost port operations, could be a decisive advantage over Ameriport on the Delaware.

whereas Interstate 80, which heads for the George Washington Bridge, offers a toll-free alternative to the turnpike, as does toll-free Interstate 70 into Baltimore from the west. Tolls cannot be avoided even by using Interstate 80 to a point north of Philadelphia, then heading south to Philadelphia, because the best route would be the Pennsylvania Turnpike's Northeast Extension. Similarly, using Interstate 70, which roughly parallels the Pennsylvania Turnpike to the south, cannot offer a toll-free alternative—the fastest highway route between Baltimore and Philadelphia is on toll roads (the Maryland and Delaware turnpikes).

A last, potential handicap to Ameriport is the possibility of the federal government's adopting a "user-fee" approach to pay for channel maintenance (by dredging) on the Delaware, rather than subsidizing this necessary work from general funds. User fees inevitably would be passed on to those who import or export via the Delaware, raising costs of shipping through Ameriport and making New York–New Jersey more appealing. It would appear that southern New Jersey's port facilities will experience, at best, slower growth than northern New Jersey's. Associated industrial-site advantages will favor more expansion of industry sensitive to the port-location advantages that are also in the north.

NEW JERSEY IN THE AIR AGE

New Jersey was an early beneficiary of the air age, thanks to the state's longtime asset—land near great cities that was relatively cheap, reasonably accessible, and certainly flat. For some of the same reasons that many oil refineries, railroad classification yards, and long-term storage facilities are in the New Jersey portion of metropolitan orbits, the first major airports for both New York and Philadelphia were in New Jersey. In the 1930s, Newark Airport was the busiest single airport in the United States, handling an estimated 20 percent of total air-passenger traffic. Camden Airport (no longer in existence) served as the major terminal for Philadelphia. The youthful commercial air-transport industry, which expanded quickly in the 1930s with the development of aircraft with larger capacity, more reliability, and greater cruising distance, demonstrated the real economic assets of airports.

It is possible that New Jersey satellites of the two metropolitan centers were permitted to host major air terminals only as long as disadvantages of terminals outweighed the advantages. When airplanes were exciting curiosities that could carry only a handful of passengers, the otherwise unproductive space they used as landing fields and the not unreal danger of crashes suggested that airports should be located in the near but somewhat expendable suburbs. The realization that airports were increasingly busy places that had the potential for generating considerable income suggested recapturing the airport function for the metropolises' home jurisdictions. Newark Airport's supremacy in the New York metropolitan area lasted from 1929 to 1939. Camden Airport was moribund by the end of World War II.

Factors Working Against New Jersey Airports

Normally, the earlier-established transport facilities are able to build upon this head start to maintain a competitive edge over their later competitors. Two important factors, however, helped overcome New Jersey's head start and shape the rise of LaGuardia and Kennedy airports on the New York side of the Hudson. Travel time between the central business district's hotels, offices, and public transit termini and the airport is critical, but it was not the sole determining factor. Compared to Kennedy and LaGuardia, Newark Airport is closest to midtown Manhattan in time-distance, about twenty-five minutes by car. Perhaps more important was the combination of land and money, both available "up front"—ahead of revenues to be generated by the improvements. Ample space was needed as more and bigger aircraft were used at busy airports. Longer runways and more runways, however, had to be matched by the latest in electronic guidance systems and foul-weather navigation gear. Newark Airport's outdated navigational aids were blamed, fairly or unfairly, for contributing to crashes. Between December 16, 1951, and February 11, 1952, two outbound airplanes and one inbound airliner crashed into the congested streets of Elizabeth; a total of 117 dead caused the understandably terrorized Elizabeth citizenry to argue for closing Newark Airport until runway extensions could be completed. It was closed until November 1952.

Despite its high degree of accessibility from downtown Philadelphia, Camden Airport, hemmed in by urban-suburban growth, could not hold its business against the Philadelphia Airport built in the marshlands to the southwest of the city. As aircraft became much larger, they could no longer use small airports—small in area or small in passenger volume. Larger passenger payloads meant that operators of these larger aircraft increasingly preferred the largest air-passenger markets within a region as their landing sites. Other airports, even if serving sizable cities, will not be served by the larger, long-distance aircraft because these aircraft will not be used efficiently if they take a series of very short hops between nearby airports. Takeoffs and landings consume more fuel than cruising; more important, they consume the airliner's prime advantage—saving time over other means of transport. Passengers prefer direct, nonstop flights and are aware that takeoffs and landings are the most dangerous part of any air trip.

Just as in seaports, and for much the same reason, traffic is progressively concentrated in the busiest airport—which then becomes still bigger. Nearby airports are then in the "shadow" of this large airport, not attracting the air service that would be proportionate to the hinterland population they serve. The larger the airport, the more frequent is the interconnection to a greater variety of destinations and the greater the likelihood that competing airlines will offer special services and reduced rates.

Successful New Jersey Airports

There are counterforces to this shadow effect of the metropolitan region's largest airport, as Newark Airport's advancing prosperity would indicate. Newark Airport, taken over on a long lease by the Port of New York and New Jersey Authority in 1947, received a major renovation and expansion in the 1970s. Now an international airport, Newark has facilities capable of handling 750 people per hour in customs and immigration processing. This new significance of Newark Airport is due to the continuing decentralization of the metropolitan area's population and to the very serious congestion at John F. Kennedy International Airport (JFK). It is not uncommon for Kennedy-bound airliners to circle in holding patterns for an hour or more, awaiting permission to land. This waste of time and fuel, not to mention increased risk, argues for the decentralization of a metropolitan area's air traffic—if Newark Airport did not exist, it would have to be created. Charter traffic prefers the diminished congestion (and thus lower operating costs) of Newark over JFK, and ten scheduled airlines serve Newark to JFK's thirty and LaGuardia's six. Air cargo could be greatly expanded at Newark Airport to relieve the pressure at JFK (see Table 6.4). Helicopter passenger service links all of the New York and northern New Jersey commercial airports.

Leading air-cargo imports at Newark Airport include clothing, shoes, machinery, printed materials, scientific apparatus, toys and sporting goods, telecommunications equipment, and office machines. Leading exports include office machines and other machinery, scientific instruments, telecommunications equipment, pharmaceuticals, photo supplies, aircraft, and aircraft parts.

FIGURE 6.10. *Terminal A at Newark International Airport.* Handling nine and one-quarter million commercial passengers a year, this largest airport in New Jersey is served by five charter airlines in addition to ten scheduled airlines, plus an additional thirteen commuter air services and five air-cargo carriers. (Courtesy of Port Authority of New York–New Jersey)

TABLE 6.4
Relative Importance of New York-New Jersey Region Airports

	Air Cargo, Domestic & Overseas, Short Tons[a]			
	1950	1960	1970	1979
Airports				
Kennedy	7,811	138,055	759,546	1,269,533
La Guardia	43,712	30,672	39,815	43,462
Newark	51,447	58,313	157,301	118,427

	Passenger Traffic, Domestic & Overseas			
Kennedy	394,344	8,803,665	19,096,705	26,976,675
La Guardia	3,631,275	4,227,755	11,845,141	18,391,035
Newark	1,055,406	2,935,613	6,460,489	9,296,942

Source: Aviation Department, Port Authority of New York-New Jersey.

[a]Formula to convert short tons to metric tons is: 1 ton equals .907 metric ton.

Other New Jersey airports with scheduled passenger service are Mercer County (Trenton), Bader Field (Atlantic City), and Cape May County (Wildwood and Cape May). This last-mentioned facility is open only seasonally. Teterboro Airport is the state's leading "general aviation" (private and corporate-private) airport. Only LaGuardia handles more takeoffs and landings in the metropolitan area.

CHAPTER 7

AGRICULTURE

LOCATIONAL FACTORS

Agricultural patterns in New Jersey should be viewed both in their relationships to the physical capabilities of landforms, soils, drainage, and climate and in their even more complex, and continually evolving, relationships to market factors. Farmers' decisions on the optimal land use for their farms thus reflect more than an assessment of the potentials and limitations of the physical resource base. Decisions on which crops and animals will be raised—even on which *varieties* of crops and domestic animals—are influenced also by such cultural factors as land value, taxes, accessibility to market, perishability, cost of labor, transport costs, and the availability of canneries, packing plants, dairies, produce auctions, or cooperative wholesalers.

New Jersey's farmers operate in a farmland region that is one of the highest priced (and with the highest potential value for development) of the United States. To remain in business, they must use their land relatively *intensively*. In *intensive* land-use systems, relatively large inputs of labor, capital, and energy are matched by high productivity and, with luck, high returns per land unit. In *extensive* land-use systems, relatively little human effort, capital (use of machinery, irrigation systems, fertilizer, pesticides) and energy is "invested" per land unit, and proportionally lower productivity and lower profits per acre are acceptable, especially when coupled with much larger farms than in intensive sys-

tems. Rising land values in the vicinity of metropolitan areas mean that farmland must be highly productive in order to compete with potential suburban uses for that land. "Raising" shopping centers, industrial parks, or housing developments can be far more profitable than raising vegetables, grains, or chickens.

The proximity to expanding cities can be a negative factor in the continuation of farming, but the superior accessibility to large markets for farm products also can be a tremendous advantage. In agriculture, as in its overall economy, New Jersey's more-important geographic assets are locational rather than in the qualities of the natural resource base. From the late colonial period on, New Jersey farmers have benefited from their relative accessibility to expanding, prosperous, urban markets. The farmers of the Garden State early earned that nickname by producing fresh fruits and vegetables so conveniently close to the consumers that perishability—the destroyer of crops and profits—was minimized. New Jersey farmers have proven to be highly innovative, open-minded entrepreneurs, capable of shifting land use to respond to changes in markets, transport costs and technologies, food preservation technologies, and new sources of competition.

To understand the transformation of New Jersey agriculture, it is necessary to view the changing consensus on land use and crop specializations within the context of changing transportation economics and

FIGURE 7.1. *A Reminder of Agriculture's Importance.*

land value. The evolution of New Jersey agriculture has been a startling exemplification of a theory of the interrelationship of transport cost, land value, and land use first advanced more than 150 years ago (Zimolzak and Stansfield 1979, 246). German economist J. H. Von Thunen theorized an *isolated state* in which a sizable town was located in the center of a uniformly productive agricultural plain. In this theoretical situation, the normally significant variables of soil fertility, drainage, and slope were all held constant. Also considered constant was the efficiency of transportation. Von Thunen stipulated that a navigable river would alter his theoretical land-use pattern, as would any modern transport system, for example. In his theoretical model, Von Thunen envisioned a pattern of concentric circles like a practice target. The town, or market, was at the center, surrounded by concentric rings of differing land use. All of the hinterland population would like to be immediately adjacent to this market for convenience and lowest transport costs. In a competition for these close-in locations, the successful high bidders would be either those with high potentials for profits or those who simply could not function at all farther away. In Europe a century and a half ago, the closest "ring" around the town was one of market gardening—the production

of fresh fruits and vegetables for the urban market. These market gardeners could pay top price for the closest locations to market because it would make no sense for them to settle for cheaper land farther away and then have their produce spoil en route to market. Also, they were using the land intensively by concentrating a great deal of effort on comparatively small plots of land. Von Thunen placed woodlots fairly close in also, because of high transport costs, then grain farming farther out from the towns, as grain was not particularly perishable nor did it generate as much income per land unit as fresh produce. At the outermost extremes of his isolated state (isolated from other markets and their influences) were those farmers involved in grazing economies, producing wool or meat. Because wool was not perishable at all and meat animals were not perishable until they were slaughtered—which would be in the market itself, these extensive land-use systems that required large amounts of cheap land were located at the peripheries of the hinterland.

For two centuries, New Jersey farmers and their choices of crops and animal production have reflected the applications of Von Thunen's economic theories on land use. Accessibility to great cities, which we now recognize poses a long-run threat to persistence of agricultural land use in a suburbanizing milieu, has been the opportunity of Jersey farmers throughout the history of the state. In 1807, pioneer U.S. geographer Jedidiah Morse observed of New Jersey that,

> The orchards, in many parts of the state, equal any in the United States and their cider is said (and not without reason) to be the best in the world. The markets of New York and Philadelphia receive a very considerable proportion of their supplies from the contiguous part of New Jersey. These supplies consist of vegetables of many kinds, apples, pears, peaches, plums, strawberries, cherries and other fruits—cider in large quantities, butter, cheese, beef, pork, mutton, and the lesser meats. (Morse 1807, 184)

These products remain important with the modern exceptions of mutton, butter, and cheese, for New Jersey is typical of Von Thunen's inner ring; this was true and has in fact intensified with the years.

Unfortunately for the persistence of farming without undue pressures from more intensive urban-suburban land-use competition, New Jersey's best agricultural soils tend to lie in the two major metropolitan areas and in the central corridor where the competition of urban uses is most intense. The economic pressures on farmers within the suburban orbit, which seems constantly to expand outward, can become almost unbearable.

HISTORICAL DEVELOPMENT

Land. Good land, cheap land—this was the lodestone for early farmers in New Jersey. The soils of the Newark Basin Piedmont and the inner coastal plain, especially the rich alluvial (water-deposited) soils of the valleys of the Passaic, Hackensack, Raritan, and Delaware rivers, were highly attractive to European immigrants and to New Englanders and New Yorkers looking for good land to call their own. These pioneer farmers had twin goals: self-sufficiency (as far as practicable) and cash income from supplying markets. Those early markets were relatively distant in terms of transport cost, whether to a growing town 20 mi (32 km) distant or to really far-off Europe. After the initial compact, nucleated settlements established by transplanted New Englanders and Long Islanders, later East Jersey farmer-pioneers roamed far from towns, preferring the isolated farmsteads to the "towns" of New England heritage. West Jersey never did emphasize towns of farmers, and so New Jersey's early agricultural pattern quickly came to resemble the now-common U.S. rural landscape of individual farmsteads.

The Short-lived Frontier

The great majority of New Jersey's farmers were not working within an isolated frontier milieu for more than a few decades. The frontier, in an economic sense, did not persist very long for most Jersey farmers, for two sets of reasons. For one thing, fairly large-scale European in-migration was late, compared to New England and Virginia. When the English finally took the settlement of "The Jerseys" seriously, the non-Indian population surged upward. Not only had a "land hunger" developed in the older, established English colonies, but the new English governors had the wisdom to confirm, without quibbling, existing Dutch land grants and deeds. They thereby encouraged the Dutch to stay and even increase by migration from the middle Hudson Valley, attracted by equitable treatment.

The other factors supporting a quick "filling in" of settlement in farming areas were considerations of physical geography. The expanding farm frontier was confined on the south-southeast by the much less desirable outer coastal plain, which was early—and generally accurately—perceived as having poor soil. Pockets and strips of usable soil exist within the Pinelands, but their being imbedded within an agriculturally sterile matrix certainly discouraged exploitation for a long time. Similarly, the rugged, glaciated ridges of the Appalachian Highlands and Kittatinny Mountain ran at right angles to the outward-spreading farm frontier. The valleys of the northwest included some highly desirable land, but were surrounded by steep, heavily wooded terrain. When settlement did progress there, it took the form of relatively quick clearing of all usable valley lands, which maintained the pattern of successive saturation of good land and ended the frontier rapidly.

The commercial crops, such as they were in the short-lived "frontier," emphasized corn and cattle, although a much greater variety of plants and domesticated animals flourished as subsistence for farm families. Agricultural historian Hubert Schmidt credits the Dutch with having been disproportionately important in introducing new plants and animals into New Jersey

FIGURE 7.2. *A Burlington County Farmstead in the Late Nineteenth Century, as Glamorized in a County Atlas.* County atlases of the 1870s and 1880s featured pictures and stories about subscribers to the atlas. This prosperous-appearing traditional farm apparently emphasized livestock within a "general farm" frame. New Jersey farmers have specialized in producing for nearby urban markets for most of the state's existence. (J. D. Scott, compiler, *Combination Atlas Map of Burlington County, New Jersey.* Philadelphia: J. D. Scott, 1876, p. 34)

(Schmidt 1973, 45–46). Cabbage, lettuce, carrots, radishes, parsnips, beets, spinach, and onions helped "keep body and soul together," while Dutch varieties of tulips, lilies, and roses fed the soul. Fruit trees of all kinds thrived here, sometimes amazing visitors with their rapid growth and heavy yields. Apple, pear, cherry and peach trees created spectacular spring scenes. The yields were so great that at least some New Jerseyans complained of the monotony of apple pie, apple sauce, and apple butter at three meals a day!

During the early phase of agriculture in

New Jersey, which Schmidt takes to about 1810, livestock were raised rather casually. Although sheep, highly vulnerable to various wild and domesticated predators, were usually carefully penned, other farm animals were allowed to forage for their food, roaming about the neighborhood unrestrained but bearing ear-crops, brands, or tattoos to establish ownership. Controlled breeding attracted little interest or concern, except in the case of fighting cocks and riding horses. Provincial laws required farmers to enclose crops against animals (rather than fence animals *in*) with fences at least 4 ft 3 in. (1.28 m) high (Schmidt 1973, 53). The first fences in the then wood-surplus areas were "worm fences" or "Virginia fences" (an indication of their possible origin), made crudely of split rails laid in a zigzag pattern. The worm fence could be built high enough to restrain livestock and required no nails, a major advantage in the days of handmade, expensive iron nails.

Random breeding resulted in poor-quality livestock. Cows, pigs, chickens, and horses were frequently of inferior size; although a law required that inferior males of domestic species be castrated or fenced in, it was widely ignored, and by the end of the colonial period livestock were distinctly smaller and of lower quality than their European progenitors.

In this early period, urban markets were small and readily supplied by nearby farms that produced livestock as a sideline. Dairying did not become a commercial specialization until the late eighteenth century. The favored breeds of dairy cattle, before the Revolution, were from the Channel Islands (from "old" Jersey to New Jersey!); they produced a high-butterfat-content milk preferred for butter and cheese. Britain forbade export of pedigreed farm stock to the United States after the Revolution, apparently without complete success.

An unintended, but unpleasant, gift to the New World was the wheat-attacking Hessian fly that seems to have arrived in a load of wheat straw used as bedding by German troops during the Revolution. Wheat had been the major crop until the Hessian fly epidemic of the 1780s; New Jersey had been a "bread" colony. The Hessian fly helped encourage a shift in emphasis to corn, which was hardier in New Jersey anyhow. Corn was consumed as cornmeal and corn mush and was very important as a livestock feed. Wheat farmers adjusted to the Hessian fly by sowing wheat in the fall rather than late summer and by selecting wheat strains more resistant to the fly. A more permanent blow to wheat acreage was to come in the form of declining soil fertility, already obvious by the Revolution.

Other crops popular on New Jersey farms before the agricultural, technological, and expanding urban-market effects of the Industrial Revolution became a major force were oats (for livestock), buckwheat, and flax. Flax was planted for both linen fiber and flaxseed (linseed) oil. Farmers also were bent on improving their pasturage by sowing timothy and red clover. White potatoes were but a minor garden crop until the Scots-Irish brought the potato back to the New World as a major crop. By the late eighteenth century, "Irish," or white, potatoes were back in favor as a commercial crop. Sweet potatoes, called Bermuda potatoes, were successful in the sandier soils of South Jersey.

Changing Agricultural Practices After 1810

The century or so from approximately 1810 to the First World War was one in which change and innovation were found not so much in new crops or animals but in care and fertilization of the soil and emphasis on more efficient, more productive varieties of plants and animals, and one in which new machinery was introduced (Schmidt 1973, 53). Farming prospered in New Jersey during the nineteenth century; the state's all-time peak farm acreage, nearly 3 million acres (1,215,000 ha), was reached in 1860. Farms actually became smaller in area in many counties later as labor-intensive fruit and vegetable production, dairying, and poultry and egg production became more widespread. The peak number of farms, about 35,000, occurred in the 1890s, before the cities exploded outward in automobile suburbs and long before steeply rising labor costs put a squeeze on truck farms. During this period of peak number of farms, 1890 to 1910, the average size of farms in the state had declined to about 75 acres (30.3 ha) from a peak of about 86 acres (34.8 ha) (Schmidt 1973).

Woodlots became a more valuable asset to New Jersey farmers by the close of the

STAFFORD FORGE CRANBERRY PLANTATION,
WEST CREEK, OCEAN CO.N.J.THE PROPERTY OF DANIEL R.GOWDY.(FOR DESCRIPTION SEE ATLAS.)

FIGURE 7.3. *Stafford Forge Cranberry Plantation,* (circa 1878). The cranberry industry is labor intensive, though this engraving suggests no shortage of labor in a crop specialization typical of the outer coastal plain. Notice the extreme flatness of the landscape in which the cranberry bogs are located. (T. F. Rose, *Historical and Biographical Atlas of the New Jersey Coast.* Philadelphia: Woolman and Rose, 1878, pp. 307–308)

eighteenth century, when firewood demands were beginning to climb in the growing towns. A 1794 report from Chatham complained that the price of a cord of walnut (today considered too valuable as furniture to burn) had risen to two dollars. Farmers usually relegated their roughest land to the woodlot, but they relied heavily on it for building materials around the farm, fencing, and cash income. Firewood brought in steady cash; farmers also sold wood to barrel makers and wagon makers and bark to tanners. The use of portable sawmills, set up in remaining stands of timber in isolated or rough country, began to eradicate virgin timber from much of the state by the middle of the nineteenth century.

As good timber and even firewood became scarce in many districts, farmers be-

gan to rely on "imported" timber (most likely from Pennsylvania) for building, and the by-then readily available anthracite from Pennsylvania for stove fuel. Some farmers were experimenting with wire fencing, while others investigated hedge plants as a solution to the perennial fencing problem. Osage orange was a popular hedge for a time in the nineteenth century, from the East Coast to the Great Plains, but was not a success in the long run. The hedges grew so large in New Jersey that they shaded field crops and sapped the water and soil minerals that could be more efficiently used by crops.

Events far from New Jersey, and totally beyond the power of Jerseyans to control or even influence significantly, had impacts upon New Jersey's agricultural economy. The ongoing transportation revolution repeatedly influenced the relative profitability of crops. Advances in food preservation—canning and freezing—hugely expanded the areas suitable to *truck farming* (the equivalent of Von Thunen's market gardening), removing some of New Jersey's location advantages. By the middle of the nineteenth century, Jersey farmers were already adjusting to grain-production competition from the developing Midwest, and their continual adjustments to changing market conditions places them surely in the vanguard of American farmers in this respect.

Unusual Crops

Casual readers of old records are sometimes startled to discover mention of a "sugarcane refinery" in Cape May County a century ago. The "cane" was not tropical sugarcane, of course, but was Chinese sugarcane, as it was then known, or sorghum. The sorghum could be pressed for a heavy syrup that some found palatable for buckwheat cakes. After housewives complained that sorghum was not an acceptable substitute for sugar in baking however, enthusiasm waned. A state subsidy kept sorghum a South Jersey crop for five years, but sorghum quickly disappeared after the subsidy ended.

Another brief New Jersey crop was the Chinese, or white, mulberry tree. Silkworm culture had been a hobby of New Jerseyans in the late colonial period, encouraged by government bounties. After all, such exotic activities are possible even in England itself, *if* high labor costs are either absorbed by the determined grower as a combination leisure-time activity and conversation piece or subsidized by a government for some misguided venture into self-sufficiency. The rapid growth of the textile industry in New Jersey supported the idea that local raw-silk production would be profitable. As silkworms insist on a wholly unadventurous diet of nothing but the leaves of white mulberry trees, the large-scale planting of trees logically preceded the large-scale production of silk. Literally millions of mulberry trees were planted as cuttings across

the state. The silk mania thrived from about 1830 to 1837, by which time enough people had discovered that the painstaking unwinding of cocoons went uncompensated—there were no eager customers. The landscape did gain a widely distributed tree that still thrives.

A happier choice of specialties was the harvest of wild "salt hay" from the tidal marshes prevalent from Newark Bay around the coast to Delaware Bay. This salt hay was very resistant to rot when damp and thus made superior bedding for stabled horses. It is still harvested for this purpose.

New Jersey farmers have produced alcoholic beverages since the colonial period, when applejack or "Jersey lightning" was famous through America. A nearly perfect "frontier crop," applejack concentrated the production of many trees into a few barrels. The popular treat had no problems of perishability and had high value per unit of weight, so that it could be shipped relatively long distances over primitive transport routes. For much the same reasons, then-remote Ireland and the highlands of Scotland had "condensed" their bulky grains into whiskey.

The New England technique of "distilling" applejack into a potent brandy was popular. In this method a barrel of fermenting apple juice was deposited on a back porch during deepest winter. Every day or so, the thirsty farmers lifted off and discarded the ice at the top, leaving a progressively more potent "jack" in the barrel. Cold winters thus produced something to "keep the cold out."

The Need for Fertilizers

Fertilizer was a nearly universal need as farmers, under mounting pressure from expanding cities, needed to use their land more intensively. The demand for fertilization came about toward the end of the colonial period, when "wearing out" land by ignorant (sometimes, arrogant) misuse could no longer be followed by moving on to fresh land, tossing away the worn-out land as today we might toss out an empty beer can. Conservation came rather late, and then not so much as a result of conscience as an outgrowth of economic self-interest. Land quickly became too expensive to treat as a throwaway.

Before scientific agriculture was made generally available through the heroic efforts of Rutgers University's experimental farms and numerous publications, farmers often effectively threw away soil conditioners and natural fertilizers. The growing numbers of domestic animals, for example, contributed a potential bonanza of manure, but it was common practice to pile up manure for an annual distribution over the fields. This unprotected storage for up to a year undoubtedly wasted much of the potential of the manure through weathering. Plowing under "green manure" like clover was an idea slow to advance at first. More than one farmer hauled "night soil" (human excrement) from cities to spread on the land. "Land plaster," or calcined gypsum (better known now as plaster of paris), was a fertilizer brought over from Germany in the late colonial period. Calcined lime was a close relative, and when farmers discovered any local limestone deposits, they would build a limekiln to process crushed limestone into calcined lime. The canals and then railroads that connected Pennsylvania anthracite with Great Valley limestone greatly reduced the cost of lime and contributed to its rising popularity.

Greensand marl was a more uniquely New Jersey natural fertilizer. The marl was obtained from pits dug into a geological formation that runs at varying depths under the interior edge of the outer coastal plain—a linear strip of fertilizer, in other words, that parallels the inner coastal plain, the most intensively farmed part of New Jersey. The marl is—or was—up to 30 ft (9 m) in thickness and lay in a belt ranging from 6 to 12 mi (9 to 19 km) in width from Sandy Hook through Marlboro, Freehold, Mount Holly, Marlton, Woodstown, and Salem. The marl was rich in marine fossils; New Jersey's marl pits also have produced some superb dinosaur remains.

Many marl pits were opened by the 1820s. The fertilizer value was rather low, so that applications had to be quite heavy—this limited patronage of marl pits to farmers in the vicinity. Farmers provided their own transportation of the marl and frequently dug it as well, hauling and spreading it in the winter. Marl applications were particularly effective on sandy soil, with which most New Jersey coastal-plains farmers were well supplied. Marl was being applied as fertilizer as late as the 1920s in at least South Jersey, but the only contemporary commercial producer of "greensand," in Gloucester County, finds that little is used as fertilizer. Now the glauconite finds a steady market as a water-softening agent.

Guano (bird manure) from Peru, rich in nitrate, was a popular though very expensive fertilizer in New Jersey just before the Civil War. Its high cost favored competing fertilizers made from urban night soil. A Newark chemist, James Mapes, successfully marketed what may have been the United States' first commercial chemical fertilizer. Mapes dissolved ground animal bones in sulfuric acid and added ammonium sulphate. New Jersey farmers have been avid users of fertilizers for a long time, reflecting their need to intensify production on valuable land and to cope with the sandy soils of the outer coastal plain. Some outer-coastal-plain farmers allege that the nearly pure sand is actually an excellent soil "base" in that any chemical properties desired can simply be added. This viewpoint, however, may be most popular with those farmers engaged in selling their farmland.

MODERN AGRICULTURE

New Jersey ranks first, nationally, in the average value of farmland and farm buildings per acre but—fortunately for its farmers—third (after Rhode Island and Massachusetts) in taxes per farm acre and third (after New Hampshire and Michigan) in

TABLE 7.1
Land in Farms in New Jersey

Year	Million Acres/Million Hectares		
1860	3.0	/	1.2
1880	2.9	/	1.17
1890	2.7	/	1.09
1900	2.8	/	1.13
1910	2.5	/	1.01
1920	2.2	/	.89
1930	1.7	/	.68
1940	1.8	/	.73
1950	1.7	/	.68
1960	1.4	/	.56
1970	1.035	/	.419
1978	1.049	/	.425

Sources: Hubert Schmidt, Agriculture in New Jersey: A Three-Hundred Year History (New Brunswick: Rutgers University Press, 1973); 1978 Census of Agriculture, State Data, New Jersey, "Land in Farms: 1945 to 1978 (Washington, D.C.: U.S. Government Printing Office, 1980).

taxes as a percentage of net farm income. Urban sophisticates and casual transients who scoff at New Jersey's appellation as the Garden State should know better— New Jersey farmers sold agricultural products worth over $359 million during 1978, the most recent federal agricultural census year. They produced those products on 1,049,000 acres (425,250 ha), a total figure that appears to have stabilized, at least temporarily, after a long and fairly steep decline (see Table 7.1). The huge decrease in the number of farms that New Jersey witnessed from 1950 to 1970, a 66 percent decline, came at a time of rapid overall population growth and surging suburbanization. The most recent data support a hope that New Jersey's enlightened farm-taxation policies may be having the desired effect. It is significant that farm acreage, as opposed to number of farms, did not drop as steeply during the 1970–1979 period.

The map of farmland as a percentage of total land area (Figure 7.4) shows the results of various physical and cultural positives and negatives. Counties that are mostly in the Pinelands, such as Atlantic, Cape May, or Ocean, have relatively little farmland for reasons of soil deficiencies, while the urban counties of the northeast, and to a lesser extent, Camden County, have many areas of good soils that are encrusted with concrete and asphalt or devoted to suburban lawns (see Table 7.2). The better soils of the southernmost outer coastal plain and of the inner plain support a high proportion of farmland in the southwest, balanced by a northwestern farm belt with more emphasis on animal products

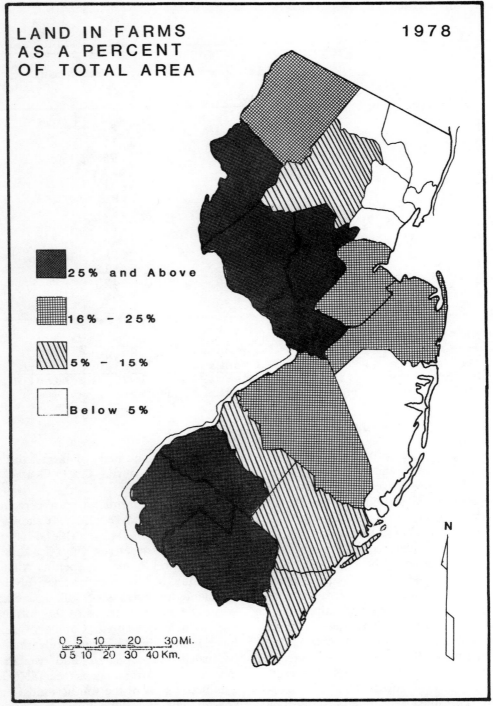

LAND IN FARMS AS A PERCENT OF TOTAL AREA

1978

25% and Above

16% - 25%

5% - 15%

Below 5%

0 5 10 20 30 Mi.
0 5 10 20 30 40 Km.

N

FIGURE 7.4. Northwestern New Jersey and the southwest are the surviving rural farm landscapes of the Garden State. Note the much larger area of suburban expansion at the expense of farms in the New York Metro area compared to the Philadelphia Metro.

TABLE 7.2
Average Size of Farm and Total Acres in Farms, By County,
1978

County	Average Size of Farm Acres/Hectares	Total Land in Farms Acres/Hectares
Atlantic	77/31	30,986/12,549
Bergen	27/11	3,866/ 1,565
Burlington	181/73	129,747/52,547
Camden	65/26	10,479/ 4,244
Cape May	139/56	15,013/ 6,080
Cumberland	137/55	83,544/33,835
Essex	49/19	1,868/ 756
Gloucester	99/40	69,661/28,212
Hudson	*/	*/
Hunterdon	111/49	122,060/49,434
Mercer	143/58	42,513/17,218
Middlesex	125/50	33,452/13,548
Monmouth	99/40	72,315/29,288
Morris	90/36	31,797/12,878
Ocean	67/27	11,530/ 4,670
Passaic	25/10	1,213/ 491
Salem	166/67	101,903/41,271
Somerset	138/56	54,034/21,884
Sussex	145/63	84,107/34,063
Union	16/ 6	*/
Warren	159/64	86,650/35,093
State	106/43	1,049,435/425,021

Source: U.S. Census of Agriculture, State Data - New
Jersey, Washington, D.C.: U.S. Government Printing
Office, 1978.

*Not disclosed due to very small number of operators.

and less on field crops. Sussex and parts of Morris and Passaic counties have glaciated terrain as an agricultural handicap.

Crop Production

Although New Jersey is not an agricultural superstar among the states, Jersey farmers have made it second in production of cultivated blueberries and summer potatoes, third in cranberry production, and fourth in production of peaches, tomatoes, spinach, and green peppers. Von Thunen would have been proud. In 1979 alone, New Jersey farms produced over sixty-million-dollars' worth of vegetables for fresh markets (but only twelve-million-dollars' worth for processing—a situation related to increasing costs of farm labor. Just under $49 million was earned by marketing fruit crops, with peaches, blueberries, and apples the leading crops.

Vegetable and fruit production requires a much greater investment in labor and capital (irrigation, cultivation, fertilization, use of machinery) than field crops such as corn, wheat, or soybeans. However, the value of vegetables and fruits per land unit is far higher. In 1979 "fresh-market" vegetables provided an average gross income per acre of over $1,300 ($526 per ha), while field crops averaged less than $200 per acre ($81 per ha). The highest gross income was earned from production of escarole, lettuce, cabbage, spinach, cucumbers, and eggplant. The cost of farm labor has risen to the point of encouraging shifts in acreage from "cannery" cropland to either higher-valued fresh market produce or lower-labor-demand pasture. An interesting response of

market gardeners on the suburban fringe has been to institute "pick-your-own" operations in which the customers make a family outing of picking strawberries, eggplant, or other fresh produce.

Although wild cranberries were present at the time of European discovery and their domestication was largely the work of New Jerseyans, the state actually is near the climatic limits for cranberries. Therefore it is not surprising that New Jersey ranks third in cranberry production after Massachusetts and Wisconsin, each producing annually over a million barrels compared to New Jersey's 254,000 barrels. New Jersey's yield, at 84 bbl per acre (34 bbl per ha), is the lowest among U.S. commercially producing states (at 150 bbl per acre or 60 bbl per ha, Wisconsin's yield is tops). Recent trends show New Jersey cranberry acreage down slightly, while Wisconsin's is up slightly and Massachusetts's is stable. As yield generally has been im-

FIGURE 7.5. *Company Housing Near Seabrook.* One of the first integrated farm-to-wholesaler freezing operations, Seabrook Farms in Cumberland County specialized in frozen vegetables grown on its own land or under contract. Operations ceased in the late 1970s.

proving in all three major producing states, New Jersey's total production is nearly stable despite a drop of 200 acres (81 ha) in the last five years.

Livestock Production

In livestock farming, cattle and hogs have shown a slight decline in number over the last five years, chickens are diminishing steadily, and sheep numbers are at a plateau. Milk cows are fewer, milk production per cow is up, and total milk production slightly down in recent years. Hog production figures are strongly influenced by a marked decline in Gloucester County, which accounts for 48 percent of the state's hog population, although other important counties are showing some sharp declines also (Burlington was down by almost two-thirds in six years). The northwestern counties are the only ones with significant increases in hog numbers. This shifting pattern may be related to suburbanization patterns. New suburban residents, who may well have purchased their new home on a crisp winter day, tend to be unpleasantly surprised by the arrival of spring in a pig-farming district, when the heady aroma of cooking garbage mixes with the sharper odor of pig manure. (Urban garbage, trucked to the pigs by farmers, must, by law, be heated to a temperature that will kill dangerous bacteria—hence, "cooking" of garbage.) Homeowners who had planned to spend a little time outdoors, or who even dreamed of open windows, are then apt to pressure for local zoning and other controls to gradually eliminate the pig farmers, who were there first.

Cattle have a different public image than pigs, which may explain something about their relative persistence in exurban and suburban-fringe counties. Warren, Hunterdon, and Sussex are the important cattle-producing counties in the north, with Salem and Burlington the main cattle country in the south. Beef cattle outnumber milk cows three to one.

Chicken and egg production have both declined rather steeply recently. The state had fewer than half as many egg-laying hens in 1980 compared to 1975. Gross income from egg sales plummeted from nearly $30 million to $13.4 million as the price per dozen eggs sank at a time when production per hen was up slightly. If the price received by the farmer had been adjusted for inflation, egg prices would have shown an approximate one-third decline. Turkey production, on the other hand, was more stable, although of much less importance in the state than chickens. In every county with egg and chicken production at all, there has been a decline over the past half-dozen years.

Characteristics of Farms and Farmers

The contemporary New Jersey "farmer" is a member of a fairly exclusive club: membership is limited to those who operate a "farm" that has annual gross sales of agricultural products of $1,000 or more. (This definition was established in 1975. Prior to then, "farm" was defined as any place of 10 acres (4 ha) or more with sales of $50 or more, or, if of less than 10 acres, annual sales of at least $250.) The 1978 Census of Agriculture showed that 2,000 of New Jersey's then 9,871 officially recognized farms had gross sales of over $40,000 (a little less than half of these farms each grossed over $100,000), while 3,187 farms each produced less than $2,500 gross value, and 1,915 farms grossed under $1,500 each.

It is obvious that there is an enormous variety among New Jersey farms in size and especially in productivity. Almost one-third of the state's farms grossed under $2,500 in 1978, while just under 10 percent grossed $100,000 or more. The 971 farms in this top economic-productivity category, however, produced 64 percent of the state's total value of farm products. The 5,460 farms that each grossed under $5,000 produced a total of only 2.4 percent of the total commercial farm production by value. Clearly, the operators of farms with very small gross incomes (net incomes, of course, must be considerably lower) must have other sources of income in addition. They are, in other words, part-time farmers. Their inclusion in agricultural statistics for the United States, not just for New Jersey, unavoidably, if incidentally, masks the true, drastic shrinkage in the *number* of farms that actually produce the overwhelming bulk of farm products.

The most recent federal agricultural census indicates that 42 percent of New Jersey farm operators did not work off the farm; that is, the farm was their full-time occupation. But 41 percent of farm operators *did* work off the farm for 200 days or more during the year, indicating that most of them held full-time jobs off the farm. (The remaining 17 percent worked off the farm from 1 to 199 days a year.) Statistics indicate that these part-time farms, which supplement their operator's income rather than being the main or sole support of the farmer, are holding their own, perhaps even increasing. Doubtless a small, part-time farm operation offers a good hedge against inflation.

New Jersey farms are predominantly individually or family owned; this category of ownership accounted for over 85 percent of the total number of farms and 69 percent of all farmland in 1978. Corporate ownership held under 6 percent of the number of farms, but 12 percent of farmland. Even this relatively small proportion of corporate control may be an exaggeration if "corporation" in this context is viewed as a huge company on the order of agribusiness in California, for example. Many of the corporations controlling farms are those in which family members are the sole shareholders: Such a family corporation can reduce the estate tax that might otherwise be due on the death of the farmer and can equitably distribute an inheritance among children without necessitating breaking up or selling the farm itself. One family member might manage the farm for a fee, and all shareholders participate in profits.

The average New Jersey farm operator is in his or her late middle age; 42 percent of all farm operators are fifty-five or older, while only 11 percent are under thirty-five years old. Farming may be losing its appeal to younger people. Additionally, the capital investment necessary effectively means that if one does not inherit a farm (or win big in the state lottery!), one must be contented with a relatively small, almost certainly part-time operation. Only 11 percent of New Jersey farms had a combined land-and-farm-building value of under $40,000 in 1978; 62 percent were worth over $100,000. Very few young people can qualify for loans adequate to start a commercial-scale farm.

Prices for Farmland

Data on farm sales for 1979–1980, the most recent available, show that the price paid per acre of farmland continuing in agricultural use varied from an average of $4,765 per acre ($1,929 per ha) in Somerset County to $943 per acre ($381 per ha) in Cumberland County. The state average was $2,134 per acre ($864 per ha); so a purchase of a very modest farm of 100 acres (40.5 ha), less than the state average, would require about $213,400, and that is before purchasing equipment, machinery, livestock, or any other capital requirements. On the other hand, agricultural land purchased for development brought a statewide average of $12,258 per acre ($4,964 per ha). Prices received ran from a high of $80,169 per acre ($32,468 per ha) in Union County to $2,987 ($1,209) in Gloucester County. (These data all represent only one year's land transfers, it must be remembered.) During that year alone, 2,045 acres (828 ha) passed out of farming and into some other, more-intensive land use. Because the troubled construction industry was at the time virtually in a depression, it would indicate that this was an abnormally slow year in demand for building lots. The general slowdown in the rate of population increase, and associated suburbanization, may have reduced developmental presures on farms.

In combination with New Jersey's Farmland Assessment Act, this may stabilize the Garden State's remaining "gardens."

THE PAVING OF THE GARDENS

Just as in the Von Thunen hypothesis the most intensive form of agricultural land use will be the successful bidder for the most desirable location, and land uses even more intensive than any form of agriculture will displace farmers. Thus there are both positive and negative economic pressures on farm owners in the path of suburban expansion. Not only does land value rise far above its realistic agricultural value, but the escalating local demands for more services require increases in local government's income from real estate taxes. In the past, as rising land values reflected potential development value, real estate taxes would rise even without a raise in rates, because the tax bill represented estimated market value multiplied by a fixed rate per $1,000. Raising *rates* simply compounded the problem. Climbing land values in the neighborhood also made it much more expensive for a progressive farmer to add more acreage to his farm to become more competitive.

Many farmers doubtless were pleasantly surprised by the new, higher value for their land, representing economic changes that they did not initiate and perhaps little understood. More than a century ago, in a "coffee-table book" more decorative than analytical, a surprisingly perceptive comment appeared among the woodcuts of nature's wonders,

In no part of the country has speculation in real estate been carried on more vigorously or more successfully than in northern New Jersey, and many a hardworking farmer has found himself unexpectedly rich through the marvelous rise in the value of the land which his father considered as only adapted to the raising of cabbages or potatoes. In the last few years, railroad communication has increased to such an extent that almost every farm in northern New Jersey enjoys the advantage of being "near the station"—a privilege which only those who live in the country can fully appreciate. (Bryant 1874, 50)

For many other farmers, however, the inexorable advance of suburban land use, with steep increases in both land value and tax rates, presented them with little choice but to sell, if at a fat profit to cushion premature or unwanted retirement.

The Transition from Farm to Suburb

Picture a rural township on the growing edge of suburbia. There are no exploitable natural resources other than good soil, adequate drainage, and minimal slope. The valuation of the land reflects its income potential for agricultural production. For the reasons noted, this value is high in comparison with the general value of agricultural land; the land has been used intensively and is well located in terms of markets. The present value is low, though, in comparison with that of suburban house lots, industrial parks, or shopping centers, but these are not yet competitors for the land. Real estate taxes, the prime source of local-government revenues, are low because the demands on local services are low. The local residents are mostly farmers, with a small village offering some basic services. The scattered farmsteads can use sanitary septic tanks and their own wells in reasonable compliance with health standards; no municipal water or sewerage systems are needed, so none yet exist. A small volunteer fire department is organized with infrequent township contributions of major equipment. A three-person local police force, operating out of a small combination township hall, police station, and library, is augmented as necessary by state police. An elementary school in an aging building serves an essentially static population; students in junior and senior high school are bused to a regional school,

FIGURE 7.6.   *Rural Landscape in Winter, Cumberland County.* The very charms of the remaining farm landscapes, mostly in the northwestern and southwestern portions of the state, are the causes of the economic pressures on those farms. The buying power of would-be "rural nonfarm" residents, the advancing fringe of galactic city, is awesome compared with farm value of the land.

if one exists, or the township pays tuition to a nearby high school in another district. The roads are mostly state and county routes, maintained by those levels of government. In a township in which almost everyone lives on a farm, with abundant open space around all, there is no pressing need for public recreational space. The school playground and some football and baseball playing fields maintained by local service clubs appear to meet recreation demands.

In the suburban pioneer stage, the first signs of the fringe of suburbia advancing from a neighboring city are observed. Farmers sell off some road frontage for building lots, particularly where road frontage coincides with wooded areas perhaps less suitable for cultivation or pasture due to soil or terrain conditions. The houses erected by the suburban pioneers are commonly custom built, but not necessarily high priced. The strings of new houses lining roads are a *false-front suburbia;* to the casual observer, it might *appear* that the area is really more suburban and higher density than is accurate, because most land

at this point is still in agricultural use. While these new arrivals are *in* the country, they are not *of* the country: their occupations, lifestyles, and viewpoints are urban, not rural. Most likely, they will perceive their school-age children as destined for colleges with competitive entrance requirements; they will start to pressure local schools for more-advanced courses, and their growing numbers will lead to a school expansion and building program, requiring higher taxes. As taxes begin to rise, more farmers sell off road-front parcels to pay the bills. Recent arrivals begin to outnumber long-term residents, and they demand more services and amenities than the "old-timers" ever thought necessary. Their washing machines, dishwashers, newly established lawns, and backyard pools are placing many demands on the local water table. Now there is talk of expensive municipal water systems and, of course, sanitary sewerage to replace septic tanks as houses are built closer together.

In a further stage of the suburban invasion, speculative builders move into the township as highway improvements decrease the time-distance from the city. Once a few farms have been transformed into tracts of new houses, the potent combination of rising land value and rising tax rates induces more farmers to sell, in turn producing higher taxes in a kind of snowball effect. The township's responsibilities and costs seem to rise every day now. A new junior-senior high school caps an expanding school system. Commuting cars have overburdened the old high-crowned rural roads with their sharp curves and occasional stop signs; new, widened, improved roads, complete with new traffic lights, are patrolled by a beefed-up police force. The recently installed water and sewerage systems are already overburdened; further expansion and improvements are necessary. Bond issue follows bond issue as the local government struggles to provide vast new capital-plant expenditures at the same time that township and school-district payrolls are soaring. The much-denser population now requires additional fire equipment, fire hydrants, and a core of paid, full-time fire fighters. There is agitation for parks and preservation of some open space as the newcomers see the rural landscape that first attracted them disappearing under an encrustation of buildings.

The cultural landscape now is overwhelmingly suburban rather than rural. A few farms persist, operated against the odds by farmers clinging to the life they prefer. These survivals in the landscape are relics of a former, now fading, land-use system.

Restraints on Suburbanization

Do farmers have any choice against the inexorable upward pressures of taxes? It would seem that farms can continue to operate on the metropolitan fringes only if tax relief is available. Fortunately for New Jersey's farmers, such relief now exists. Farmland now is taxed at its agricultural-productivity value rather than at its potential value for development. If, or when, the farm is sold for development, the state will back figure taxes for two years at the higher "development" rate, thus redressing the tax burden on the former farm's neighbors.

This restraint on previously unrealistic tax burdens on farmland came in 1964, when the Farmland Assessment Act was passed following a referendum in which voters authorized the necessary constitutional change. The act authorized assessment at farm value, rather than speculative value, on any plot of land 5 or more acres (2 ha) in size that had produced $500 or more in gross farm income per year. In 1982 the state began to purchase development rights, thus compensating farmers for giving up the option of selling their land for development.

CHAPTER 8

INDUSTRIAL DEVELOPMENT

As in the case of agriculture, New Jersey's manufacturing has moved from a subsistence level in the colonial period to more specialization. The specializations are oriented to the physical resources, including situational resources, and depend upon local and neighboring markets. As with agriculture, there has been both a high degree of diversity and a trend toward production that emphasizes quality, with specializations in finished materials ready for markets.

LOCATIONAL FACTORS

The state's present industrial mix and industrial-location patterns reflect many individual and corporate decisions on New Jersey's relative advantages and disadvantages. This can be expected to hold true in the future, because choosing the best location for any industry is rarely guesswork. Locational analysis is becoming a specialization that rests upon geographic principles; industrial-location consultants commonly have backgrounds in geography and economics.

The objective in industrial-location research is to identify that location that will have the lowest total cost of raw-material assembly, manufacturing, or processing and delivery of the product to its market. The lowest-cost location will be the most profitable and most competitive. *Direct costs* include labor, raw materials, energy and fuel, water supply, waste disposal, and cost of delivery to market. *Indirect costs* include acquisition and preparation of the building site, the building itself and movable equipment within it, local taxes, maintenance, utilities, and administration. The specific ranking of cost factors by their relative importance varies, naturally, with the particular industry. For most manufacturing industries, direct costs are most important; in sales and services, indirect costs are the primary considerations.

The four major direct costs are raw materials, power and fuel, marketing, and labor. The first three are all related critically to transportation, and even the availability of labor is sensitive to the costs of commuting. The four variables in transport costs are: (1) quantity of commodities handled, (2) perishability, (3) cost per unit of transportation, and (4) degree of concentration of producing and consuming centers (Zimolzak and Stansfield 1979, 371–375). If there is great loss of bulk of little or no value, the industrial location will be at the raw-material production site, as in the processing of magnesium from seawater at Cape May Point. The addition of low-value bulk during manufacture usually results in a location within the market to reduce transport costs, as in brewing beer at Newark. When the raw material is perishable, processing moves toward the source

139

of that raw material, as in processing fruit and vegetables or canning or freezing fish and shellfish. If the finished product, as in ice cream or fresh baked goods, is even more perishable than the raw materials, a location near consumers makes sense. Similarly, when the costs of transportation of finished products is higher than that of the parts or materials, assembly and finishing should be close to market, as in an auto assembly plant at Linden. In a highly concentrated market, as the silk industry in Paterson in the 1920s, silk machinery logically located there as well. Ports are often nearly ideal locations for industries that process materials moving long distances by cheap water transport. *Break of bulk,* that is, the making of many smaller units or packages from one large bulk shipment, is a typical port function. The port is a good place to process, refine, and package materials for distribution inland; Hudson County's coffee-roasting operations are a good example.

Labor Costs

Labor costs are almost always a critical consideration, but the relative proportion of total costs resulting from labor is highly variable. In nineteenth-century Newark's jewelry and watchmaking enterprises, labor was the single most important cost. In contemporary oil refining, a *capital-intensive* rather than *labor-intensive* industry, labor costs are proportionately small. Traditionally, the more skilled the labor, the more static it is in location, that is, the less likely to move. Therefore, skilled jobs used to come to the labor supply rather than the other way around. The continuing validity of this assumption is doubtful in that highly skilled, highly educated people are now quite mobile in their careers. Except for the necessary mobility of the least-

FIGURE 8.1. *The Thomas Edison Mansion, Llewellan Park, West Orange.* Ever the practical man, Thomas Edison bought a house completely furnished so he would not waste time shopping for furniture, drapes, or even dishes. Edison helped pioneer suburban locations for light industry and research labs, a location trend that has accelerated since. He was attracted to the suburbs of the Newark area by the varied array of highly skilled labor within the area.

FIGURE 8.2. *Paterson—"Smokestack America" Incarnate.* The traditional Manufacturing Belt industries—coal-based, often polluting, and technologically obsolescent—are in continuing decline. High-technology, research-oriented, and service industries are New Jersey's future, especially if, as projected, offshore oil and gas supplies prove inadequate to meet even present demands.

skilled labor (farm labor), lesser-skilled workers tend to have less savings to support moving about in search of jobs. For this reason northern New Jersey's accessibility to incoming European immigrants was an important factor in industrial growth for nearly a century, and the attractiveness of the greater New York area to contemporary flows of migrants from the Caribbean remains an advantage for industrial location there.

Both the increasing interstate mobility of highly skilled labor and the much-lower mobility of recently arrived immigrants have positive and negative implications for New Jersey. The old industrial cities are unattractive, perhaps even repellent, to highly skilled and educated workers. On the other hand, the high-amenity environments of the mountains and seashore should

help industries there attract these workers, even in competition with the Sun Belt. The ready supply of low to moderately skilled recent immigrants is a plus for New Jersey industry, except that industries emphasizing low-skilled operatives are not the ones flourishing in New Jersey, and rising unemployment rates could result.

Even the polished skills of workers do not remain a location factor if, as often happens, the skill level required of production workers decreases over time as the machinery they operate becomes more automated and more reliably free of breakdowns and frequent servicing needs. Newer, more efficient machines can be tended by much less experienced and skilled operatives, and so low cost of labor has become more important than high skill. Industry has been able to abandon its skilled New

FIGURE 8.3. Although silica sand is still in plentiful supply in South Jersey, clean-burning, high-heat energy is not; natural gas fires the glass furnaces. Recycling, which in effect "mines" the urban areas for used glass containers, produces glass at much less energy than using sand. Glass manufacture is among the "slow growth" industries of the state, largely because of the high proportion of energy costs in total costs.

Jersey labor for the cheaper labor of the South.

Energy Costs

New Jersey's poor position in regard to industrial raw materials is matched by its shortage of domestic energy resources, a shortage that has been chronic throughout the state's industrial development after 1830. Pennsylvania anthracite was an early, large-scale energy import; its modern counterparts are the gas and oil pipelines and the oil tankers bringing Venezuelan, Middle Eastern, African, and Mexican crudes, directly or indirectly, to New Jersey. New Jersey does not have any local sources of *cheap* energy. Even when offshore gas is brought ashore, it will not be a cheap fuel, nor would potential offshore oil be available in sufficient volume surplus to present demands so as to attract energy-intensive industries. New Jersey industries most likely will continue to pay relatively high costs for energy and so will be attracted by other location factors, if at all. (The petroleum-refining industries are market oriented at a break-of-bulk point within the market; chemical industries are attracted to locations near the refineries as raw material sources, not because of energy costs as such.)

Even a significant proportion of the electrical energy New Jersey consumes is generated outside the state. According to a study in *New Jersey Economic Indicators* in 1977 (June 30, 8–15), New Jersey's installed electric-generating capacity was 2.25 percent of the national total, while New Jersey had 3.25 percent of the national population and a higher-than-average proportion of industry. The average annual growth rate in generating capacity within New Jersey had been slightly lower than the national average between 1956 and 1975. Pennsylvania, on the other hand, with many energy-consuming industries, had 7.5 percent of the nation's installed generating capacity, but 5.23 percent of the population. New Jersey electric utilities not only import coal and oil to generate electricity but also continually "import" electricity from both coal-generated and nuclear-generated sources in Pennsylvania. Of 130 generating units producing electricity for consumption within New Jersey, 115 are within New Jersey and 15 are in Pennsylvania. Small amounts of power are supplied to northeastern New Jersey from points in New York State, and there are periodic, seasonal, and emergency long-distance interchanges of electric power throughout the region, particularly imports from Quebec Hydro.

The high cost of importing both fuels for electric generation and electricity generated elsewhere encouraged New Jersey utilities to shift the fuel mix of coal, oil, and nuclear sources toward nuclear. The oil-price increases of 1973, quadrupling oil-fueled generating costs within a few months, were an obvious spur. In 1974, four nuclear steam units provided 14 percent of New Jersey's total electricity consumption, but three of these units were located in Pennsylvania and partly owned by New Jersey utilities. Since that time, the two units in Salem County have been completed to join New Jersey's first, Oyster Creek in Ocean County, which opened in 1969. The Forked River plant near Oyster Creek will be the fourth nuclear plant; two more projected

FIGURE 8.4. This major refinery on the Delaware River has a strong market orientation, located as it is within the Philadelphia metropolitan region. Each of the great deepwater estuaries and harbors at either end of New Jersey has developed a market-oriented petroleum refining–petrochemical complex. That serving the northern New Jersey–New York metropolitan region sprawls along the Arthur Kill–Kill Van Kull–Newark Bay district, while this refinery is part of a complex from Deepwater to Paulsboro along the Delaware River. (Courtesy of Wayne Stansfield)

for Hope Creek near the present Salem units on the Delaware have been postponed by a combination of declining rates of energy-use increases and environmental concerns. Nuclear energy now supplies 27 percent of New Jersey's electric consumption.

The generation of approximately 17 percent of New Jersey's electricity requirements in Pennsylvania is an interesting example of "exporting" pollution. New Jersey's air-pollution rules are quite strict; these rules, in combination with an emotional response to the near tragedy at Three Mile Island near Harrisburg in 1979, make it likely that New Jersey's import of electric energy is a desirable alternative. Certainly Pennsylvania's coal resources can support more generating capacity than Pennsylvania needs, and few expect it to become easier, politically or technologically, to build

additional, reliably safe nuclear plants in New Jersey.

EARLY MANUFACTURING

Doubtless the first "manufacturing" in New Jersey was the production of household consumables in the homes of most pioneer families. Soap, candles, textiles, and tools were produced in small quantities for home consumption rather than for sale. Not every family could grind its own grain, however, so milling became one of the first industrial specializations, followed by tanning.

Three needed industrial raw materials were found in the twin colonies in sufficient quantity and quality to support industrial specialization; the triad of iron ore, timber, and glass sand was to dominate New Jersey's early industry. The 1807 Morse geography reported that "the manufactures of this state have hitherto been inconsiderable, not sufficient to supply its own consumptions, if we exempt the articles of iron, nails and leather. A spirit of industry and improvement particularly in manufactures, has however greatly increased within a few years" (Morse 1807, 184). Morse was, however, quite impressed with the New Jersey iron industry,

> The iron manufacture is, of all others, the greatest source of wealth to the state. Iron works are erected in Gloucester, Burlington, Sussex, Morris and other counties. The mountains in the county of Morris give rise to a number of streams necessary and convenient for these works, and at the same time furnish a copious supply of wood and ore of superior quality. In this county alone are no less than seven rich iron mines, from which might be taken ore sufficient to supply the United States. . . . (Morse 1807, 185)

As it turned out, of course, this was a very shortsighted view of the growing appetite for iron in the United States. That New Jersey *was* a major iron-producing state at the time, though, is documented by Morse's statistics on its annual output: 1,200 tn (1,088 t) of bar iron, 1,200 tn of pig iron, 80 tn (72.5 t) of nail rods, and various castings and hollow ware, "of which vast quantities are made" (1807, 185).

In addition to Morris County iron (magnetite ore), many local deposits of bog iron (limonite) were worked in the Pinelands. Iron in solution was precipitated in bogs and lake bottoms; early iron makers recognized the sedimentation of ore taking place and even attempted to encourage it by damming streams. Bog iron had the reputation, apparently accurate, of being very slow to rust, so it was prized in kitchenware. The early iron industry utilized the vast forests of both the Highlands and the Pinelands as fuel. Charcoal was made by baking timber in earth-covered mounds, watched carefully by a worker who regulated air flow to roast the wood in insufficient oxygen. The resultant charcoal was then burned to produce the high heat necessary to iron making. The flux was often oyster shells rather than limestone. Water wheels powered the bellows to "blast" oxygen into the furnace.

Other early industries included copper mining near New Brunswick and pottery and steel at Trenton. In the 1760s, the discovery that marl or "greensand" deposits could be mined and applied as fertilizer boosted a new industry at many points along the inner-outer coastal plain transition (towns such as Marlboro and Marlton). Allowaystown in Salem County was the site of New Jersey's first glass factory in 1740; by the Revolution, Salem County was already a leading producer of bottles, pitchers, and other glassware. The

FIGURE 8.5. *The Great Furnace at Allaire.* Allaire, in the northern Pinelands, was typical of the isolated company towns built on charcoal, bog ores, and glass sand. The industrial exploitation of the Pinelands was relatively short-lived as the resource base was narrow and restricted in quantity and quality.

FIGURE 8.6.   A typical company town, Quinton, in Salem County, featured company-built housing (complete with outhouses in the back gardens). Notice the evident pride in smoke in this 1876 engraving designed to please the company—reassurance to people of a century ago of industrial progress and power. (D. J. Stewart, compiler, *Combination Atlas Map of Salem and Gloucester Counties, New Jersey*. Philadelphia: Everts and Stewart, 1876, p. 29)

heat source for glass manufacture was charcoal.

The successful conclusion of the American Revolution presented great opportunities to these infant industries. The harsh, all-encompassing regulations of the British, designed to keep the American colonies in a submissive, tributary position in trade, were gone. The Americans had been ingenious at circumventing the spirit of the Navigation Acts, which stipulated the manufactured articles that could only be made in England for the American market. Making crude pig iron (the "pigs" were formed by pouring molten iron into sand molds) was permitted in America under the Navigation Acts, but the "pigs" were to be sent to England, as ship ballast, to be refined and used in fabricating consumer goods. The New Jerseyans, with their many successful iron furnaces, managed to cast "pigs" that looked remarkably like firebacks (large iron plates bolted to the back of fireplaces to reflect heat out to the room), pots and, when the time came, cannon balls and musket shot. After the Revolution, not only did restrictions disappear, but the new governments, federal and state, actively encouraged U.S. manufacturing to foster economic, as well as political, independence.

Alexander Hamilton, first secretary of the treasury, advocated an industrializing United States; he did not share Thomas Jefferson's vision of a nation of sturdy, independent farmers on family-owned and -operated farms. Hamilton understood that we needed our own factories to counter cheap British factory-made goods; small-scale "cottage industry" would not do. Hamilton wanted to establish a planned industrial town with a cluster of factories. The energy source, in this early phase of the Industrial Revolution, would be direct waterpower. The general location, or situation, was to be in "New York, Pennsylvania or New Jersey"; Hamilton did not make his actual choice, the Great Falls of the Passaic, known at first, so that he would not discourage support from people who did not live near the falls. The Society for Establishing Useful Manufactures (SUM) was chartered in 1791 and promptly chose northeastern New Jersey, stating that "it is thickly populated—provisions are there abundant and cheap. The state having scarcely any external commerce and no waste lands to be peopled can feel the impulse of no supposed interest hostile to the advancement of manufacture. Its situation seems to ensure a constant friendly disposition" (Vecoli 1965, 71). No doubt the legislature's action in voting SUM perpetual exemption from county and township taxes and giving it the right to hold property, build canals, and raise money by lottery aided the decision. The Great Falls of the Passaic, 70 ft (21 m) high, was chosen as the site of the new industrial city, to no one's surprise.

No less than Major Pierre L'Enfant, a noted French architect, was hired to plan the millraces for the new industrial city to be built on a 700-acre (283-hectare) tract at the falls. L'Enfant's plans for waterpower distribution seem to have been followed, but New Jersey's chance to have a grand baroque city plan—influenced by Versailles' grand vistas, radial avenues, and wide streets (all the better to stage a good parade)—was lost. The SUM simply could not afford to allocate land for public streets on a monumental scale, and so L'Enfant took his grand city-planning ideas to the suitably grandiose vision of a new federal city on the Potomac. For better or worse (how does one get around a traffic circle in rush hour?), L'Enfant's designs materialized as Washington, D.C., rather than as Paterson, New Jersey.

The Society for Establishing Useful Manufactures had problems from its birth, but these problems were not due to any deficiencies in the site of its planned mill town. Only half the proposed capital was subscribed, and skilled workers were scarce until some arrived from the British Isles on invitation of the new manager for SUM, one Peter Colt. SUM's short life ended in an embezzlement scandal, but the falls site did become a great manufacturing city, vindicating Hamilton's advocacy. The basis for its future success lay in the attraction of skilled textile workers from Britain. By 1810, Paterson was known as the Cotton City. Later in the nineteenth century, practically the whole silk industry—both machines and workers—was exported from Macclesfield, England, to Paterson.

Thus, industry in the late eighteenth and early nineteenth centuries was located largely at the sites of raw material or energy resources (charcoal or waterpower). The transportation revolutions of the first half of the nineteenth century—canals and then railroads—changed the rules, reorienting industry to the growing commercial cities with their transportation advantages.

THE EARLY NINETEENTH CENTURY

A state chamber-of-commerce publication presented an interesting, characteristically optimistic portrait of New Jersey as a manufacturing state in the 1920s. Then, New Jersey was seventh in manufacturing among the states (it still is), and the report boasted, "New Jersey is a state of destiny by virtue of the permanence of its established (industrial) assets. It can never be the geographic center of American territory or population, but it will continue to be the heart of the world's most intensive and highly developed industrial life" (Parsons 1928, 401). By 1925, only 4 percent of the Garden State's population lived on farms, less than the national average then, and

147

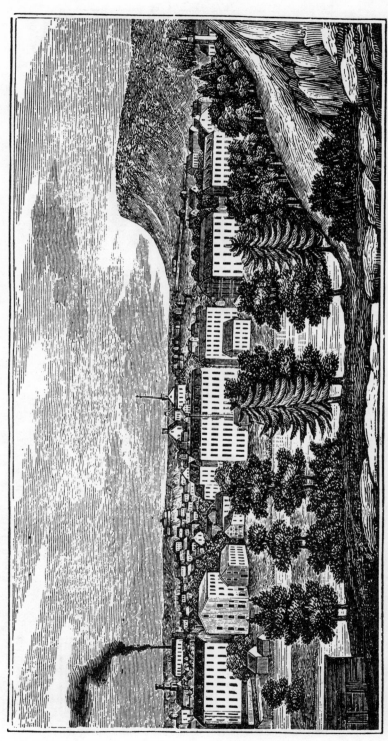

FIGURE 8.7. After SUM's failure, Paterson went on to become a prosperous mill town, especially after the Morris Canal began delivering coal to the city in the 1830s. By 1844, when this woodcut was made, Paterson was already producing silks, lo-comotives, and Samuel Colt's first production models of his revolver. (*Early Woodcut Views of New York and New Jersey.* New York: Dover Publications, 1975, p. 110)

148

FIGURE 8.8. *The railroad crossing the Delaware and Raritan Canal with industrial smokestacks in the background.* This 1844 woodcut epitomizes the early Industrial Revolution in New Jersey. Queens College, originally chartered in 1766, was reborn as Rutgers College in 1825 and has helped sustain New Brunswick since. (*Early Woodcut Views of New York and New Jersey.* New York: Dover Publications, 1975, p. 102)

already there was talk of changing the state's official motto to the "manufacturing state."

The industries of 1925 of which the chamber of commerce was so proud were somewhat different than now. Silk ranked first in number of employees, followed by electrical machinery (we can thank Thomas Edison for that), then textile dyeing and finishing, foundry and machine products, worsted textiles, chemicals, transportation equipment, oil refining, cotton goods, and rubber goods. In a ranking by value added (and with different industrial groupings), textiles were first, then chemicals, machinery, iron and steel, food processing, transportation equipment, paper and printing, stone, clay and glass, metals and metal products, and "musical instruments and phonographs" (Edison again!).

New Jersey's economy now has moved further into more sophisticated industries emphasizing research, although the location advantages of both its immense ports and market keep oil refining and industrial chemicals a major factor. Diversity was, and remains, a hallmark of the state as well. The outstanding decline of textiles, among the relative industrial rankings, is typical of the northeast as, indeed, it is typical of highly industrialized societies the world over. Just as in New England (which has also experienced a sharp decline in textiles), the textile industry in New Jersey was one of the first industries to be developed. As such, it was the oldest and the most obsolescent; lower-cost, much more efficient plants with more modern machinery were being built in the South, particularly the Carolinas and Georgia, by the 1920s. Lower labor costs (nonunion) were only part of the story. The aging plants in such cities as Paterson could not easily expand, embedded within the city as they were. Their energy costs were high, and their labor had become understandably militant after decades of poorly paid piecework in tenements.

FIGURE 8.9.   *The Restored Rogers Locomotive Works, Paterson.* A large part of the old factory district of Paterson is now on the National Register of Historic Sites. The locomotive works shown here, one of several, is being converted to a museum.

Still, the 1920s industrial structure did hold the seeds of the future mix of manufacturing activities. New Jersey had more than its proportionate share of a declining textiles industry, but also more than its share of more-dynamic industries—chemicals, metal products, rubber products, and "miscellaneous"—the diversity that defies easy compartmentalization.

THE CHANGING ECONOMY, 1950 TO 1980

New Jersey's unique blend of location factors is accurately reflected in its changing industrial structure. Table 8.1 lists employment by standard industrial classification (SIC) categories for the years 1950, 1960, 1970, and 1980. The data portray a state economy moving toward the *post-industrial,* high-technology, service-oriented employment structure. Although total nonfarm employment increased by over one and one-third million in thirty years, total manufacturing employment is in decline.

Until the middle of the twentieth century, New Jersey was a preeminently industrial state, one that had been among the top-ranked industrial states since before the Civil War. Indeed, in the first half of the twentieth century, New Jersey experienced a twentyfold increase in the value of its manufacturing output. This was an astounding achievement in that New Jersey's growth came on top of an already impressive base in 1900 (Flink 1958, 192–193). New Jersey, in fact, had successfully outpaced the much-slower growth trends of the whole Middle Atlantic region, of which New Jersey is a part. The Middle Atlantic region is one of the mightiest industrial concentrations in the world, but its rate of growth since 1900 has been below the national average; New Jersey's growth in manufacturing output surpassed the national average through 1950. The industrial growth of New York and Pennsylvania, the other states of the Middle Atlantic region, was very low in comparison. There is clear evidence now, though, of New Jersey having joined the Middle Atlantic region, or, more accurately, the northeastern seaboard megalopolis, in shifting emphasis from manufacturing to services employment. This shift toward services is considered a sign of economic maturity within a heavily urbanized region and, to some extent, reflects that very high degree of urbanization.

Classification of Economic Activity

The traditional threefold classification of economic activity identified primary, secondary, and tertiary categories in ascending order of supposed sophisication and average wages and in descending order of direct reliance on the local physical-resource complex. *Primary* industries are those in which raw material is produced or acquired. Mining, agriculture, quarrying, logging, hunting, and fishing are primary activities in two senses, historically and technologically. Historically, they include the means of supporting oneself directly from the resources of the environment. In the most primitive of societies, hunting and gathering, including fishing, would occupy virtually everyone. Agriculture was a significant advance for human societies, but it remains a primary activity. This category of activity is primary in a technolial-industrial-services chain of dependencies also. There would be no manufacturing without raw materials and little without fossil fuels, nor would the most sophisicated research or services be possible without the production of food and the availability of raw materials to be processed, shaped, transported, and serviced in support of all more-advanced activities.

Secondary economic activities are processing and manufacturing. The growing of peaches is primary; their canning, secondary. Producing iron ore is primary, but the steel industry is secondary. Secondary activity transforms raw materials into more usable forms, reshapes them, adds new qualities, and preserves them for future use.

TABLE 8.1
Total Employment by Selected Major Industries, Wage and
Salary Workers (thousands) for New Jersey

	1950	1960	1970	1980
Total Nonfarm	1,657.1	2,016.8	2,608.6	3,043.5
Total Manufacturing	756.4	808.4	863.0	780.8
Contract Construction	81.2	98.1	119.2	110.7
Services	166.8	252.0	410.4	599.5
Government	171.0	242.2	374.8	532.5
Fabricated Metals	44.2	54.2	66.4	61.9
Nonelectric Machinery	49.9	61.0	72.8	75.1
Electric Machinery	97.2	122.3	116.9	91.9
Transport Equipment	40.1	48.5	26.3	18.7
Instruments	17.8	31.7	33.2	36.5
Printing & Publishing	22.8	32.3	44.8	54.5
Chemicals	73.7	86.4	122.3	129.4
Petroleum	16.5	11.5	9.9	12.1
Rubber & Plastics	26.4	29.2	40.0	36.4
Finance Insurance Real Estate	68.3	88.6	117.7	155.2
Transport, Comm. & Public Utilities	135.4	149.5	182.2	184.2
Mining	4.3	3.5	3.2	2.7
Primary Metals	40.5	42.6	37.2	25.4
Food	56.5	62.9	63.5	48.7
Trade	273.7	374.6	538.2	677.9
Textiles	58.2	31.4	29.6	20.2
Apparel	89.0	77.7	72.3	57.2

Source: New Jersey Economic Indicators, State of New Jersey, Department of Labor and Industry, Division of Planning and Research, Trenton, various issues.

NOTE: Partial Tabulation--minor industries not presented. Post-1972 data for workers in chemicals, rubber, services, and instruments industries not precisely comparable with pre-1972 data due to SIC revisions.

The old *tertiary* category was a general, residual one; anything that did not fit into either of the first two categories was tertiary. Essentially, tertiary activities were all services. If one did not produce raw materials or harvest them from nature and did not process or manufacture these materials to change their utility, then one was in a tertiary activity. A problem with the tertiary category was that it included such a wide and growing variety of occupations. Truck drivers are in tertiary employment, but so, under the old categorization, were bankers. Stockbrokers, insurance adjusters, and psychiatrists were tertiary, as were rest-room attendants, janitors, and garbage collectors.

The geographer who identified "megalopolis" and studied it in detail, Jean Gottmann, also observed that the types of jobs that were growing fastest within megalopolis were services, or tertiary, but especially certain types of tertiary. Gottmann identified a fourth category as *quaternary*. These were nonroutine services that required extensive, specialized education or training to perform and that usually did not involve a tangible or physical service. The tertiary category, now quantitatively reduced, remained residual; it included all activities that were not primary, secondary, or quaternary (Gottmann 1961, 567–582).

Thus, postal carriers, typists, store clerks, short-order cooks, bartenders, and television repairers would be tertiary. Judges, lawyers, tax accountants, physicians, teachers, and bankers would be quaternary: they have long periods of special training and perform largely intangible services. They are being compensated for their knowledge, experience, and professional judgment and advice rather than for a physical service. Both tertiary and quaternary services are increasing in importance in New Jersey's economy, although quaternary-type jobs seem to be increasing at a faster rate. The general employment categories used by most statistical sources do not support, however, an accurate division of these two categories.

Recently there has been talk of identifying a fifth category of economic activity—*quinary*. Quinary occupations would be those positions that are almost entirely administrative. If a college professor were considered to be in quaternary employment, a college dean or president would be quinary. Quinary thus would represent top-level bureaucrats and administrators.

As a particular region of the earth moves through a sequence of stages of development, economic activity—and thus employment—will shift in emphasis from primary to secondary to tertiary. Whether any sizable region can successfully shift toward quaternary or even quinary is more problematic.

A Shift in Activities

In 1950, with a total state population of 4,835,329, there were 1,657,100 nonfarm jobs in New Jersey. Total manufacturing employment was 756,400, or 46 percent of nonfarm employment (Table 8.1). By 1980, total nonfarm employment had risen to 3,043,500, an increase of 84 percent (see Table 8.2). State population, in the same interval, had increased by 52 percent. The net total of manufacturing jobs had risen to 780,800, an increase of only 3 percent. Total nonfarm jobs had risen faster than overall population, by a healthy margin, but manufacturing had barely maintained the same number of jobs as thirty years earlier. If the secondary-employment component was essentially static, then primary or tertiary jobs must account for the great increase in nonfarm employment (farm employment continued to drop during this period also). However, the only clearly primary category reported in the SIC groupings by the New Jersey Department of Labor and Industry, "mining," declined from 4,300 to 2,700. It has not been important in modern New Jersey and has become even less significant in state totals recently. The general category of "services," however, rose by an astounding 259 percent, 1950 to 1980 (see Table 8.2), while "government" (all levels) zoomed 211 percent and "trade" 147 percent. "Finance, insurance, and real estate" managed a 127 percent gain.

In fact, as Tables 8.1 and 8.2 document, employment categories most likely to be predominantly tertiary (transport, communications and public utilities, construction, and trade) have grown, as a group, much faster than most secondary categories. The categories most likely to have significant numbers of quaternary (and even quinary) workers (services, government, finance, and so on) enjoyed an even higher growth as a group. Among more purely

TABLE 8.2
Winners and Losers: New Jersey Employment, by Major Industry
Categories, 1950 to 1980 (Percentage Change in Thirty Years)

Winners, in order of percentage gain		Losers, in order of percentage loss	
Services	+259%	Tobacco	-89%
Government	+211%	Textiles	-65%
Trade	+147%	Leather	-57%
Printing & Publishing	+139%	Transport Equipment	-53%
Finance, Insurance, Real Estate	+127%	Mining	-37%
Instruments	+105%	Primary Metals	-37%
(Total nonfarm)	+84%	Apparel	-36%
Chemicals	+76%	Petroleum	-27%
Nonelectrical Machinery	+50%	Miscellaneous Manufacturing	-25%
Fabricated Metals	+40%	Food Processing	-14%
Rubber & Plastics	+38%	Lumber, Wood	-9%
Construction	+36%	Electrical Machinery	-5%
Transport, Communications & Public Utilities	+36%		
Paper	+31%		
Furniture & Fixtures	+9%		
Stone, Clay, Glass	+6%		
(All Manufacturing)	+3%		
(Durable Goods)	+3%		
(Nondurable Goods)	+3%		

Source: Compiled from data presented in New Jersey Economic
Indicators, State of New Jersey, Department of Labor and
Industry, Division of Planning and Research, various issues.

secondary categories, it was the more-sophisticated industries (chemicals, including pharmaceuticals; printing and publishing; instruments, nonelectrical machinery; fabricated metals; rubber and plastics) that outpaced the more-basic, more raw-material-oriented industries (stone, clay, glass; tobacco; leather; primary metals; food processing; lumber and wood).

The ethical drug industry is one of New Jersey's largest single industries (*New Jersey Economic Indicators* June 30, 1978, 9–13) and is typical of the continuing shift toward *high-value-added,* research-oriented industry in the state. Drug manufacturing is highly concentrated in the United States, with about 50 percent of total output generated in the Middle Atlantic states and 25 percent in New Jersey alone. The drug industry accounts for over 11 percent of the total state value added by manufacturing, although it employs only about 5 percent of manufacturing employees. The nation's drug industry spends over a billion dollars on research and development per year, and about 50 percent of this is spent in New Jersey. The United States ranks second in the world in drug exports, and New Jersey's accessibility to air-freight terminals is an advantage in this export industry. New Jersey's most important advantage is location, both relative to the chemical industry that supplies raw materials and to consumer markets. Many multinational drug firms—Swiss, German, and Dutch—have chosen New Jersey as the location of their U.S. facilities.

Implications of the Shift

Within manufacturing, then, we can see a relative demotion of industries that emphasize raw materials (primary metals, petroleum), while those emphasizing skill and research become more important. The implications for New Jersey are far-reaching. The shift to services, particularly quaternary and quinary services, and to highly skilled precision industries has positive and negative aspects for New Jersey's growth and for its present population. For a century, most New Jersey industry has not been based on local supplies of raw materials. The lack of a sufficient quantity and quality of industrial raw materials in the modern industrial age, excepting only glass sands, and the early proximity to huge markets and generally excellent transport facilities helped the state achieve a reputation for diversity. This diversity, epitomized by late-nineteenth-century Newark, helped preserve New Jersey's manufacturing against the earlier declines

of its neighbors in the Middle Atlantic region and the northeastern quadrant of the entire United States. For half a century, New Jersey defied regional trends. Now, as the postindustrial transition becomes more obvious, New Jersey is in a position to play a leading role. The negative aspect of this shift to services and high technology is that these are the jobs that require highly trained people. The help-wanted columns will continue to feature computer programmers, electrical engineers, research chemists, machinists, technical writers, editors, and accountants, with few attractive opportunities for garment workers, auto assemblers, textile-machine operators, or food-processing workers. There are likely to be many very frustrated would-be unskilled or semiskilled workers in the aging cities. What New Jersey will have to sell to the rest of the world will continue to shift toward ideas, discoveries, new techniques and new application of existing technology, experienced advice, sophisticated high-technology items, and recreational services. As research-oriented, high-technology "brains" industries are notoriously "footloose"—that is, able and willing to relocate in the interests of amenities, lifestyles, and relative tax burdens—New Jersey's "image problem" can have economic consequences.

CASE STUDY: THE SKI INDUSTRY

Although its status is difficult to document statistically, tourism and recreation appears to be one of New Jersey's largest industries. New Jersey's national repute as a resort area lies largely in its seashore resorts, the nature, location, and season of which are opposite those of skiing. Less well known, but of considerable regional importance, are the mountain resorts and their functions. Although a list of renowned ski areas in the United States generally would not include New Jersey, the state does have a viable and growing ski industry, one that reflects apparent changes and trends

FIGURE 8.10. *Exxon Research and Development Labs, Florham Park.* Quaternary (and quinary) employment represents New Jersey's brightest hope for its future economy. "Brains" industries are highly desirable; they are seldom polluting, and their relatively affluent professional employees pump money into local and regional economies. Note the spacious campuslike setting here in the suburbs in contrast to the congestion of central city sites. (Courtesy of Exxon Research and Engineering Company)

in the social and economic nature of skiing in the United States. The ski-resort component of recreation-related industries is particularly interesting because of its relationship to advancing technology and its increasing market orientation—a major shift in location requirements.

Classifications of Recreation Areas

In the classic categorization of recreation areas (Clawson and Knetsch 1966), Marion Clawson identified three types of facilities. The first of these was *user-oriented* recreational facilities, whose primary attraction is high accessibility and whose natural amenities may be quite limited in nature. An example would be an urban park, a suburban reservoir, or a roadside picnic area. Clawson placed at the opposite extreme the *resource-oriented* recreation site, which may or may not be highly accessible but which features unique, highly attractive recreation environments, such as spectacular landforms, spacious ocean beaches, or mountain lakes. Yellowstone National Park would be a good example of a resource-oriented recreation site. Yellowstone's location relative to the major concentration of population, and therefore of recreation demand, is hardly convenient. But ease of accessibility is largely irrelevant in that example; it is the justified fame of Yellowstone's unique scenery that attracts visitors, not the degree of accessibility from, say, Newark, New Jersey. Clawson's second category, *intermediate,* was essentially a compromise between the two extremes; it is an area that is less accessible than user- or market-oriented ones and perhaps less naturally attractive than resource-oriented sites.

In the past, skiing was considered an inherently resource-oriented activity: One envisioned spectacular mountains and heavy snowfalls as necessary ingredients in successful ski operations. The location of ski resorts apparently reflected physical geography. However, the ski industry in areas where prime physical resources are far distant from market demand is experiencing a definite shift toward market orientation rather than resource orientation. Physical geography, in other words, is becoming relatively less significant in influencing the location of new ski resorts. A number of social, economic, and technological factors have been involved in this shift in location requirements. One of the many facets of the continuously evolving geography of the ski industry is the development of ski slopes in New Jersey, which in climate and—to a degree—topography is definitely marginal for such an activity. It is becoming apparent that mediocre slopes that have hazardously unpredictable local climate conditions, if easily accessible to population centers, can be transformed into a successful ski recreation area.

Characteristics of Skiers

As implied in Clawson's threefold categorization, consumers of recreation services and experiences will spend short vacations or relatively brief periods of leisure time in the closest-available, reasonably attractive site. For the major, extended vacation periods those who have both adequate money and time may be attracted by a more-remote, more-expensive-to-reach, natural-resource-oriented site. Skiers are likewise choosing among ski sites in terms of the length of time and amount of money available for the enjoyment of this recreational activity. Another factor, that of relative expertise, enters into the choice of ski resorts. A moderate, short slope that satisfies the novice may be entirely too inadequate a challenge for the more-experienced skier.

The changing nature of skiers is proving quite significant in the expanding location patterns of the ski slopes (Stansfield 1973, 6–10). It has been estimated that two-thirds of all skiers in the United States are thirty years old or under; one-fifth to one-third are eighteen years or younger. There is a general trend reported toward skiers being younger as a group; there is a shift toward unmarried skiers and toward more women. The average skier may enjoy an income 25 to 30 percent higher than the median, and except for students, roughly half of the skiers are in professional occupations, implying a higher-than-average education. Most skiers, about 80–90 percent, never go away overnight to ski, and those who do seldom go for more than three nights; skiers generally do not travel great distances for their sport.

The average U.S. skier visits over four areas within a year; 57 percent of long-term vacationing skiers went to Vermont, with all other states far behind (Stansfield 1973, 8). Interestingly enough, over 79 percent of skiers interviewed assume that the snow reports issued by resorts are inaccurate. Resorts in climatically marginal areas, known to rely on snowmaking equipment, may pose no more potential risk to the wary ski enthusiast than resorts in higher-snowfall areas. The type of area that is highly dependent on daytrippers for its clientele may have a severely limited terrain but benefit from the fact that it is highly accessible from population centers. Such areas generally have snowmaking equipment to supplement meager snowfall and elaborate lighting for night skiing in order to attract customers who live within a few hours time-distance and come out on weekday nights.

Ski Areas

The minimum set of requirements for a ski resort would include a fairly long, smooth slope cleared of trees and most obstacles and covered by at least 6 in. (15 cm) of snow. Additionally, some type of mechanical lift capacity must be provided for the skier as well as equipment rental, restaurant, lodge, and parking facilities. These very specific site requirements tend to distort any broad association between markets and ski-resort loation. In terms of these minimal site requirements, New Jersey lies in a very marginal position for ski-resort development. The topography of more than half of the state has no natural potential for long ski slopes. The largest number of potential ski slopes would be found in the Highlands, that belt of relatively resistant metamorphic rock that crosses the state in a forty-mile (64-kilometer)-wide swath in a northeast-southwest trend. The Great Gorge ski area, whose vertical drop of 1,033 ft (314 m) is the greatest of any ski slope in the state, is located within this region (see Figure 3.2). Great Gorge is undergoing the most extensive development of any ski area in the state, highlighted by the 1971 opening of a 100-room hotel complex in Great Gorge North and another set of ski runs using the same ridge. The two next-largest ski areas in the state, Vernon Valley and Snow Bowl, each with a vertical drop of 600 ft (182 m) or more, are located in the vicinity of the Great Gorge. Of the seven ski areas situated outside the Highlands, most have vertical drops of 200 ft (60 m) or less and are considered generally inferior in terms of lift capacity and supporting facilities (see Figure 8.11).

Although the New Jersey slopes do not attract the expert skier, some of them provide sufficient challenge to those of the intermediate level of skill and, of course, to the novices who constitute the majority of skiers. As the number of skiers among the population increases (it is expected to double within ten to fifteen years), the proportion of intermediate and novice skiers will of course increase.

In most parts of the state, natural snowfall is not sufficient to keep a resort open continuously throughout the winter. The winter season is quite short in comparison to other ski areas, Vermont, for example. The ski season in New Jersey opens in mid-December and generally ends toward the end of March. As a result, all of the ski areas in the state, with the exception of the small Peapack ski area, use snowmaking equipment to supplement the natural accumulation—only 40 to 50 in. (101 to 127 cm) per winter in the hillier regions. The technological advance of efficient snowmaking equipment thus bears most of the responsibility for facilitating a viable ski industry in New Jersey.

Skiing as an Industry

The ski industry in New Jersey is a quite recent phenomenon. Only one resort, Craigmeur, was operating in 1958. Most of the ski slopes have opened within the past ten years. New Jersey ski areas generally fall into the day-trip category, with the probable exception of the Great Gorge and Vernon Valley resorts; these two qualify as weekend resorts, servicing many more out-of-state skiers than the other smaller and less well equipped facilities.

The New Jersey ski areas do have the advantage of being readily accessible to both the Philadelphia and New York metropolitan areas. Vacation or long-term skiers are not normally attracted to New Jersey from other states, because there are intervening opportunities within their own states in the northeast that provide superior ski and lodging facilities. Most daytrippers, on the other hand, can only make a skiing trip on the weekend. Ski resorts such as those of New Jersey, which are primarily dependent on daytrippers, experience a heavily peaked demand on Saturdays and Sundays and very low patronage for the remainder of the week. The weekend overflow is a phenomenon common to all kinds of resorts and recreation facilities, but when this situation is placed in the context of a short, three-month-long skiing season and an uncertain natural snowfall, the New Jersey ski resort is placed in a potentially precarious operating condition.

The New Jersey State Division of Economic Development estimates that 35 percent of all skiers using New Jersey slopes are from out of state. In addition to attracting nearby residents from out of state, much of the advertising by the state is directed toward keeping New Jersey resi-

158

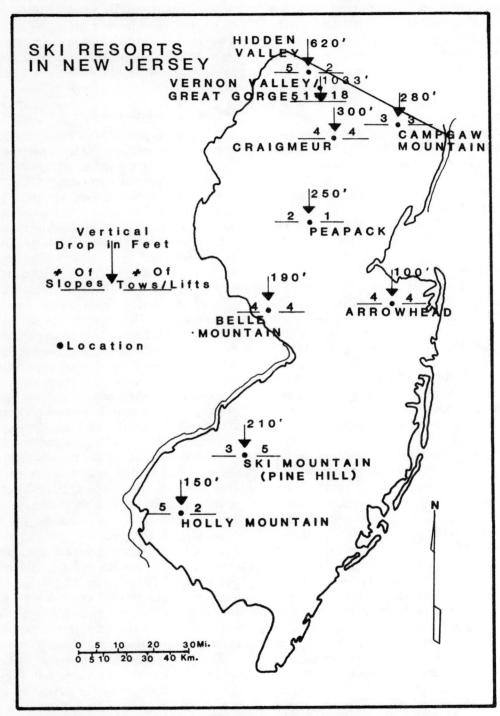

FIGURE 8.11.   Skiing in New Jersey—the impossible dream meets technology.

dents within the state instead of going to Pennsylvania's Poconos or New York's Catskills, areas seen as the major competitors for New Jersey skiers.

The growth of skiing in New Jersey, with its distinctly marginal physical environment for this type of activity, must be viewed as a response to heavy market demands within this area. While recognizing New Jersey's less-than-ideal physical environment compared with Vermont or Colorado, local residents are compromising for the less elegant but more readily accessible slopes. In attempting to simulate the conditions of more-famous ski resorts, New Jersey operators are forced to rely upon artificial snow. Trails are frequently given names that appeal to the assumed thrill-psychology of the skier, such as "Suicide Run." Base lodges are generally decorated in Alpine motif, and ski instructors are encouraged to develop an Austrian accent. In some areas where the demand for skiing facilities is great but mountains are in short supply, even a slight rise in elevation will make an acceptable ski slope. An example that would stimulate ridicule on the part of ski enthusiasts in Vermont, Idaho, or Switzerland is Ski Mountain in Pine Hill, Camden County, southern New Jersey. This is situated on the highest ridge in the southern part of the state, which provides a natural slope of 187 ft (57 m). South Jersey's other ski slope, Holly Mountain, is said to be the result of a township government experiencing a sudden surge of tax revenues as a result of the construction there of the Salem nuclear plant.

The rapid and continuing growth of ski slopes in New Jersey, until recently regarded as a high-risk natural environment, illustrates a dramatic change in Americans' perception of recreational opportunities in the natural landscape. The geography of recreation, formerly intimately associated with natural physical resources—particularly in a highly specific set of site requirements such as those imposed by skiing, is increasingly influenced by location of demand rather than the location of natural recreational resources. Surging demand for recreation facilities, coupled with increasing diversification and sophistication of recreational activities, is apparently capable of creating a largely artificial recreation landscape in the environs of large population centers. Contemporary user-oriented recreation sites are becoming characterized by man-made facilities and landscape modifications that attempt to compensate for observed deficiencies in the natural environment. The demand for recreation amenities of maximum accessibility is reshaping significant areas of the U.S. landscape; this transformation is especially visible in densely urbanized New Jersey's ski industry's success in overcoming physical-environmental handicaps.

CHAPTER 9

THE METROPOLITAN STATE

THE HIGHLY CENTRALIZED CITY

The contemporary scene in some of New Jersey's largest cities bears a disturbing similarity to old newsreels of World War II era destruction and its immediate aftermath. Whole blocks of cities like Newark, Trenton, and Camden have been leveled. Sometimes the rubble has been cleared, sometimes not. Broken sidewalks line empty rectangles that may be used for parking, if close enough to what remains of the central business area (see Figure 9.1). Fires of "unexplained origin" (arson that has not been proved) have gutted homes and apartment buildings, sometimes whole blocks of them (see Figure 9.2).

Often, brick row homes—the fancier of them faced with Jersey brownstone on their lower front walls, as if they were survivors of some mysterious chocolate flood—are still there. Their windows are broken; their copper pipes and wiring looted; their interiors frequently are burned out. The graffiti-covered walls persist, however, because they are solidly built of enduring materials. Their builders expected them to last, and they did. The rest of the house should have lasted, too, as should the neighborhood; in other cities and communities, perhaps even close by, that generation of homes and neighborhoods is still viable, still occupied by owners proud of them, maintaining them, enjoying them. The urban blight sometimes seems like a capricious garden blight—destroying formerly healthy areas while ignoring the same species of neighborhood, the same approximate age, a mile or so away. Because the causes of blight and urban decay are complex, and perhaps ultimate blame can never be fixed, the frustrations of both individuals and governments are high.

Cities often have been compared with living organisms. It is common to refer to the "birth" or "infancy" of cities and, sadly, now many refer to the "death" of cities. If the ultimate question is why are those particular cities dying, then the first question should be, why did cities grow where they did in the first place? The process of dying is as obviously related to geography as is growth. One may hear (possibly premature) reports of the impending death of Newark or Camden, but not of Houston, Atlanta, or San Francisco. If only *some* cities are in trouble, is this trouble related to their *site* (immediate location) and *situation* (general, relative location)?

The Importance of Situation

Why do great cities arise where they do? Why did a Newark or Jersey City not arise in the Pinelands or in the Southwest Farm region? The generally meteoric rise in land values and business opportunities as a city develops from open, rural land is surely motivation enough for at least some local

FIGURE 9.1.   *The Landscape of Urban Violence—A Theater in Downtown Newark.*
The plight of movie theaters within the old central cities is a microcosm of the
diminished value of centrality. Elaborately decorated, the sumptuous "first-run"
theaters downtown depended on crowds arriving by public transit. Now the central
business district is almost abandoned at night, and many theaters are closed or
devoted to violence or pornography.

residents to try strenuously to make a city
of every hamlet. In some cases, founding
a city was not a goal at all, yet a city grew
just the same. At the other extreme are
many would-be metropolises that never
made it, despite high hopes and gaudy
promotional brochures.

In probing the secrets of successful cities,
as in dissecting their sometime decay, it
will become apparent that site and situation
are both important, but situation is critical.
On a quite different scale, but just as
realistically, real estate salespeople joke that
the "three most important considerations
in real estate are location, location, and
location!" The qualities of site are significant, but a poor site—that is, one handicapped by poor drainage, hilly terrain, or
the like—can be overcome by a good situation. The dynamic economic development attracted to a superior situation can

pay for engineering to correct site handicaps.

Transport Technology as a Situation Factor

The significance of location relative to
the larger region, state, and world is related
intimately to accessibility, and thus to
transport technology. When transport technology changes, so does the relative efficiency and cost of accessibility of any place.
These changes can affect locations within
the city as well as the relative success of
the city itself. What has happened within
metropolitan areas, and among them as
well, is that the rules have changed.
The goals remain the same—minimizing
cost, maximizing profit, but the means—
transport and communications technologies, availability and cost of energy—have
changed.

FIGURE 9.2. *Inner-City Destruction and Abandonment, Newark.* The decline in population of the old central cities is related—as cause and effect—to the decline in habitable housing stock. It is alleged that some landlords arrange insurance fires as the only way to retrieve their investment in deteriorating property in the inner city.

Throughout most of history, there has been a clear, direct, and obvious relationship between degree of centrality and population density. Central locations were the most valuable when the cost of transport was high. *Friction of space* describes the costs—in time, labor, energy, and capital—of overcoming distance. With primitive transport facilities—inefficient vehicles or ships and inadequate roads or port facilities—the friction of space is high, favoring progressively higher concentration of economic functions and of people. Technological advances in transportation efficiency, lowering time-distance and cost-distance, "lubricate" the friction of space—distance can be overcome more easily, and centrality loses some of its appeal. Relatively high-cost and slow transport favors centripetal characteristics of economic lo-

FIGURE 9.3. *The Failure of High-Rise Public Housing, Newark.* Built in the late 1950s, these public housing towers were abandoned by 1980. The need for public housing remains, but this style has not worked, either in Newark or elsewhere. All the windows are boarded up.

cations, while faster, cheaper transport becomes a centrifugal force, or at least makes possible "centrifugal desires" for many people.

It is not accidental that most of New Jersey's great cities, as well as most of the world's, are on navigable water. Virtually every early settlement was on a waterway of some sort, although some of the small rivers on which early ports were located are not now navigable by any commercial-scale craft. In the early nineteenth century, where navigable waterways were not provided by nature, they were built, if economically feasible, to connect existing cities and to foster growth in developing cities. Turnpikes and then railroads first supplemented, then supplanted, canals, as new modes of transport were applied to accessibility problems and potentials.

In New Jersey, as always, situation relative to New York and Philadelphia was key to the growth of cities. It was not a one-way relationship, of course; New York's and Philadelphia's prosperities were linked to their access to New Jersey's various physical, cultural, and economic resources and to its markets. Newark's early growth was linked to its port functions and to its connection to the Pennsylvania anthracite coal fields via the Morris Canal; other New Jersey cities fattened on their positions astride canals, railroads, harbors, or turnpikes or various combinations of these transport facilities. By 1840, on the eve of New Jersey's era of great expansion in population, urban growth, and manufacturing, all but one of New Jersey's future large cities were linked to either New York or Philadelphia or both by natural waterway, canal, rails, or turnpikes. The exception, Atlantic City, did not exist in 1840; it was created, literally, by a railroad from Philadelphia in 1854.

Transport Modes as Centripetal Forces

Canals and railroads were obviously *fixed-route* transport systems. Their routes were commonly expensive to construct and maintain, and their profitability was based on high-density use of these spatially fixed investments. Railroads, in particular, were most efficiently operated between relatively concentrated distribution-collection-sorting yards and freight depots. Every point along a rail line, in other words, did not benefit directly in accessibility, especially in terms of bulk-freight movements. The railroad could not serve efficiently a very large number of sidings or short branch lines per mile. Very large customers could negotiate these special services, of course, and probably arranged them first before locating there, but smaller customers depended on accessibility to yards and depots. In this sense, the railroad was a *centripetal* force, that is, its operation favored reasonably centralized, compact groupings of activities dependent on the rails. In passenger traffic, the railroads were more flexible, to a degree, but even here the location advantages of rail transportation were confined to a series of stations or nodes along a linear route. The railroad suburbs, which were an early form of urban decentralization, were more like a loose string of beads, with the dispersal of the beads on the string related to the efficiencies of steam railroads (later, electrified lines) at stopping and then building up speed before slowing for the next station.

Within cities, congestion was the norm until the evolving technology of horsecars, then electric streetcars, made commuting a working-class option. Although the wealthy minority of urbanites has always had the ability to pay for daily transportation to work and so could spatially separate residence and work place, average urban dwellers at first had to walk. This "walking-scale city," in Sam Warner's phrase (Warner 1971, 1), was a necessarily congested one. Too few working-class commuters could be carried at low fares to make carriages or coaches an economic option, and so only the rich could afford to travel daily from suburban locations. Putting the coach on smooth steel wheels on smooth steel rails greatly reduced friction and thus multiplied the number of passengers a horse could pull. Strips of new neighborhoods followed the streetcar lines radiating from cities, because the horsecars and electric streetcars could stop and start with ease every block. However, like the railroad, they were fixed routes of fairly high investment requiring heavy patronage. It would make little sense, then, to duplicate streetcar lines on every street. The expanding city began to take starburst form, with urban development following the radial streetcar lines, leaving wedges of undeveloped or less densely occupied land between.

Just as the railroad era for industrial location emphasized centripetal forces for industry and urbanization, the streetcar era fostered centripetal location factors for shopping. The central business district or "downtown" was at the center of a spider's web of streetcar lines. While there were always some crosstown connector routes, the more heavily traveled routes with more frequent service were the direct lines to downtown. The downtown convergence of public transit routes (where streetcars sometimes were augmented by subway or elevated lines) meant that downtown was the zone of *maximum accessibility* within the expanding metropolis. Because urban expansion outward was directly linked to the public transit lines, new neighborhoods were connected efficiently with the center, until the auto age changed the rules.

The Automobile as a Centrifugal Force

The centripetal city, with a neat association of land value and access via public transit lines, no longer exists. The old streetcar lines have all but disappeared from U.S. cities, including most of New Jersey cities; public transit is now overwhelmingly performed by the more flexible buses. The effect of mass ownership of cars has been a clear and continuing trend to *centrifugal* location forces, scattering new investment in retailing, wholesaling, industrial, and even office functions to the suburbs. The ideal department-store location has shifted, for example, from the

center of the one-time streetcar net, the central business district, to a suburban mall preferably located where a major radial highway from the city crosses an encircling "bypass" route. This location should also be in a middle to upper-middle income portion of suburbia, one in which new home construction is continuing and in which the "demographics" are right—families with school-age children and, probably, both adults working out of the home. For the residents in this ideal market, the suburban mall serves as an intervening opportunity or "interceptor"—it is closer to them than is downtown, and it is far more convenient to use. Shoppers take their cars to shop; they avoid public transit if at all possible, and so the centrality of downtown is no longer an advantage. Instead, the congestion of narrow downtown streets is a disincentive to drive downtown, where free parking is very unlikely and where any parking at all may be both inconveniently located and expensive.

The subsidiary position of New Jersey's cities within the urban "solar systems" of which New York and Philadelphia are the central stars has meant that New Jersey's cities lost their retailing functions even faster than most U.S. cities. The central business districts of cities like New York and Philadelphia have adjusted to the diminishing significance of their centrality; they have shrunk, relative to their one-time dominance. No longer the exclusive suppliers of "shopping merchandise" (items in which price comparison and style variety are important enough to bring shoppers out of their home neighborhoods where they shop for convenience goods such as fresh food) for the entire metropolitan population, the "survivor downtowns," like Philadelphia, have shifted emphasis. They now function as the department-store and specialty-store "mall" for inner-city residents, as they are more convenient than suburban malls for those people. Prestige shops for the sophisticated market of the urban elite can persist in New York and Philadelphia because those cities, unlike

FIGURE 9.4. *Deptford Mall, Deptford.* The large regional mall, serving as the "downtown" of many suburban communities, typically offers two or three major department stores along with fifty or more specialty shops and restaurants. As more social functions follow economic ones out of the deteriorating downtown business districts to the malls, the huge shopping centers find themselves adding many new functions beyond retail stores. This mall recently pioneered the northeast's first shopping-mall branch police station.

Newark, Hoboken, Trenton, or Camden, still have some sizable wealthy enclaves on the edge of their central districts. Lastly, only the largest of the traditional downtowns—New York and Philadelphia again—can maintain their highly specialized functions as the logical location of unique goods and services. If there is but one outlet or supplier of a particular item within the entire metropolitan region, there remains the location advantage of *the* downtown: central Manhattan or central Philadelphia. Even in the streetcar era, this was so, and it remains valid. New Jersey's satellite downtowns thus do not have the specialized and elite markets to sustain them through the transition imposed by the situation that fostered the suburban malls.

GROWTH DYNAMICS OF MEGALOPOLIS

In 1961, geographer Jean Gottmann enriched Americans' vocabularies with *megalopolis*—a new definition, within a different context, of a Greek word meaning "super city" or "giant city." There is an original Megalopolis in Greece, a small town that never achieved the size or importance of its founders' dreams. Gottmann applied the term, redefining it as he did so, to not *one giant city*, but rather an unprecedented *urbanized region*. Great cities had expanded outward before, certainly—London, Paris, Moscow, and Los Angeles among them. Along the northeastern seaboard of the United States, however, there was a phenomenon that was new in the immense scale on which it was taking place. A handful of cities—each a great city in its own right—was in the process of growing not only outward, but *concentrating* that expansion in the direction of neighboring great cities. This was creating a polynucleated (many-centered) urban-dominated region stretching, Gottmann said, from southern New Hampshire's suburbs and satellites of Boston to Northern Virginia's sprawling suburbs of Washington, D.C. Later redefinitions of the dynamically expanding megalopolis have placed its southern fringes at metropolitan Richmond or even Norfolk–Newport News, as pointed out in Chapter 1.

New Jersey is central to this northeastern megalopolis; it is central in the contemporary extent of the urban region and in the historical context as well. The geographic center of megalopolis lies in south-central New Jersey, the midpoint of a line drawn from Boston to Washington, D.C. New Jersey lies astride the New York City–Washington, D.C. axis; along with southeastern Pennsylvania and northern Delaware, it thus lies between two of the most important cities—two of the most important decision-making centers—in the world. Washington's government nerve center is balanced by New York's financial and corporate control center and its still valid, if relatively declining, claim to being the United States' cultural capital. When the United States was younger, and the future megalopolis was still a series of spatially distinctive and discrete cities, New Jersey lay between the first and second cities of the day—New York and Philadelphia—and already was being influenced profoundly by this interposition. The New York–Philadelphia corridor was the earliest example of the growth dynamics of the future megalopolis—it was the nursery of many megalopolitan phenomena.

The attractions of the expanding urban fringe have always emphasized land values, balancing decreasing accessibility from the city's center against lower-cost land as the land is converted from a previously *extensive* land-use system to *intensive* land use. As land is developed and built upon for urban uses, the efficiencies of transport and communications facilities must be improved. New transport *infrastructure* (physical facilities complex supporting development) is built, and improvements and advances in the basic technology of transport and communications frequently combine to decrease the *time-distance* and *cost-distance* to the center of the urban area. As this happens, the fringe of expansion continues outward, converting another concentric zone of rural land to urban uses, and what was a frontier may be subjected to another wave of building and intensification of urban land use. This pattern of urban growth at one time resembled the outward-moving concentric rings created by tossing a rock into a pool of water.

Of course, the actual pattern of expansion would not be that simple and regular. More accurately, the expansion might resemble an irregular ink blot, with the city expanding farther, faster, along already established transport lines. Accessibility has always overridden distance from the core as a consideration in land-use conversion to urban uses. Holes or voids in the fabric of urbanization may persist where topographic barriers (steep, irregular terrain or swampy, flood-prone areas) or even political barriers (jurisdictional disputes, legal restrictions, zoning, even boundaries with other political units) exist. Scenic resort amenities, deep-water port facilities, or some other resource may "pull" the developing fringe in one direction more than others.

In the case of the megalopolis, however, the strongest pulls are toward other great cities, concentrating on the already-dense webs of transport arteries that connect them. Here, in the evolving corridors of metropolitan interconnection, the growth dynamics of the fringe are doubled and redoubled. The synergistic energy of a location not only on the expanding fringe, but *between* two cities (and perhaps on the linear axis of many big cities thus interconnected) is a powerful attractant to urban-suburban expansion. Two sets of factors, one positive and one negative for the state, are at work in the dynamics of megalopolis's "corridor" growth. The aging central cities of megalopolis, including those in New Jersey, have some megaproblems; New Jersey's broadly defined suburban corridor has some megaadvantages.

The rise of a modern highway-based long-distance trucking industry, greatly accelerated by the interstate highway program, has led to new rules of location for most economic activity. The crowded, congested central cities have many *diseconomies of scale*—they are too densely occupied and movement on their narrow, obsolescent street systems is too nearly paralyzed to appeal to many new industrial ventures. The once-familiar pattern of railroad-oriented urban industrial locations is being replaced by suburban locations on high-speed highways, preferably where interchanges link radial routes from core cities to the circumferential bypass routes. In this manner, suburban locations become more convenient than central city ones, which are buried within a dense web of narrow streets intersecting at time-consuming traffic lights. This overturns the old rules of higher accessibility near the center of the urban area and less at the edges.

As Mark Twain observed of his premature obituary, the death of central cities has been "greatly exaggerated." Cities are not dead, but the nineteenth-century image of the city *is* dead. The *form* of the city has changed radically. The changes have not always been swift or large scale but have continued with only temporary interruptions since the advent of the automobile age. The cumulative effects have certainly been dramatic. At the same time that significant changes in transport technology, energy systems, and communications technology have accelerated the outward movement of many urban functions, along with many urbanites, the political fragmentation of the metropolis (and, of course, the megalopolis) has contributed to the decentralization of activity and jobs from the aging cities at the metropolitan cores.

New Jersey's megalopolitan corridor contains both "winners" and "losers" as the rules of economic locations change. The fact that New Jersey never developed a metropolitan center on the scale of its near neighbors, New York City and Philadelphia, has meant that New Jersey lacked the concentrated financial power of its out-of-state "central cities." It has the disadvantages of aging industrial satellites coupled with the advantages of being in the suburban expansion ring, receiving many facilities outbound from either big city. Growth appears to be somewhat greater in the southern portions of the northeastern seaboard megalopolis than in its northern extremities; New Jersey will retain its centrality but can logically be expected to experience proportionately greater growth in South Jersey and in central Jersey. This sense of southern New Jersey's time for growth having arrived, coupled with a degree of boosterism and dark suspicion about the intentions of the (northern) majority has fueled the rising sense of South Jersey regionalism explored in a case study in the next chapter.

FROM PLANETARY CITY TO GALACTIC CITY

The interrelated factors of land value, land use, and population density in the classic city resembled an archery target—a bull's-eye pattern of concentric circles with the highest values in the center, the lowest at the outer edge. Within the classic model of what goes on where and who lives where, within the city, the center would be occupied by commercial, administrative, and institutional land uses. Public transit (railroads and trolleys) increased the value of central locations. Population-density averages corresponded closely to the archery-target model as well, with high density in the inner circles and progressively lower densities toward the periphery. As cities grew larger and their cores became more specialized in function, their central areas had declining population densities because residential uses could not compete for the highest-valued land. Thus a "dead-heart" phenomenon became common, a center empty of permanent population. Daytime population densities were highest, however, in this center.

The edge of this classic city, the common form until at least the middle of the nineteenth century, was a fairly sharp transition from high-density urban uses to open country: the urban-rural dichotomy was clear. The "sharpness" of this boundary was blurred only by the suburban residences of the wealthy. These people, and their suburban residences, were the exception, not the rule.

This earlier form of the city resembles the planet itself, with its high density nickel-iron core, its lighter mantle, and the lightest materials riding the crust. This "planetary" city—compact, sharply defined, with an internal gradation of density—was early the center of a miniature "solar system" as satellite communities developed within its economic gravity field. These satellites, definitely tied to the central city's economy, were typically highly specialized in functions that complemented those of the central city. A mining or heavy-industry satellite might grow atop a nearby mineral or energy resource, or a resort satellite might appear at a recreational amenity such as an ocean beach or mountain lake.

By the middle of the twentieth century it was apparent that metropolitan systems were developing on a grand scale. Urban populations and urban functions were dispersing from the old congested cores. A *constellation* of cities, satellites, and suburbs was forming, the original megalopolis. Gottmann believed that this northeastern megalopolis was the forerunner of many others, and he was right.

The most recent phase of centrifugal tendency in urban functions and among urbanites is that examined in northeastern

New Jersey, but present throughout the state and nation. Geographer Peirce Lewis terms this highly dispersed phenomenon the *galactic city*, an intermingled sprawl of urban functions and urban-economy participants with open countryside. In this galactic city, there is a virtually universal dispersal of characteristically urban activities and people through low-density rural areas as well as medium- and high-density, more traditional, urban-suburban forms. The once tightly bounded, compact city appears to have exploded outward, flinging people and functions into its outer hinterland and, at the same time, loosening up the former concentration in the core. The line between city and countryside, in the process of blurring for more than a century, is now almost invisible. Rather than a line, there is a very wide, and widening, amorphous zone of transition. If the urban-rural boundary *could* be objectively identified, it would have little significance, economically or culturally. Pieces of the city, or rather the functions of the city, have been flung far out from the old cores; manufacturing enterprises, warehouses, various services, retailing, and resort activities are found scattered, seemingly randomly, over a huge urban-suburban hinterland. While commuting is still a way of life, commuting is much less certain to be from suburb to central city. Just as likely, commuting takes place from suburb to suburb, countryside to suburb, and even city to suburb.

Imagine a simple diagram of average population density showing density changes from the central core to the furthermost suburbs. In the early nineteenth century, the density curve would have been more vertical than horizontal, with a steep decline in population density outward from the center. This curve would have begun to flatten when the trend toward suburban residence, pioneered by the wealthy, was democratized by the horsecar and electric trolley, producing compact, high-density suburbs at the same time that railroad commuting permitted more affluent urbanites to move to more-distant suburbs. The eventual drop to low rural densities would occur farther away from the city center.

The rapid spread of medium- to low-density suburbs facilitated by automobiles accelerated after World War II, further flattening the once almost vertical density-average line. Still, most of the jobs were in the cities, along with much of the cultural activity of the metropolis. Commuters tended to focus on the city or at least the densely built-up inner suburbs. The core city "pinnacle" of the population-density curve had stopped growing upward and, in the most overcrowded core cities, had begun a slow decline. The outward spread of diminishing density into the older suburbs was not obvious until the 1980 census. Now, thousands of odd bits and pieces of urban functions float in "rural" landscapes with a much less clear relationship to one another than they once had back in the compact city of yesterday. The inner-city peak of the population-density curve is in definite, apparently inexorable decline (see Table 9.1).

Population losses, overall, have been startling in some cases. For a few cities, the decline in population is more reminiscent of the Middle Ages' bubonic plague or a disastrous war than mere suburbanization. The effect on municipal tax rateables (real estate on which property tax is levied and paid), budgets, ethnic neighborhoods, public-employee makeup, and other social economic characteristics can only be described as earthshaking. With some notable exceptions, New Jersey's major cities suffered population losses from 1960 to 1980 (see Table 9.1) of one-fifth to one-third of their 1960 levels. Union City managed to grow, as did several large suburban townships, while Paterson, Passaic, Elizabeth, and East Orange were able to contain their losses at a low level.

The density curve is now at its least-vertical, most-horizontal orientation. Galactic city has arrived on the horizon, and New Jersey is in the vanguard.

CASE STUDY: A GALACTIC CITY

The northeastern section of New Jersey provides a good case study of the trends affecting the state, the northeastern seaboard megalopolis, and much of the rest of the country. Bergen, Hudson, Essex, Passaic, Union, Morris, Middlesex, and Somerset counties form the geographic base for a detailed study of population changes as urban dispersal moves beyond megalopolis toward an even more far-flung, decentralized form (see Figure 9.5).

Although the population decline of some older core cities was apparent back in the 1930s, few then could imagine that these inner-city or core-city declines would continue for four decades and more, or that the "blight" of formerly healthy cities would someday expand outward to include the older generation of suburbs. For many decades, wavelike ripples of population growth and increasing population density moved outward from the high-density cores. Now it is apparent that a second outward-moving ripple of population change is in motion, this time of *decreasing* population densities. This second, negative wave is very slowly following the earlier, positive-change wave, which is still advancing further into the countryside.

Population density in 1950 for the eight counties being examined would have closely resembled such a density map for 1930. The westernmost townships and municipalities in Passaic, Morris, and Somerset counties had fewer than 100 people per sq mi (258 per sq km), while Newark actually topped 18,000 per sq mi (46,620 per sq km) in 1950. East Orange had over 19,000 per sq mi (49,208 per sq km); Passaic City, in Passaic County, over 18,000 per sq mi; Paterson, over 16,000 per sq mi (41,438 per sq km); and Jersey City, over 20,000 per sq mi (51,798 per sq km). West New York, in Hudson County, at 41,870 per sq mi (108,400 per sq km), was tops in crowding that year. Population change from 1940 to 1950 (Figure 9.6) shows suburbanization

TABLE 9.1
The Declining Populations of New Jersey's Cities

City	Population 1960[a]	Population 1970	Population 1980	% Change 1960-1980
Atlantic City	59,544	47,859	40,199	-33
Camden	117,159	102,551	84,910	-27
Irvington	59,379	59,743	61,493	+ 4
Newark	405,220	382,417	329,248	-19
Bloomfield	51,867	52,029	47,792	- 8
East Orange	77,259	75,471	77,025	-.3
Bayonne	74,215	72,743	65,047	-12
Jersey City	276,101	260,545	223,532	-19
Union City	52,180	58,537	55,593	+ 7
Hamilton Twp.[b]	65,035	79,609	82,801	+27
Trenton	114,167	104,638	92,124	-19
Woodbridge[b]	78,846	98,944	90,074	+14
Clifton	82,084	82,437	74,388	- 9
Passaic	53,963	55,124	52,463	- 3
Paterson	143,663	144,824	137,970	- 4
Elizabeth	107,698	112,654	106,201	- 1
Union Twp.[b]	51,499	53,077	50,184	- 3

Source: U.S. Census, 1960, 1970, 1980.

[a]Limited to cities of over 50,000 population.

[b]Communities of over 50,000 in 1960, but not organized as cities.

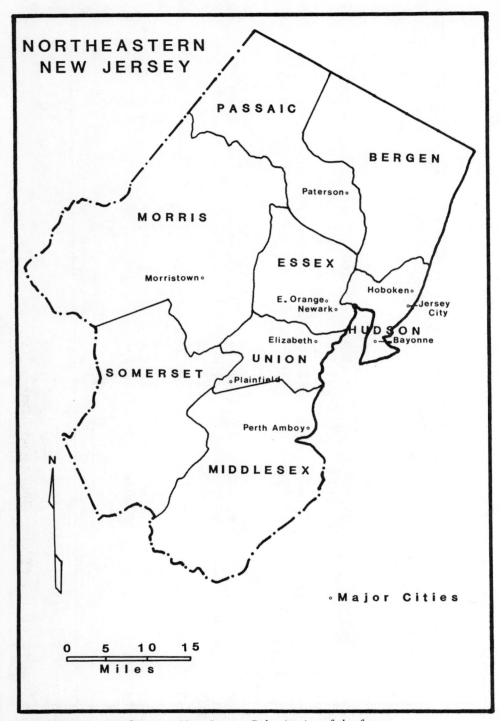

FIGURE 9.5. *Northeastern New Jersey: Galactic city of the future.*

173

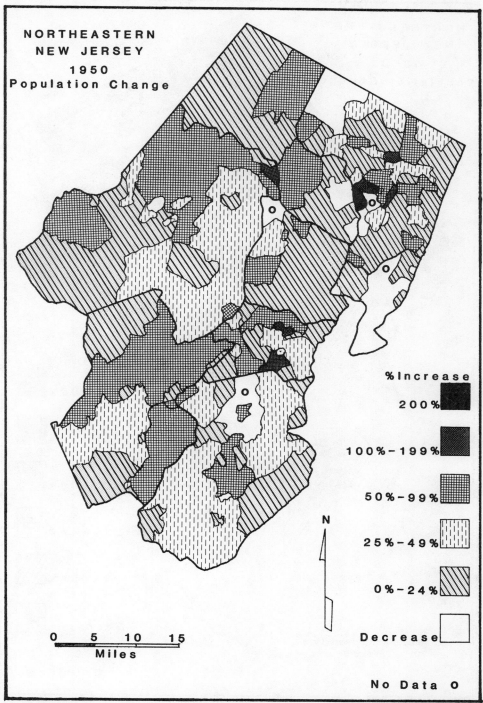

FIGURE 9.6. In 1950, few municipalities in the eight northeastern counties had experienced population loss, and suburban expansion was underway.

174

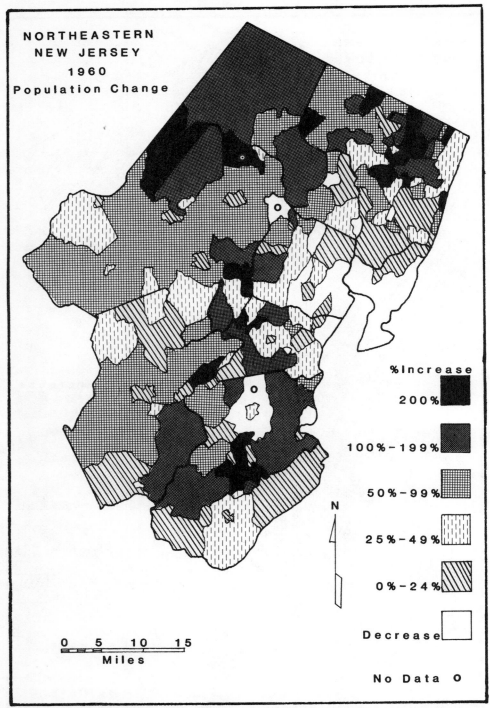

FIGURE 9.7. Suburban growth is evident as New Jersey completes its greatest numerical population growth. Only the aging central cities lost people.

well under way as every township or municipality in these eight counties was growing in population except the cores. Even then, only the highest-density core cities declined, and not all of them did—Newark posted a slight gain. (Throughout this series of maps, occasional local-government boundary changes and/or deficiencies in census data unavoidably result in a few instances of "no data".)

The map of population change from 1950 to 1960, Figure 9.7, shows a literal explosion of population after New Jersey's premier suburbanization decade. The old core cities, this time excepting Paterson, were losing people, but at least some municipalities of every county except Hudson showed population gains of over 100 percent. In Bergen, Morris, Union, Middlesex, and Somerset counties, intercensal gains of 200 percent or more were recorded in some localities. Losses were confined to most of the old core cities and a few older, high-density suburbs of the railroad and trolley era. Newark lost 7.6 percent of its people and Orange, 5.9 percent. Hudson County's continuing slide was paced by East Newark's 13.8 percent drop; Elizabeth lost 4.5 percent.

The map of population change for 1960–1970, Figure 9.8, shows the advancing "positive wave" clearly; the heaviest percentage gains are among those local jurisdictions furthest removed from the old cores, which were still in decline. A rather neat pattern of growth is obvious, with increasing distance from the cities generally correlated with increasing rates of gain. The otherwise concentric circles of increasing population gains are modified by major highways more than any other factor. Decreases were still largely confined to the aging cores. The 1980 map (Figure 9.9) documents the outward-moving ripple of declining populations.

Suburban densities have risen dramatically over thirty years of suburbanization. No township had fewer than 100 people per sq mi (258 per sq km) by 1980 (see Figure 9.10). It is in the *changes* in pop-

ulation totals that 1980 marks a significant change from past patterns, and a portent of the future form of the "city"—if indeed we can continue to use the term as it has been understood until now. Only tiny Plainsboro, in Middlesex County, had experienced a gain of over 90 percent, and in that instance the actual numerical gain totaled only 3,957.

Between 1970 and 1980, Bergen County's fastest-growing municipality posted a gain of only 16 percent, Essex's top was 19.7 percent, Passaic's was 31.5 percent, and Somerset's top township had a gain of 72.3 percent. Hudson County's ongoing population hemorrhage was countered by tiny Guttenberg's gain of 27.6 percent, but Guttenberg has but 1.3 percent of that county's total population. Union County had population decreases in every municipality.

The 1980 map of population change (Figure 9.9) shows losses through core cities and older, inner suburbs; these losses more than balance gains elsewhere in five of the eight counties in the sample area. Only outer-suburban-ring Morris, Somerset, and Middlesex manage an overall population gain. Now population *decreases* are being experienced by older, relatively high-density suburbs, with one interesting category of exception (see Figures 9.9 and 9.10). Aging crowded suburbs like East Orange are receiving enough black in-migrants to overbalance the "white flight" to lower-density suburbs.

The rules are changing; the traditional form of the city has changed almost beyond recognition. Centrality is out, dispersal and diffusion are in. Onetime centripetal economic forces are countered by new centrifugal social and economic forces. The outward explosion of people from the central cities has not just populated the suburbs; it has begun to depopulate the cities and their older, inner suburbs. The 1980 pair of maps indicates that the advancing frontier of suburbia has reached the outermost edges of the study area and is well into Sussex, Warren, Hunterdon, Mon-

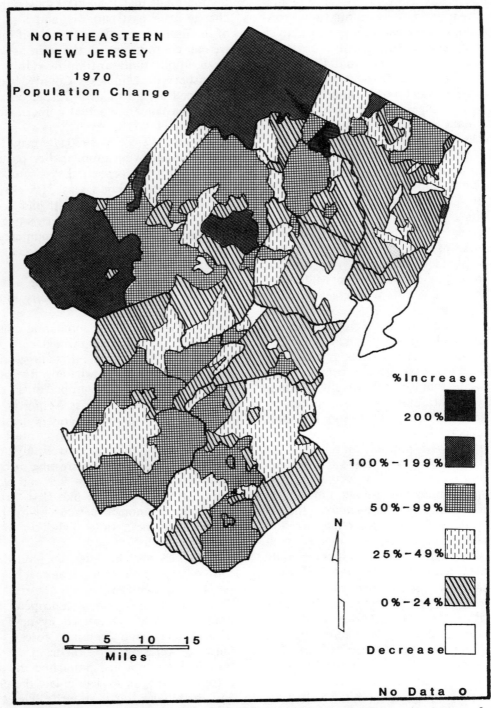

FIGURE 9.8. By 1970 the very high rates of suburban growth were in the past for these counties, and many of the inner, older suburbs were essentially stagnant in terms of population.

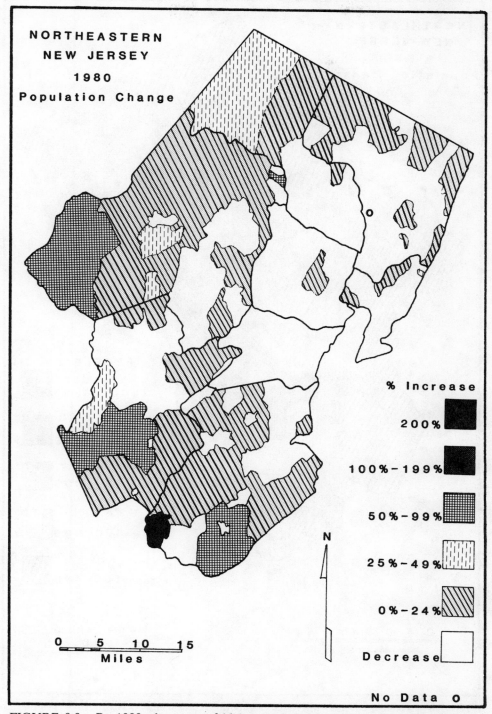

FIGURE 9.9. By 1980, the areas of high growth had moved beyond these counties, westward to Sussex, Warren, and Hunterdon counties and southward toward Monmouth and Ocean counties. Population loss, formerly associated with the decaying cities, had spread to the older generation of suburbs.

178

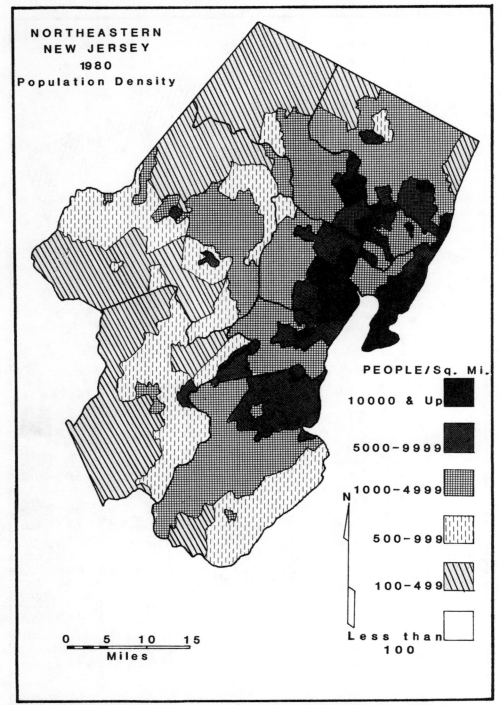

FIGURE 9.10. Apparently there is a general relationship between high population density and population loss, as well as between low population density and population gain. Are we in an era of diminishing contrasts in density, urban to rural?

mouth and Ocean counties, as previously shown on Figure 5.6.

CASE STUDY: ATLANTIC CITY

Approximately 120 years after Atlantic City was founded on a then-desolate off-shore sandbar, the city's economy, social health, and reputation were all in desperate condition. The once-glamorous, fabled Queen of the Jersey Shore, as it immodestly proclaimed itself, had sagged into a kind of frayed and peeling self-parody. Atlantic City's appeal—its crowd-attracting formula combining natural and created attractions—no longer symbolized the extravagant and fantastic illusion that vacationers seek as recreation environments.

Atlantic City's plight by the 1970s explains much of the determination to seek the economic salvation explicit in legalized gambling. The reasons for Atlantic City's economic and social malaise are more complex. Some of Atlantic City's problems can be viewed as yet another instance of the urban cancer affecting virtually all aging central cities of America's metropolitan areas. Other aspects of the resort's decline are related to causes and considerations unique to resorts.

Prelude to Desperation

A prerequisite to understanding the contributing causes of Atlantic City's sad decay is some comprehension of the degree of the problem. Data from the 1970 census illustrate Atlantic City's poverty. The city's census tract with the lowest mean income had less than half the county mean, while only two census tracts in Atlantic City exceeded the county mean. The percentage of families below the official poverty level,

Pages 179 through column one of 186 are adapted from an article by Charles Stansfield, "Atlantic City and the Resort Cycle," originally published in *Annals of Tourism Research* 5 (1978): 238-251, reprinted by permission of *Annals of Tourism Research*, © Department of Habitational Resources, University of Wisconsin—Stout, Menomonie, Wisconsin.

slightly under 10 percent for the entire county, varied within Atlantic City from 3.5 percent in the southernmost part of the city, adjacent to the neighboring city of Ventnor, to an astonishing 46 percent near the urban-renewal district of the north end. The percentage of family heads sixty-five years old and over, in which both the city and county rank far above state and national averages, indicates that there were virtual old-age ghettos within the city: census tracts ranged from negligible through 80 percent for people age sixty-five and over. The percentage of unemployed adults in the population, which for the city as a whole exceeded the national average, reached an incredible 20 percent in one district, with half a dozen other tracts ranking above 10 percent.

Atlantic City was an aging city, with two-thirds of its year-round housing stock built in 1939 or earlier; nearly 40 percent of the city's census tracts exceeded three-quarters of their total housing stock in this age category. Atlantic City's black population approached one-half of the total; racial segregation was fairly rigid, with eight census tracts possessing a black population higher than seventy-five percent and another ten having fewer than 10 percent blacks. Interestingly, there was no clear or absolute correlation of black-population distribution with economic characteristics, nor was there a consistent relationship between old age and poverty in Atlantic City.

In summary, the census statistics outlined a city with a set of social and economic problems that at the same time were results and causes of Atlantic City's changing resort functions. Atlantic City's history has followed a cycle of development, expansion, changing clientele, and decline that may be representative of a general resort experience.

The Resort Cycle

Phase One: Founding and Early Growth. The first phase of resort development is the "discovery" of an area's recreational possibilities, possibly focusing on an existing settlement whose economic functions are not yet particularly resort oriented or perhaps involving the conscious creation of a resort, usually by a group of entrepreneurs. Atlantic City is the quintessence of the created resort; Absecon Island was previously inhabited only by a lighthouse keeper, a few fishermen, and, seasonally, farmers grazing their cattle on the island. The economy was extractive, and the population was sparse.

Atlantic City's genesis was in 1852, when a civil engineer from Philadelphia, who had been in on the beginnings of Chicago's great boom and hence knew a few things about "town booming," led a group of local capitalists to practically empty Absecon Island. In Charles Funnel's delightful phrase, "He wanted them to get a whiff of dollars in the breezes that skirled about the untrodden sands" (Funnel 1975, 3). The scheme was to connect the market demand with a natural recreation amenity, suitably equipped with entertainment, hotel, and restaurant facilities. The demand existed, certainly, in the rapidly expanding industrial cities of the future northeastern megalopolis, particularly nearby Philadelphia. The recreation amenities were abundant in the forms of a gently shelving, broad white sand beach, clean saltwater, and cooling sea breezes. That whiffs of future dollars had not tickled noses earlier at that spot speaks to the significance of changing transport technology and patterns rather than to any lack of alertness to opportunity.

Cape May, some 35 mi (56 km) down the coast, then was a resort of national reputation, attracting over 110,000 visitors a year by 1851. The perception that a resort on Absecon Island could rival well-established Cape May was based on the realization that the steam railroad was the most efficient connector of recreation demand and recreation amenity by the middle of the century.

Before the railroad era, transporting vacationers from Philadelphia, Trenton, Wilmington, Baltimore, or even New York to the "Jersey shore" involved either the water routes or the slow, clumsy, and relatively expensive overland stages, or a combination of the two. Steamboats replaced sailing ships on the Philadelphia–Cape May route by 1830; stages or "jersey wagons"—wagons with unusually wide wheels to negotiate the soft sands of the outer coastal plain—were poor alternatives. In terms of *time-distance*, Cape May was the closest point on the ocean shoreline to Philadelphia. By the 1850s, Cape May could boast of the largest hotel in the United States and clientele from New York (with which the cape had steamboat connections for awhile), Philadelphia, and the upper south. Southerners took a Chesapeake Bay steamer from Baltimore to Frenchtown on the upper Eastern Shore, then the New Castle and Frenchtown Railroad across the narrow neck of the Delmarva Peninsula to catch the Cape May boat outbound from Philadelphia. The New Castle and Frenchtown, opened in 1832, was typical of early railroads in that it was a short link between water routes.

The infancy of railroads thus merely enhanced the utility of the water routes, but as the railroad era flowered, all-rail direct land routes to the seashore became the controlling factors in the fortunes of the various resorts and remained so until after World War I. The shortest all-rail route from Philadelphia to the surf and sand focused on the vicinity of Absecon Island. It is significant that the developers of Atlantic City first formed the railroad, the Camden and Atlantic, and then a wholly owned subsidiary, the Camden and Atlantic Land Company, to sell real estate at the seashore terminus.

Phase Two: Expansion. The Camden and Atlantic Railroad began operations in 1856; Cape May's first railroad arrived during the 1860s. Comparative costs and time-distance now discriminated against Cape May and favored new Atlantic City, at least for Philadelphians. Connecting customers with the resort is the basis of all resort development; all recreation and tourism patterns take place within a time-and-space frame. Atlantic City's time-distance and *cost-distance* relative to Philadelphia were a successful blend of shortest straight-line distance and the efficiency of the railroad. Just as the new economics and time-distance of the railroad era helped slow Cape May's growth as a resort, the railroad literally created Atlantic City and shaped its patronage base, its urban morphology, and its history.

The boom that followed completion of the railroad was impressive. Land values escalated as the tide of visitors expanded each year. A city block in Atlantic City was offered at $1,000.00 in 1865, a nice increase over the 1853 price of $17.50 per acre ($7.08 per ha), but only a feeble portent of rocketing values over the next fifteen years as population increased tenfold.

The effect of this early dominant role of the railroad upon Atlantic City was marked. As fans of the famous Monopoly game (based on the game creator's observations of real estate values in Atlantic City) will recognize, Atlantic City's grid of streets was named in a manner calculated to enable visitors unfamiliar with its street plan to find their way about by remembering two simple rules. Avenues paralleling the oceanfront boardwalk are named after oceans and seas, (*Pacific, Atlantic, Arctic,* and so on) while most of the closely spaced streets at right angles to the Atlantic Ocean are named after states in approximate geographic order from the north end's Maine Avenue through to the south end's Georgia Avenue. The simple grid pattern with its long, narrow blocks at right angles to the seafront (thereby stretching the desirable location boast, "one block to the beach") was the basis of a very compact, pedestrian-oriented resort. Atlantic City's proudest and most famous "avenue" was the pedestrians-only boardwalk.

Vacationers arriving by train expected to walk most of the time, and the dense pattern of land use facilitated this. Indeed, in Atlantic City's early years, the railroad trestle and causeway from the mainland across the marshes and bay to Absecon Island was the only island-mainland connection; a highway-bridge causeway was constructed only in 1870, as the railroad was not eager to encourage stage or wagon traffic to the new resort. Early vacationers thus could not drive their own carriages to the resort; this factor may have encouraged a seafront pedestrian promenade rather than the seafront vehicular drive for the traditional display of fancy coaches that characterized older resorts such as Cape May or even such resorts as Brighton and Nice in Europe.

This early total reliance on the railroad, and continuing dependence on the railroad during the resort's first six or seven decades, produced a pedestrian-oriented city, one in which taxis and "jitneys" (small buses, owner-operated) provided the intracity public-transit services. Wicker "rolling chairs" or "pedicabs" on the boardwalk carried footsore vacationers in stately progress. Parking, that space-gobbling city destroyer in some contemporary planners' views, was not a problem until after World War I. But by 1923 more vacationers were arriving by auto than by rail.

The railroad terminal was the cornucopia of the resort; the railroads were the umbilical cords connecting the industrial cities' pleasure-seeking hordes with the resorts. The location of the terminal was a strong influence upon real estate values in that the daytrippers who had a day to sample the resort's many delights headed directly for the seafront and were effectively tethered to the seafront within a few blocks of their arrival axis.

Obviously, all the facilities in Atlantic City's early days were new, and *new* commonly equals *desirable* to U.S. tourists. The early success of Atlantic City is illustrated by the size and plushness of its hotels. For example, the United States Hotel (see Figure 9.11), which occupied an entire city block, was described in a contemporary account as accommodating 600 guests in rooms that were "large, airy,

UNITED STATES HOTEL. ATLANTIC CITY. N.J. PROP'S. & OWNERS. BROWN & WOELPPER.

FIGURE 9.11.   The pride of Atlantic City in the 1870s. (T. F. Rose, *Historical and Biographical Atlas of the New Jersey Coast*. Philadelphia: Woolman and Rose, 1878, p. 325)

comfortable, carpeted and furnished in walnut, with gas in every room and in every respect will compare with a first class city hotel. There are also attractive billiard rooms, ten pin alleys and shooting galleries and daily morning, afternoon and evening open air concerts are given by a celebrated orchestra" (Rose 1878, 42). Host to President Grant in 1874, the hotel was one of the most successful ventures of the railroad company, but by 1894 it had been torn down, an example of the energetic drive to "keep up to date."

The expansion phase of the resort cycle is thus characterized by intensive real estate speculation, rapid construction of the expanding infrastructure of the resort, and, commonly, relatively affluent vacationers attracted by the combination of fresh and uncrowded natural recreation resources and new, plush accommodations, restaurants, and transport facilities of the latest design. The reputation of the resort, carefully nourished by enthusiastic public relations efforts, is at its height, that of an "in" place with a magnetic appeal to the trend followers and aspiring leaders of social strata just beneath that of the pioneer vacationers.

Phase Three: Changing Clientele. Atlantic City's boosters polished the image of Atlantic City as a resort cutting across all class lines and attracting the social elite; the resort perpetrated, and then perpetuated, a glamorous aura of a saltwater taffy Newport, but this was not an accurate description. Funnel's study of social columns and hotel registers indicated that Atlantic City was essentially a working-

and middle-class resort with very infrequent appearances by social registerees. But the myth—the cherished notion that shop girls were sharing the beach with the elite—was important.

As leisure time and disposable income were democratized, successively lower-income groups arrived to sample Atlantic City's well-publicized delights. This trend toward a broadening of the social strata patronizing the resort is intimately related to the progressive lowering of the time and money costs of travel to the resort. The socioeconomic orientation of a particular resort is often closely associated with its relative accessibility, as it exists, and as it has developed through the history of a resort.

By World War I, Atlantic City had reached a false stasis. It appeared that all was well, that the tried and true formulas still worked. But by that time, most of the resplendent and extravagant seafront hotels had been built; few more on the truly grandiose scale would be added. The railroad was still fulfilling its dominant role, although motorists were beginning to clog the highways in summer. The costs of reaching Atlantic City were decreasing. The railroad, whose speed made day trips feasible, was carrying more of the lower economic groups to Atlantic City, and the entertainment complex increasingly reflected their tastes. This shift in emphasis towards working-class tastes was both a cause and a consequence of the upper middle class's declining allegiance to Atlantic City.

The mechanical amusements, cheap vaudeville theaters, and garish entertainments that so thrilled the working classes helped to drive away the upper middle class from the ornate hotels and high-class restaurants. The "takeover" of a resort by a lower-income group than had originally dominated it may be partially explained, however, by the upper-income group's desire for new recreation environments.

Thus, in the third phase of the resort cycle, the resort has been abandoned by most representatives of the "founding" or pioneering social classes. The physical complex of hotels, restaurants, and the more-expensive, higher-class entertainments is allowed to slowly deteriorate. No new investment is attracted due to diminishing patronage, at least of the higher-priced facilities.

Phase Four: Decline. Changing transport technology and consequent changes in transportation geography and relative location were instrumental in Atlantic City's founding and rapid rise. Unfortunately, Atlantic City's fortunes were tied to the passenger trains in both their ascendant and eclipse phases. The last excursion trains were phased out after World War II, leaving Atlantic City with only minimal, commuter-oriented train service. Limited-access, high-speed highways and jet airplanes—the replacement of trains for tourists—both favored other resorts over Atlantic City. Relative location, in terms of convenient accessibility to the vacationers' homes, had changed again, and Atlantic City was the loser under these new rules. Although Atlantic City's Bader Field, one of the first commercial airports in the nation, is convenient to downtown, the air age has not greatly benefited Atlantic City. Other than convention trade, few visitors arrive by air. The time-distance by air from most of megalopolis to other resorts, such as those of southern Florida, is not all that much greater than that to Atlantic City. Moreover, Atlantic City's situation within megalopolis places it, and the neighboring small resorts, within the "traffic shadow" of New York and Philadelphia. Short-haul service to Atlantic City from Philadelphia Airport has not been very successful, although it is continued.

The mobility of the automobile led to a style of vacation quite different from that of the old railroad resorts; the railroad had conferred only point-to-point mobility on its users, so that the vacationers' dollars were spent mostly within the confines of a particular resort. Private automobiles had major impacts upon recreation patterns, which did not really benefit Atlantic City. Vacationers arriving in cars wanted to be able to park conveniently and preferably free of charge. However, crowded, densely built-up Atlantic City was firmly oriented to pedestrians, not cars; by the auto age, most of the city's buildable land was occupied by multistory structures packed tightly together. The narrow streets of an earlier era could not accommodate both heavier traffic and curb parking on both sides. Relatively few large motels were constructed in a city where many hotel rooms were empty except in peak season and where the fixed investment in aging hotels argued against large-scale new construction. Frugal vacationers could stay "offshore" (on the mainland) at cut-price motels constructed along the highways and drive in daily to crowd Atlantic City's beaches and streets, but leave little money behind. The much-sought-after middle-class "family trade" increasingly preferred the smaller resorts that were less crowded, less expensive, quieter, and less garish. The new highways that brought vacationers to Atlantic City also facilitated their going to other resorts or their commuting into Atlantic City from less expensive locations. Highway improvements ever increased the day-trip hinterland of the city.

The automobile age also affected Atlantic City in much the same manner that it affected cities with other economic bases. The nuclei of most seashore resorts had been established by 1880, in a frenzy of real estate development that optimistically attempted to reproduce Atlantic City's early and spectacular success on every sandbar. Rail tentacles had ventured across bay and marsh to each aspiring resort and then had extended the length of each barrier beach. By the 1950s, most of the islands had been built up, and new construction of second homes, retail areas, and motels had shifted emphasis to the mainland. Confined to its offshore island, Atlantic City was unable to expand its corporate boundaries to either its island neighbors or its "offshore" mainland satellites that were growing rapidly in the period after World War II. Non-tourist-oriented retailing shifted to cheaper real estate on the mainland, as did new, upper-income residential construction.

By 1970 Atlantic City was the central city for a linear urban area that occupied the ocean shoreline and a strip of mainland behind the bay-fringing marshes. In common with other metropolitan areas, the aging city's functions were migrating to the suburbs, leaving behind the poor, the aged, and the minorities. The physical plant became obsolescent, from the street grid through to public and private buildings. The population had been shifting to the barrier beaches from the mainland portions of the shore counties since the middle of the nineteenth century, but by the middle of the twentieth century the population balance was shifting back to the mainland, reflecting the suburbanization of the resorts' permanent populations. The mainland-island population ratio was in approximate balance around 1970, with future gains anticipated entirely in the mainland communities.

An indication of Atlantic City's decline and the obsolescence of its infrastructure was the loss of about 3,500 hotel rooms (to demolition, mostly) between 1964 and 1969, accompanied by a loss of 2,500 "guest house" rooms. Although motels did add approximately 1,000 rooms in this period, the net decrease in transient rooms available was nearly 20 percent of the total stock in just five years. In this last phase of the resort cycle, the natural amenities that led to the founding of the resort were of deteriorated quality, with environmental pollution a serious and intensifying problem. For example, the once-popular annual "around the island swimming race" was abandoned due to "lack of interest," a lack of enthusiasm possibly related to the presence of raw sewage discharged from pleasure craft in the back bay.

Commonly, resorts attempt to modify their appeal to vacationers in this final phase of the resort cycle. As a result in some measure of uncontrollable or unforeseeable changes in leisure patterns, transport technology, and fashion and because of environmental pollution and plant obsolescence, the resort can no longer rely on its original set of attractants. The resort may choose to emphasize its historical and cultural uniqueness rather than its deteriorated, less-attractive physical-site amenities. In other words, superior climates, lower costs, relatively comparable degrees of accessibility in changing transport technology, more modern and glamorous facilities, less-crowded beaches—all of these assets may characterize other and newer resorts. Some unique quality of the artificial or man-created environment can, conceivably, be emphasized to lure tourists—for example, the huge stock of accommodations and entertainment facilities that are available at lower rates in attracting conventions.

A notable example of capitalizing upon the historic landscape is Cape May's largely successful preservation of its Victorian townscape. Cape May's stock of architecture from the 1850s through the 1890s helps draw visitors to an otherwise out-of-the-way and unprepossessing physical site with eroded beaches.

Atlantic City's architecture, while flamboyant and varied in the few remaining great hotels of the period from the turn of the century through the 1920s, is not yet quite old enough to draw the full interest of the preservationists and nostalgia buffs who have made a pet of Cape May. Great gaps in Atlantic City's oceanfront skyline resemble broken or missing teeth in a smile—a reminder of senescence and neglect. While small-town Victoriana at Cape May is charming, turn-of-the-century Atlantic City, what there is left of it, seems more isolated in a sea of slums and consequently dreary. Atlantic City simply cannot be another, larger Cape May. It must be reassessed in terms of its remaining assets in the perspective of changing times.

Gambling as Panacea

Las Vegas is many things that Atlantic City is not. Las Vegas is an automobile-oriented city in structure, a jet-plane–oriented resort in vacationer hinterland.

Las Vegas is new glitter and frantic pace; Atlantic City is fading gilt and leisure. The contrast of Las Vegas's "strip" and Atlantic City's "boards" sums it up neatly. By the 1960s, Las Vegas was enormously successful; Atlantic City was in deep trouble.

The recreation geography of Las Vegas does, however, resemble that of Atlantic City in important respects. Each, in its way, was the closest point to a metropolitan area at which a major recreational resource was available; an ocean beach in Atlantic City's case; a permissive, indulgent political-cultural environment in Las Vegas's instance (Las Vegas was the closest oasis of legalized gambling to metropolitan Los Angeles). In common with Atlantic City, Las Vegas was "boomed" by a significant change in time-distance and relative cost of transportation, which in each case eventually extended the "vacationer hinterland" beyond the major metropolitan area that at first supplied most of the customers and is still the most important single source of customers.

The social and economic plight of Atlantic City spurred a variety of efforts to revitalize the city by the 1960s. A new high-speed toll highway, the Atlantic City Expressway, was built between Philadelphia's New Jersey suburbs and the aging resort. A new state college was built on the mainland nearby. There was talk of extending a suburban high-speed commuter railway from Philadelphia all the way to Atlantic City. The most intriguing (and, initially, controversial) suggestion was to legalize gambling. New Jersey had already followed the lead of some neighboring states by instituting a state lottery. Travel agents throughout the state routinely organized group charters to Las Vegas or the Bahamas so that Jerseyans could gamble legally. Legalization was at first opposed on the ground that it might attract organized crime into the presumably pristine state; some cynical Jerseyans are still laughing. A referendum on gambling casinos that appeared on the November 1974 ballot was resoundingly defeated, three to two. The defeat was attributed to well-organized opposition ("no dice on casino gambling"), particularly from church groups. However, the 1974 proposal, supposedly designed to help Atlantic City, would have made casinos a matter of local option anywhere in the state. Clearly, the possibility of a casino in everyone's hometown was unpopular.

A 1976 ballot proposal was restricted to legalized casinos in Atlantic City only. A million-dollar campaign fund was contributed by Atlantic City's businesses (including $125,000 from Resorts International— a Bahamas casino operator that had already purchased controlling interest in a 1,000-room hotel). In the 1976 proposal, state revenues from casinos were to be devoted to property-tax and utility-bill relief for the elderly poor—a maneuver that attracted many votes. The campaign of the Committee to Rebuild Atlantic City succeeded, despite a warning from the superintendent of state police that the load on law enforcement would be "unbearable." Important in the vote was the claim that over $800 million would be generated through new construction and renovation; 21,000 permanent new jobs were to be created, with $205 million in new wages.

The revitalization of Atlantic City was to be accomplished by emphasizing a unique (for the region) political-cultural location advantage that would attract the necessary capital for major modernization as well as the return of the golden hordes of affluent tourists. The grand old resort could rise again, once again possessed of a desired recreational amenity in the new set of recreation assets. It clearly is essentially market oriented within the northeastern megalopolis. Americans' values and lifestyles are changing, and at Atlantic City the artificial amenity supplements the natural amenities in attracting vacationers. The cycle will recycle.

Have the Casinos Fulfilled Their Promises?

The casinos' impacts on Atlantic City and its region have been mixed. When New Jersey's governor participated in the opening of the first casino on the Memorial Day weekend of 1978, there were great expectations about "turning around" the fading old resort with its impoverished, declining employment dominated by high seasonal unemployment. Between 1968 and 1977, average monthly employment declined by over 40 percent in hotels and motels, and Atlantic City's seasonality, that is, the inverse of its ratio of low-season (winter) employment to high-season (summer) employment, increased. In 1968, winter employment in the lodging industry was at 65 percent of the summer peak; by 1977, the last "B. C." (before casinos) year, winter employment was only 47 percent of summer. There was an average seasonal shift of 12,500 jobs each year. While seasonal migrants held some of those summer jobs (college students as well as managers and chefs who regularly shift from Florida to the Jersey shore in season), permanent residents in the job market put in twice as many unemployment claims in winter as in summer (Hamer 1982, 3–16).

Clearly, Atlantic City needed not only more jobs, but less seasonality in its employment structure. The jobs have increased. Employment in hotels, motels, and other lodging places was 1,711 during the last months before the first casino opened (data not seasonally adjusted). With the first casino open, Resorts International, this employment category soared to 4,065, although this coincided with normally increasing seasonal employment. By April 1981, with a total of seven casinos in operation, there were 25,243 employees of casino hotels alone in Atlantic City. An eighth casino, the Tropicana, opened in November 1981. Overall employment in services in Atlantic County increased 44 percent from 1980 to 1982. Seasonal fluctuations in Atlantic City employment, while still evident, are far lower now than in the years before casinos. Unemployment claims have fallen by at least 3,300 compared to projections made before casinos made their debut. Seasonal fluctuations are running at about 82 to 88 percent of summer, a major

FIGURE 9.12. *On the Boardwalk at Atlantic City: The Old and the New.*
The Blenheim (*above*), a landmark since 1908, was built using a reinforced-
concrete technique developed by Thomas Edison. It was demolished in 1978
to make room for the new casino (*below*). Although the valuable oceanfront
properties are being transformed by the casino industry, much of the rest
of the city remains in deteriorated condition.

FIGURE 9.13. *Atlantic City Beach.* The superb ocean beaches were the first attraction in the growth of New Jersey's seashore resorts. Atlantic City remains one of the few resorts not imposing a beach user fee, as casino revenues and related activity here support maintenance, cleaning, and patrolling costs. (Courtesy of Atlantic City Press Bureau)

accomplishment in Atlantic City. In 1979, Atlantic County led the nation in personal-income growth rate.

Providing more jobs, however, was not the only goal of casino legislation as envisioned by New Jersey voters when they approved legalization. Jobs for Atlantic City *residents*, particularly the poor and minority groups, were to be provided by casinos. This apparently has not happened.

A recent study of casino-employee migration showed that about 25 percent of them lived in Atlantic City, about 30 percent commuted from outside the county, and most of the rest lived in Atlantic County outside the city (*New Jersey Economic Indicators* March 16, 1982, 8–14). In 1970, only 10 percent of those employed in Atlantic County commuted in from out of county. Now, about 1,800 casino workers

commute from Cape May County, 1,360 from Ocean County, and 1,350 from Camden County. Fewer than 8 percent commuted from other counties in the state. However, only 53 percent of casino-hotel employees lived in Atlantic County one year before they applied for a hotel-casino employee license. Almost one-fifth of the successful applicants for a license had lived out of state one year before application: almost 1,000 had lived in Puerto Rico, 6,500 in Pennsylvania, and 1,700 in New York State. Nevada was the past residence of 686 employees; the casino industry is a very specialized one, and management as well as floor personnel must be experienced in the business. For this reason, many "foreign" immigrants to Atlantic City casino employment were from the Bahamas and the United Kingdom, where, as in

FIGURE 9.14.   Atlantic City's rejuvenation based on casinos is evident in this aerial view looking northward along the seafront. All but one of the new casinos are located directly on the famous boardwalk. (Courtesy of Atlantic City Press Bureau)

Nevada, casino gambling had been previously legalized.

In addition to experienced personnel, another component of immigration has doubtless been young adults. The same 1982 study showed that almost two-thirds of hotel-casino employees were between the ages of twenty and thirty-four; only 3 percent were over sixty years old. At least in positions that require meeting the public (which is virtually all of them in a service and entertainment business), this is a "youth and beauty" business—personal attractiveness is an important, if not explicit, consideration in hiring. Minority representation in casino employment is commendable; almost 48 percent of total hotel-casino employees are female; over 25 percent are nonwhite. However, when employment data are characterized by "key casino" (managerial and supervisory), "casino" (gaming-floor workers), and "hotel" (non casino service—chambermaids, bellboys, maintenance workers, and other services), the picture is somewhat different. Nonwhites are 16 percent of key casino employees, but 40 percent of the hotel category.

In the meantime, the increase in real estate taxes has helped drive out lower-middle-class Atlantic City residents at the same time that rental housing is deteriorating and being sold for casino-related development. Many small retail businesses in Atlantic City have not benefited from casino-bound crowds. Apparently casino patrons tend to regard the casinos as individual islands of appeal, entertainment factories set along the boardwalk or inlet, but backed by a swamp of hazardous and unsightly slum. This view is not without foundation.

Although seasonal employment fluctuations have been reduced, the experience of Nevada's gambling-oriented resorts suggests that seasonality cannot be eliminated by introducing gambling into a resort that, climatically, has an obvious off-season. Mild Las Vegas does have a nearly constant level of operation; Lake Tahoe and Reno, which have severe winters, experience sizable seasonal fluctuations. However, Atlantic City's market orientation has meant that it already surpasses Las Vegas in number of casino gamblers, and soon may exceed Las Vegas's gambling grosses.

The rather mixed effects of casinos on Atlantic City's economy and residents suggest a comparison with those developing nations in the Caribbean that also host casinos. Atlantic City's plight, as described above, was not dissimilar to, say, the Bahamas. Income averages among Atlantic City's residents were not only lower than state averages, but heavily dependent on seasonal service jobs in an economy increasingly dominated by outside sources of capital. The coming of casinos accelerated the trend toward "outside" corporations controlling the larger, more-profitable operations. Casino operation requires both heavy capital investment (in effect, a casino functions as its own bank) and expertise in this specialized activity, requirements not likely held by typical Atlantic City residents before the coming of casinos.

It is an interesting coincidence that the operator of Atlantic City's first casino had operated one in the Bahamas after losing a Havana operation in the Castro revolution. The top management and experienced floor supervisors come in from outside, as noted, and the corporate profits flow back to shareholders, most of whom are not among Atlantic City's largely unskilled, poor, aged, black, or Spanish-speaking population. The jobs likely to be filled by precasino Atlantic City "natives" are the relatively lower-paying service jobs, in return for which Atlantic City residents are being priced and taxed out of their homes. Economically, Atlantic City has been colonized by casinos in a manner not unlike the Bahamas. Small, locally owned hotels, guesthouses, and restaurants tend to benefit only from the high-season "spill-over" (demand surplus to the major hotels' capacities), while the heavily advertised casino hotels attract near-capacity business in the lengthened season. The blame for this situation does not rest upon the casinos, but rather on the unrealistic expectations generated by their advent.

CHAPTER 10

REGIONS

REGIONALIZATION

Two basic organizational approaches characterize geography. In *systematic,* or topical, geography, study is focused on the phenomena rather than on area. In a *regional* study, the focus is upon a specific portion of the world; *all* physical, cultural, economic, or political factors that can help achieve an understanding of that region are studied.

New Jersey *is* a region; the state has been explicitly defined as a region, one of fifty for the United States. Within New Jersey, there are impressive, and significant, variations; New Jersey is anything but homogeneous. The character and qualities of the widely different faces of New Jersey can best be interpreted by regionalizing New Jersey.

Two general categories of regions are studied by geographers. The state of New Jersey is an example of the *formal* region, one relatively uniform throughout in terms of its identifying criteria. For purposes of voting for governor or filing a state income-tax return, for example, any part of New Jersey is exactly like any other part. Other political regions share this characteristic.

In the other type of region, a *functional* region, there is a definite center or node. An interaction system or network implies a definite pattern of relationships within the functional region. A good example would be the daily commuting hinterland region of a city like Paterson. There would be a rhythmic cycle of interaction between Paterson and its surrounding area; Paterson would be the node or center for this interaction system.

In any type of region, the criteria for identifying the region, and bounding it, are chosen by people for their own purposes. Even physical regions, such as climate or soil regions, are determined by applying criteria of measurement that people find significant or important to them in some way. The phenomena being described and measured may not necessarily be the product of human action, but the selection of salient details of phenomena to use in regionalization schemes is definitely a human decision. In other words, regions exist only after someone chooses criteria that seem appropriate.

A key to regionalizing is the careful choice of significant criteria on which to base the identification and boundaries of regions. Too much detail would cloud the picture, not illuminate it.

Everyone already has a sense of the meaning and usefulness of regionalization; people perceive regions even if they do not always call them regions. From childhood we are aware of neighborhoods, which are, of course, local-scale regions. There would be a surprising degree of agreement among a neighborhood's residents as to the existence, boundaries, and cores or centers of their neighborhood. An urban neighborhood might correspond generally with a voting district, the area served by a fire station, a church or synagogue, or an elementary school. The neighborhood will be understood as having a character, an identity different, at least in some details, from other neighborhoods. Similarly, a shopping district, church, playground, park, or even an industrial complex could form all or part of the core or focus of the neighborhood. Neighborhood boundaries are commonly major "breaks" in the patterns of a neighborhood resident's daily or weekly round of activities. An unusually wide or busy street, a ravine or cliff, a railroad line, a freeway, or sometimes a large park or open space can become an accepted boundary, perceived as such by many local people.

Just as neighborhoods within urban, suburban, or even rural localities show identifiable characteristics and thus make logical regions, the different sections of New Jersey become associated in many minds with certain characteristics and are thus widely perceived as regions. Because regions are intellectual creations—products of human curiosity, understanding, and the apparent need to bring a sense of order to a complex and occasionally chaotic world that humans experience—there are as many different possible regional schemes as there are regionalizers. Additionally, the precise boundaries chosen for regions are essentially arbitrary. There are seldom really sharp, obvious boundaries between geographic regions of any but the very smallest scale. Perhaps everyone has had the experience of watchfully approaching some type of region—a resort area for example—and suddenly becoming aware that one has entered the region already, without any conscious notice of a boundary. The boundary was not abrupt, but rather there was a zone of transition, of change. So it is with most of the boundaries between the regions selected for New Jersey. Also, the boundaries are not permanent—they shift and change over time.

The seven regions of New Jersey (see Figure 10.1) were determined to highlight the qualities of the cultural landscape. The features of New Jersey's landscapes that were considered most significant to re-gionalization include a wide variety of physical, cultural, and economic phenomena. Terrain, drainage, soils, vegetation, and climate are each fundamental to the historical and contemporary perceptions of usefulness, and thus to land use, economy, population density, and general flavor of landscapes. The human population—its density, age- and sex-ratio characteristics, mobility, ethnic or racial makeup, and its economic and social variables—is the second major category of general landscape components and modifiers. The type and intensity of economic development forms another set of landscape molders. Types of natural resource exploitation; land-use systems; transport routes and technologies; energy production, transferral, and utilization; and industrial activities are all of obvious importance, as are the scale and influence of urbanization on the landscape.

THE SEVEN REGIONS

The seven regions represent a series of compromises and generalizations designed to communicate the rich variety of cultural landscapes within the state without overly fragmenting an understandable pattern.

The seven regions include two sprawling metropolitan-oriented regions, the central corridor (including Trenton), the Highlands of the northwest, the Pinelands "empty areas," the southwestern agricultural area, and the unique environment of the seashore. The boundaries are not really sharp lines as necessarily indicated on a map but rather are zones of transition. Also, several of the boundaries are definitely unstable as one region expands at the expense of another. This instability is related to metropolitan expansion within both the New York–oriented area and the somewhat smaller greater-Philadelphia sphere.

The Highlands

The Highlands region includes the physiographic province known as the Appalachian Highlands, together with the Kittatinny Ridge and Valley and a large,

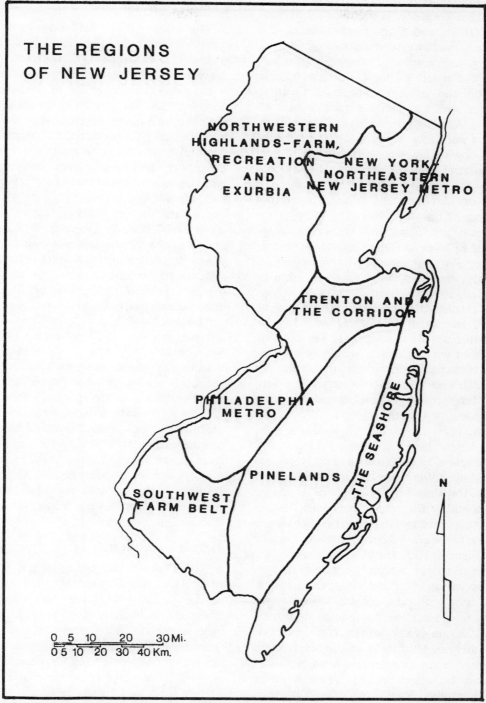

FIGURE 10.1. The seven regions are based on population density, economy, and—to a lesser extent—landforms, soil, and natural vegetation. In detail, each region could be further subdivided, but this would obscure more than it revealed of the varying character of the state.

northwestern portion of the Newark Basin Piedmont Province. It includes all of Sussex, Warren, and Hunterdon counties, the extreme northwestern corner of Bergen County, the northern "hourglass" projection of Passaic County, western Morris County, and most of Somerset County, together with the northern part of Mercer County. Although the valleys of this mountainous and hilly region, such as the Musconetcong Valley, were settled early, much of this land remains relatively lightly settled.

Resort development was early of importance, from the Delaware Water Gap to the beautiful natural lakes now augmented by lakes created by damming stream valleys. Portions of the Highlands more strongly resemble New England than a crowded, industrialized portion of megalopolis; this region is perhaps least typical or representative of New Jersey in the perceptions of non-Jerseyans. The eastern fringes of the Highlands are under continuing suburbanization pressures from the adjacent New York–Northeastern New Jersey Metropolitan region as galactic city continues its growth.

New York Metro

The New York–Northeastern New Jersey Metropolitan region, or New York Metro for short, includes all of Hudson, Essex, and Union counties, lower Passaic County, the easternmost part of Somerset, and the northern half of Middlesex County (see Figures 10.2 and 10.3). This region has experienced a significant overall loss of population over the last two decades; its decaying central cities are in the trauma of decline, abandonment, and attempted revitalization of varying degrees of success. Its industries tend to be of the older, basic type with a strong orientation toward market and the superb transportation facilities of this region. New York Metro is most representative of the decline of the long-established, too frequently obsolescent Northeast or the U.S. Manufacturing Belt.

Central Corridor

The Central Corridor includes metropolitan Trenton and the inner coastal plain to the Raritan estuary. This is part of the main axis of the northeastern megalopolis; it has been dominated by an intensifying corridor function, northeast to southwest, that has linked the developing New York and Philadelphia metropolitan areas since colonial times. Its good-quality farmlands are under intense pressures from suburbanizing extensions of the New York Metro and Philadelphia Metro regions; indeed, the commuting or daily interaction hinterlands of New York and Philadelphia merge in the vicinity of Princeton. A startling microcosm of this suburban-oriented state is the suburbanization of the state capital's functions. Trenton, an old and once-prosperous industrial town, has been virtually abandoned. The office-building complex housing state workers is still there, but the after-hours socializing and politicking that is so important to any bureaucracy is carried out in Princeton rather than Trenton. The governor's official residence is in Princeton, surely the only example in the United States of the governor's mansion not being located in the state capital. The Central Corridor includes major portions of Mercer and Middlesex counties, together with relatively smaller sections of neighboring Monmouth and Burlington counties.

Philadelphia Metro

The Philadelphia Metropolitan Sphere, or Philadelphia–New Jersey Metro region, is the smallest region in territory, and distinctly second to New York Metro in size and overall influence across state boundaries. This region includes the northern halves of Camden and Gloucester counties with the northwestern sector of Burlington County. The commuting hinterland of Philadelphia has not extended so far across the New Jersey border as has that of New York, and within New Jersey the

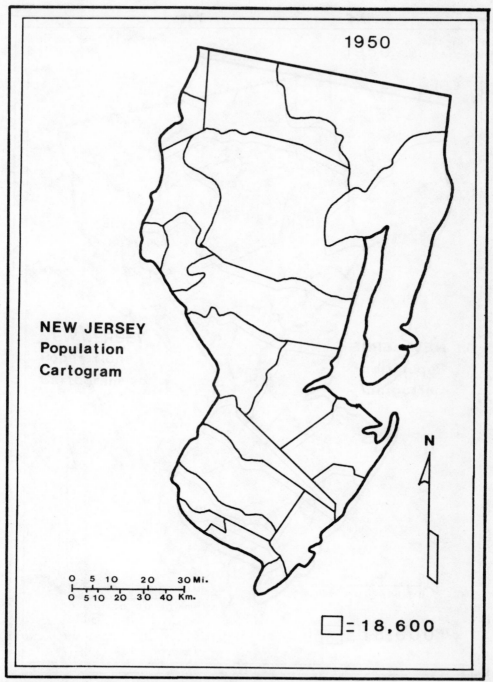

FIGURE 10.2. This 1950 cartogram shows New Jersey's counties in proportion to their share of the state's population rather than their geographic area. The densely populated northeastern urban counties dominate the state and its politics.

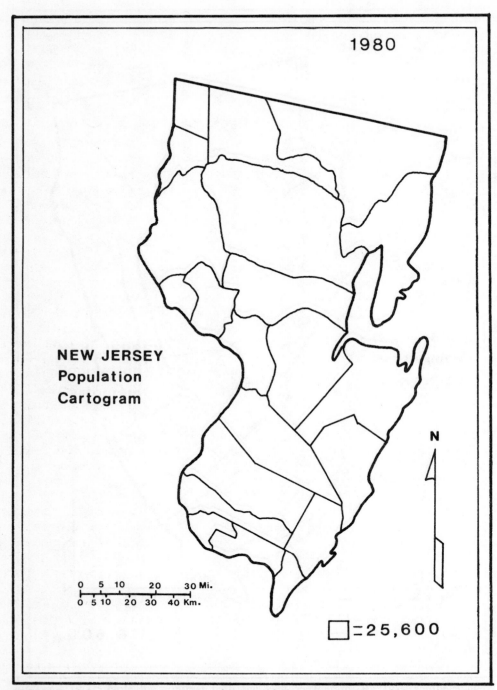

1980

NEW JERSEY
Population
Cartogram

0 5 10   20   30 Mi.
0 5 10   20   30   40 Km.

N

☐ = 25,600

FIGURE 10.3. Note the contrast with the 1950 cartogram. By 1980 southern New Jersey and the northwestern counties were much more significant within the state's population distribution, although the majority of New Jerseyans still reside in the counties north of Burlington and Ocean.

metropolitan area never has had its "own" large central city. Even the satellites of a large out-of-state metropolis, on the order of Newark, Jersey City, or Paterson, do not meet this criterion. In the future, the Philadelphia Metro region will be far more effectively restrained in its further penetration of New Jersey hinterlands than will that of the New York Metro region, because of the virtual elimination of future expansion into the Pinelands.

The Pinelands

The Pinelands, like the Highlands, is one of the larger regions in territory, but it is very small in population. It is least typical of New Jersey in this respect, but paradoxically, outside of New Jersey it is becoming one of the best-known regions. It is probably the least-understood region of New Jersey as well as that least discussed in general terms in the earlier systematic chapters on agriculture, industry, urban growth, and so on. The Pinelands region is the subject of a case study in this chapter for these reasons.

Part of Monmouth County, the bulk of Ocean County, central and eastern Burlington County, most of Atlantic County, the easternmost parts of Camden and Gloucester counties, and small portions of Cumberland and Cape May counties are included within the Pinelands. Historically, the Pinelands were settled quite late, and their overall population density has remained much lower than the rest of the state. The region is a curiosity in the northeastern United States—an almost empty land, not mountainous, and highly accessible from great cities. Its bog iron and timber resources attracted exploitation in the colonial and early federal periods, yet populations based on these resources have repeatedly expanded suddenly and as quickly collapsed owing to the changing economics and technologies of industry. This is now the most controversial region in New Jersey as a result of the state's determination to preserve this unique biotic region in as pristine a condition as possible.

There is little doubt that the Pinelands have been under increasing pressure from the encroachment of suburbia from both the Philadelphia Metro and Seashore regions. There is also little doubt that the Pinelands Protection Act is quite unpopular in South Jersey.

Southwestern Farm Region

The Southwestern Farm region is the southern survival of a once continuous and prosperous farm region in the inner coastal plain. It is separated from its northern outlier, the Central Corridor, by the Philadelphia Metro's encroachment into the Pinelands. The southwestern portion of the outer coastal plain has somewhat better soil, supporting an agricultural settlement that goes back to the early colonial period. This region is experiencing a steady suburbanizing pressure from both the Philadelphia Metro to its north and the greater Wilmington, Delaware, metropolitan area to its west. The building of the Chester-Bridgeport bridge and the twin Delaware Memorial bridges has accelerated the industrialization and suburbanization of this farming area. Southwestern Gloucester County, all of Salem County, and a large portion of Cumberland County make up the Southwestern Farm region.

The Seashore

The Seashore region—*the Shore,* as it is known to millions of visitors from the nearby megalopolis—is constituted of the eastern coastal areas of Monmouth, Ocean, and Atlantic counties, together with a tiny tip of Burlington County and the bulk of Cape May County. It is an ocean shoreline without a single important port; its shallow waters, shifting inlets, and dangerous shoals are mostly unusable by any but the smallest of fishing boats and pleasure craft. Even for those, vigilance and the timely investment in public-works engineering are all that make safe ports available.

This is a region whose utility has been perceived very differently throughout its modern history. Most of the shore area south of Point Pleasant all the way to Cape May was virtually uninhabited until a century and a quarter ago. Although two of the nation's earliest and most-successful seashore resorts, Long Branch and Cape May, were in this region, the urbanization of the bulk of this shoreline is a creation of nineteenth-century railroads and twentieth-century highways. The seashore has proven so popular with summer residents and tourists that a smaller-scale version of the great northeastern megalopolis has evolved here. Paralleling the main axis of the megalopolis, this leisure-oriented string of resorts, a *leisureopolis,* has formed along the coast. It includes both the offshore barrier beaches and the nearby "mainland" communities that parallel the beaches across the marsh-and-bay belt. Almost all of the shoreline is now encrusted with summer cottages, hotels, motels, and entertainment complexes, with the exceptions of Sandy Hook (Gateway National Recreation Area), Island Beach State Park, and Brigantine National Wildlife Refuge.

FIGURE 10.4. *The Pinelands of the Outer Coastal Plain:* One of the last few "empty areas" of the urban-industrial northeastern United States. Valuable as a huge underground reservoir of clean water as well as a recreational area, the Pinelands have been designated a national preserve.

CASE STUDY: THE PINELANDS

Are the Pinelands the least-understood region? The common designation "Pine Barrens" tells much about popular perceptions of this region. *Barren* means unproductive, which is only partly true and even then only in a narrow economic sense. There does not seem to be a consistently accurate descriptive term for this unique biological and cultural region. Pinelands would seem more objective and less negative than Pine Barrens, but probably there are more oaks than pines in the area now. Along with a dozen species of oak among the pitch pines, cedar and maple appear to signal water close to the surface.

While the Pinelands are relatively empty, especially when viewed in the context of the neighboring northeastern seaboard megalopolis, they have never really been quite empty in terms of human settlement. They still show many, if sometimes subtle, signs of human use, management, and mismanagement over thousands of years.

Timber Management

That the Pinelands have as many pines as they do at present seems to reflect human activities, particularly logging and the setting of fires. The natural succession of vegetation here would lead first to pines and then to hardwoods on the upland (better-drained) sites. These upland sites feature a mixture of pitch pines and shortleaf pines with various oaks. Shallow muck layers in swamps support Atlantic white cedar, with some red maple, blackgum, and sweetbay. On the poorly drained soils between upland and swamp biotic communities, almost pure stands of pitch pines flourish (Sinton 1979, 105–118). If human intervention is eliminated, hardwoods succeed pines on upland sites because the hardwoods tolerate shade far better than pines do and can grow up in the shadow of pines, whereas pines would not thrive under a mature hardwood (mostly oak) forest. Also, the large heavy acorns can fall through the dense litter of pine needles and other organic debris on the forest floor, while the tiny seeds of pines can best take root in a bed of exposed sand with little or no debris.

White cedar also is intolerant of shade compared to oaks. White cedar has been a highly valued wood since early colonial days. Highly resistant to rot, it makes superior roof and siding shingles, weathering to a soft silvery gray that is very attractive as well as durable. Cedar was cut so enthusiastically by early New Jerseyans that at least one European observer, Peter Kalm in 1749, expressed fear that cedar was being exterminated (Studley 1964, 17–46). White cedar, however, not only has survived 200 years and more of exploitation, but probably benefited from clearing of competing hardwoods. Almost pure stands of cedar have sprung up in swamps that were "logged out"—cleared of hardwoods as well as cedars—as long as "seed" cedars were left, deliberately or accidentally.

Just as human intervention has favored the prized cedar, so human manipulation of fire has favored pines, which produce more usable wood than would oaks on the same plot in the same time span. Fire favors pines, as the pines can sprout from the trunk after a fire and sprout from stumps as well. A fire that burns off the carpet of floor litter also favors the seeding of pines on the exposed sandy soil. After fires, pines form a larger proportion of total trees than before.

The right kind of fire can be beneficial—one that occurs in winter to minimize danger of too-rapid spread, one that burns out quickly to avoid damage to the crowns of mature trees, and one that affects stands of pines at least 2 in. (5 cm) in diameter (thick enough not to burn through in a light fire). However, the protection of the Pinelands from deliberate fires and the quick extermination of natural fires from lightning can have the effect of setting the stage for a really disastrous eventual fire.

The accumulation of dry pine needles on a forest floor long untouched by fire (pine needles are slow to rot into soil humus) fuels a hot fire when one finally does occur. Some huge forest fires occur from time to time in the Pines (as the Pinelands are also called). There are several hundred forest fires in this region every year, and an occasional one really gets out of control. The uncontrollable ones develop in areas long unburned, where, in addition to floor litter, a whole understory of bushes has grown since the last fire. This spreads fire into young trees' crowns and on up into branches, then crowns, of mature trees. (In light fires, the lower branches of trees are burned off, helping prevent the next fire from spreading to the crown.) For these reasons, about 6,000 or 7,000 acres (2,430 to 2,835 ha) of the Wharton State Forest's 96,000 acres (38,880 ha) are control-burned every winter. Although many arsonist-set fires occur, it is widely believed that most are set by "outsiders," not local residents who know all too well how quickly the fires can spread. At one time, locals did start fires to harvest more wild blueberries, as the wild bushes produce more berries after a fire than before, but this practice, still done in Maine, is now illegal.

Enormous fires have occurred repeatedly in the Pines. A fire in 1755, for example, burned along a 30-mile (48-kilometer)-long line. In 1930, eight fires burned over 170,000 acres (68,850 ha), and in 1963, 161,000 acres (65,205 ha) were burned in one weekend (Sinton 1979, 107).

The Groundwater Resource

The freshwater resources of the Pinelands have often been cited as the major attraction of the region to the "outside." Indeed, part of the controversy surrounding the Pinelands National Reserve and the preservation plans of the state's Pinelands Commission (formally the Pinelands Planning and Management Commission) is the general suspicion in South Jersey that north Jersey thirsts for the Pinelands' water. The history of the Pinelands, specifically the Wharton Tract, bolsters these suspicions.

Between 10 and 17 trillion gal (37 and 64 trillion l) of potentially usable fresh water lie beneath the Pinelands, specifically in the Cohansey sand formation. This layer of quartz sand underlies nearly 2,200 sq mi (5,698 sq km), varying in thickness from a "featheredge" on the west to more than 300 ft (91 m) along the ocean shoreline. The sand serves as a filter only in terms of filtering out solids. Water moves so readily through the poorly consolidated sands that contaminants in solution disperse quickly through the aquifer (water-transporting rock or other earth materials). Almost 90 percent of the stream flow in the Pinelands is fed by groundwater discharge. This means that significant withdrawals of fresh water from the subsurface sands will quickly be reflected in diminished stream flow. Heavy withdrawal via wells thus would have a drastic effect on plant and animal communities in lakes, stream areas, and swamps. These effects would be further magnified in normal drought years, when stream flow would be reduced to levels unacceptable to any conservation-minded Pinelands management philosophy. As one scholar observed, "The extent to which the public is willing to allow such ground water level, streamflow and associated biotic changes is a political, not a hydrologic question" (Sinton 1979, 8).

Assuming that the public would not knowingly tolerate destruction of the present Pinelands environment by ruthless "water mining" (extracting water at a rate above the natural recharge rate, and the rate at which stream flow would not be significantly affected), the water resource thus defined is relatively small. According to a study by David Robertson, water withdrawal at an ecologically acceptably low rate, allowing for anticipated expansion of water supply in the Atlantic City area, would barely meet the projected shortfall (of water supply relative to water demand) in Bergen County. "In fact, the reserves

probably would not justify the capital costs of land acquisition and pipe installation to transport any water out of Southern New Jersey" (Sinton 1979, 35).

If the public cares little about the ecology of the Pinelands, or values a good water supply more than a unique ecological area, the water would be "mined"—withdrawn and transported to the cities and their thirsty suburbs. In his classic regional portrait, *The Pine Barrens,* John McPhee likened the Cohansey aquifer to "a lake seventy-five feet deep with a surface of a thousand square miles" (McPhee 1971, 13). This "lake" is, so far, very clean—the groundwater is almost sterile, odorless, and clear. It is uncontaminated, owing not to any natural filtering but to so few people living atop the great underground reservoir. The sand is so easily penetrated by water that it is said to absorb up to 6 in. (15 cm) of rain in an hour. About twice as much of the total precipitation enters the groundwater supply (as opposed to running off the surface or evaporating) as is average in the United States.

South Jerseyans suspicious about "water mining" to benefit the water-short north are likely to remember Philadelphian Joseph Wharton and his scheme to send Pinelands water to Philadelphia. Financier Wharton (for whom the prestigious Wharton School of the University of Pennsylvania is named) acquired nearly 100,000 acres (40,500 ha) of Pinelands between 1873 and 1890. He planned to set up around thirty shallow reservoirs on his land and pipe the pure water under the Delaware River to Philadelphia, which certainly needed, and still needs, pure drinking water. The New Jersey legislature foiled this innovative plan by passing a law forbidding the "export" of drinking water, and the Wharton estate sold the tract to the state in 1955.

The state would have bought it earlier, but when the question of the state's purchasing the Wharton estate (to maintain it as a watershed and low-density-usage recreation area) was first put on the ballot, in November 1915, it was defeated. The referendum drew 103,456 in favor, but 123,995 were opposed. North Jersey favored the purchase, but South Jersey was strongly in opposition. Burlington County, in which much of the tract is located, was especially vehement, along with Camden and Atlantic counties, also containing Wharton lands. Nine townships in the tract were particularly threatened by the loss of taxable real estate that would follow state acquisition. In one township, 40 percent of tax revenues were paid by the Wharton heirs (Pierce 1957, 35–40). By 1955 increased recognition of the biotic and recreational value of the Pinelands resulted in passage of a similar referendum.

Piping Pinelands water *under* the Delaware River to Philadelphia's water mains is a concept that should lead logically to the question: why pump water under a river that is, after all, a freshwater supply in itself? It sounds like carrying coal to Newcastle or carrying sand to the Pinelands. Actually, it *is* logical, but only in the context of a world of pollution, greed, and politics. It is logical in the same sense that it is logical to pipe a good part of New York City's water supply from the upper Delaware River under the Hudson near West Point. The lower Hudson, like the lower Delaware, is one of the Northeast's great rivers by volume of flow, but it is not used as a municipal water supply in its lower valley except in direst emergency. (The Delaware is used by the City of Philadelphia, though.) The Hudson flows past New York City unused as a water supply because it already has been much overused and abused as a municipal and industrial sewer. While it would be possible to clean and filter the water and dose it with disinfectants to reach minimum standards for human consumption, it is simply cheaper for New York City to tap the pristine upper Delaware. Cleaning up pollution in the Hudson also would require political pressure on corporations and towns and cities upstream from New York City; hence the tunnel under the Hudson was cheaper in political terms, too.

New York City's competition for upper Delaware River water and the high cost of purifying the Hudson to acceptable standards put additional pressure on northeast New Jersey's communities to consider the potential of the Pinelands water supply. Thus, if the Pinelands water is ever "mined" for export north, the blame should be shared by the polluters of the upper and central Hudson River.

The preservation of the Pinelands in their present state and the preservation of the subsurface water supply in its present high quality for eventual use as a water supply both require strictly limiting the further development of the area. Large-scale water "mining" would defeat the ecological preservation objective, of course, but in any case the purity of the water resource is in imminent danger. The high porosity of the Cohansey sands allows contaminants to move freely through the subsurface supply and to travel large distances. Septic-tank systems and cesspools allow quantities of nitrates to travel into the soil and soil water. Phosphates enter the water supply, along with ammonium compounds and bacteria that can cause disease. Related disturbances of soil acid/alkaline balance could harm the blueberry and cranberry industries. The present low density and low concentration of settlement in the region is related directly to water purity; increases in population can be expected to be reflected in decreases in water quality, which is undesirable whatever the fate of the water itself.

The Pineys

A considerable amount of misinformation, misinterpretation, and unadulterated nonsense circulates, within and without New Jersey, about the alleged peculiarities of the "natives" of the Pinelands. Piney, until recently a derogatory nickname when applied by outsiders, has become a generally positive self-identification and symbol of prideful acceptance. By the mid-1970s, green-and-white buttons proclaiming "Piney Power!" were being worn at Stockton State College and other Piney-frequented Pinelands centers. The Pineys have been libeled so repeatedly that one could understand a certain reticence toward the world outside the Pinelands, though Pineys freely interact with everyone else in the area. The Pineys are a good deal more sophisticated than many of their detractors imagine and are much less "different" than even their admirers believe, or wish to believe.

The myth that Pineys are a tightly inbred group of shiftless, poverty-stricken people with high rates of mental retardation and criminal behavior seems to have been the result of an unprofessional oversimplification and sensationalism, by the researcher's superior, of a 1913 report on subnormal intelligence among some Pinelands residents. The original research report had honestly and compassionately recorded some case histories that would not have surprised psychological case workers anywhere in the United States. The sensational, abbreviated, and "fictionalized" version became a staple of psychology textbooks under the fictitious family case history of the "Kallikaks."

Like any society or region, the Pinelands and Pineys are not without unfortunate cases, but their incidence here has never been demonstrated as above average. There are really two related myths prevalent about the Pineys. One is that they are an isolated, homogeneous culture, crystallized in a time past by isolation and so a living museum of life-styles long dead outside the Pines. Another is that they are of inferior mental ability, morality, and ambition.

Portions of the myth have some relationship with reality in the central "heart" of the Pines—the area of the Mullica River watershed. In the nineteenth century, the population was of predominantly Anglo-Scottish-Irish heritage, mostly born in New Jersey to second- or third-generation New Jerseyans. Most were Methodists, with a small minority Roman Catholic. This cultural homogeneity is perfectly understandable in view of the *extensive* land-use sys-

tem that characterized the Pines. The southern portions of the Pinelands do contain some areas of soils capable of agricultural use when scientifically analyzed and properly fertilized. For those reasons, the southern Pinelands supported an agricultural frontier in the second half of the nineteenth century, an interesting story in itself. But in the north-central Pinelands, where the Mullica River watershed is located, the sandy, highly porous soils with little humus or soluble minerals were traditionally used for forest-based industries. The land was used very extensively (large tracts, which were but lightly or sporadically productive, were needed to support each family) for the excellent reason that it would not, could not, support any more *intensive,* or concentrated, land use.

In Arthur Pierce's classic study, *Iron in the Pines,* he calculated that about twenty forges and furnaces operated in the Pinelands between 1800 and 1850. An average-size furnace would consume 12,000 bu (423 kl) of charcoal fuel each year, requiring the production of about 12,000 acres (4,860 ha) of pine woods. The woodcutters and colliers ("coalers," or charcoal makers) successfully managed the woods for maximum production of pine trees. At a ratio of at least 12,000 acres per furnace, somewhere between 100,000 and 200,000 acres (40,500 and 81,000 ha) of woods (all twenty furnaces were seldom "in blast" at the same time) would have been required to support the iron industry, to say nothing of glass furnaces, shingle making, and boat building (these latter two industries used cedar, not pine) (Pierce 1957, 37–39). That extensive a land-use system clearly could not support a very dense population, and so the region then attracted few permanent in-migrants. As the furnaces surrendered to the economic competition of Appalachian coal and upper Great Lakes ores, the Pineys either drifted into cities or maintained their extensive forest-exploitation existence. They gardened, sometimes selling surplus produce to the fringing resorts to the east or fringing suburbia to the west. They hunted and gathered wild food, probably sold moonshine, and sold holly branches, pine boughs, and mistletoe in the Christmas season to urban dealers. Sphagnum moss, sold to florists as a moisture-retaining wrapping for cut flowers, was a less-seasonal sales item. Industry abandoned the Pineys, it should be noted, not the other way around. When the furnaces, glassworks, and paper mills were operating, their labor forces were largely Pineys.

Piney family life never differed significantly from national experience. Even back in the nineteenth century, Pineys were predominantly a literate society that sent their children to school, visited towns regularly for business and cultural reasons, and were very much aware of what was happening—in their region, state, and country (Sinton 1979, 171).

The Piney society obviously was a flexible one to have survived a series of economic dislocations, each induced by changes in industrial technology, raw-materials base, and scale of enterprise—changes brought about beyond the control of the Pineys or of anyone else in New Jersey, for that matter. Pineys are not, and have not been, isolated in any real meaning of the term; they could drive, or walk if necessary, a maximum of 20 or 25 mi (32 or 40 km) to an urban place of 20,000 or 30,000 or more. So if Pineys differ in life-style and attitude from other Americans, they do so from choice, being fully aware of their urban-industrial contemporaries in New Jersey. Many Pineys have traveled widely, have lived in metropolitan areas (technically they *do* live in metropolitan counties as part of SMSAs), and have chosen a rural but definitely not isolated life. Some relish the outsider's assumption that they are bumpkins and enjoy elaborate word games in local taverns at the expense of city people.

The Southern Pinelands: An Ethnic Archipelago

Cultural geographer Elizabeth Marsh characterizes the southern portion of the Pinelands as an "ethnic archipelago"—a series of "islands" of better-drained upland separated from one another by swampy headwaters of streams and occupied by a broad variety of ethnic groups, many of which arrived in the latter nineteenth century (Sinton 1979, 192–198). The curiosity of a late-nineteenth-century agricultural frontier, roughly coincident with the advance of the more-famous western frontier into the intermontane area between the Rockies and the Sierra Nevadas and the Cascades, can be explained by changing perceptions of the utility of soils and economics of a South Jersey location relative to markets. The "best of the worst"—those soils of the outer coastal plain with some natural components besides sand—were ripe for settlement by the middle of the nineteenth century.

The Pinelands' not totally deserved reputation as an "empty" land had an important corollary, the lack of a well-developed transport system through it. The interposition of the Pines between the expanding cities to the west and the rapidly developing seashore resorts to the east, however, meant that the area was crisscrossed by railroads between 1854 (when the Camden and Atlantic was established) and the 1880s. With appropriate fertilization, the pockets of land with somewhat better potential for cultivation could be farmed. It would not be easy and would require enough financial backing to persist a few years without much production as crops, fertilizers, and farming techniques all went through an experimental phase. Organized group pioneering, a type not seen in New Jersey for some time, had some obvious advantages over individual pioneering attempts. Power pumps to irrigate the droughty soils were another necessary adjunct, as water naturally drained into these soils too quickly for many shallow-rooted crops.

Because the land of the southern Pine Barrens had been usable only in an extensive land-use system (lumber, paper, charcoal—all marginal enterprises, economically—were there by the Civil War period), the land's value reflected this and was consequently cheap. The expense of experimentation with fertilizers and irrigation was thus counterbalanced by low land costs. Middle-class Germans, with their own investment capital, arrived at Egg Harbor and Folsom (then New Germany) in the 1850s. Yankees from New England, looking for affordable land near urban markets, settled Hammonton in the 1860s and also brought their own financial resources. Some of the most interesting agricultural colonies, certainly unusual in many respects, were the Jewish farm communities of Salem, Cumberland, Atlantic, and Cape May counties, founded in the 1880s as refuges for Jews driven out of Russia by the infamous pogroms of the time. Mizpah, Rosenhayn, Norma, Brotmanville, and Woodbine were the sites of organized group colonization with investment capital supplied by the Hebrew Emigrant Aid Society and individual philanthropists like Baron de Hirsch. As each group cleared land and established prosperous farms, orchards, and vineyards, it recruited another, more-recent immigrant group to do the heavy labor involved. The vineyards of Atlantic County, for example, were started by German and French immigrants, who later brought in Italians. The Italian pioneers of the Vineland area later were joined by Puerto Ricans as the "move-up" sequence continued (Sinton 1979, 196).

Control of Development

The "empty" Pinelands have proven positively magnetic to the eyes of would-be developers. Nearly twenty years ago a grandiose plan surfaced to build a huge jetport in the Pines—a New Jersey version of the Dallas–Fort Worth Regional Airport. The sprawling jetport, it was claimed, could serve the central megalopolis from metropolitan New York to metropolitan Philadelphia and attract the many economic activities that flourish within easy reach of such airports. In terms of the economics

of location, the proposal had merit; in terms of single-handedly wiping out the largest remaining nonurbanized area of New Jersey, it was viewed as a threat by many citizens. Unfortunately for the jetport enthusiasts, the Pinelands Regional Planning Board (predecessor of the Pinelands Commission) already existed and responded vigorously to the proposal.

Two counties including large tracts of Pinelands in their jurisdictions, Ocean and Burlington, took an active role in planning for preservation of the Pinelands, and federal government interest was becoming apparent by the 1970s. A mid-1960s State Planning Office report on shaping future growth (the assumption was, as it usually is, that then-current population growth rates would continue) mentioned the concept of a large planned "new town" in the Pine Barrens, but then quickly downplayed the idea in favor of preservation. The eventual passage of the state's Pinelands Protection Act in 1979 underlined the longer trend toward state government moving into what had been largely the province of local and county government—land-use planning and zoning.

The Pinelands Protection Act resulted in the designation of 1.1 million acres (438,534 ha) in which future development would be strictly circumscribed. The *Preservation Area* is the core of the Pinelands; within it, development is effectively prohibited. The *Protection area* has less-stringent restrictions but still strongly channels and regulates growth. The *Pinelands National Preserve* is a still-broader, overlapping region with fewer restrictions. Table 10.1 lists the acreage of the three classes of control by county.

Two major discrepancies exist between the *pinelands* (the soil-vegetation association natural region) and the *Pinelands,* the officially designated preservation and protection area. Some portions of the natural region, notably in northern Ocean County and nearby Monmouth County, are not within the official Pinelands. Two pinelands areas near Atlantic City, slated for

TABLE 10.1
Protecting the Pinelands: Acreage Totals for Counties

County	Protection Categories (in thousands of acres[a])		
	Pinelands Preservation Area	Pinelands Protection Area	Pinelands National Preserve
Atlantic	21.3	246.4	243.6
Burlington	232.4	336.4	346.6
Camden	14.4	54.6	54.6
Cape May	0	34.2	85.6
Cumberland	0	45.6	55.7
Gloucester	0	33.2	33.2
Ocean	100.7	183.0	263.5
TOTAL	368.8	933.7	1,082.8

Source: State of New Jersey Pinelands Commission, Draft Comprehensive Management Plan for the Pinelands National Reserve and Pinelands Area, New Lisbon, New Jersey: State of New Jersey Pinelands Commission, 1979, Vol. 1, p. 4.2.

[a]Formula for conversion of acres to hectares is: one acre equals .405 hectare.

major development investments, are exempted from control at any of the three levels of varying stringency. On the other hand, salt marshes and offshore barrier beaches, never before considered "pinelands," are inexplicably included (Currier 1981, 2–4).

A variety of planning and development-control techniques are being used in the Pinelands National Reserve. These are discussed in Chapter 11.

CASE STUDY: WHERE IS SOUTH JERSEY?

Historical, physical, economic, cultural, political, and geographic factors are related to the recent movement advocating the secession of South Jersey as a separate state. While a successful secession is extremely unlikely, its serious consideration, at least in the south, indicates a significant cultural, economic, and political division within New Jersey. South Jersey commonly has not been accepted as a *formal region* by geographers studying the state (although the U.S. Postal Service uses a "South Jersey" cancellation on all material posted south of Trenton). However, there is intriguing evidence that it is a *vernacular,* or *folk,* region, that is, a commonly understood, if unofficial, region.

The Multifocused State

New Jersey is said to have an identity crisis. Many allege that the poorly defined self-image of the state is further diffused by the two huge interstate metropolitan regions whose hinterlands meet in New Jersey, but whose centers are in New York State and Pennsylvania. Northern New Jersey's economy, popular culture, and mass media tend to reflect a New York orientation. South Jersey (never "southern New Jersey" to its residents) just as clearly has intimate ties across the Delaware to Philadelphia and, to a lesser degree, Wilmington. Northern and southern New Jersey are satellites, if important ones, of systems whose central stars lie across state boundaries.

The majority of New Jersey's counties are officially recognized by the U.S. Bureau of the Census as part of *interstate* metropolitan systems involving each of New Jersey's three neighboring states. In a nation in which state boundaries have progressively less practical significance to people's daily economic and cultural lives, New Jersey stands out as an extreme example. The daily connections of New Jerseyans, in their economic and cultural lives, are likely to cross state lines; intrastate ties, or unifiers, seem comparably weak. In Jean Gottmann's perceptive interpretation of the factors of *iconography* (the set of symbols of loyalty, common experience, and common goals that tie a people together, culturally and politically) and *circulation* (the set of communications and transport systems that literally tie an area economically and that have significance to cultural and political interactions as well), New Jersey would have a relatively weak iconography and a circulation system in which ties to the "outside" challenge intrastate ties for supremacy (Gottmann 1973).

South Jersey and Secession

New Jersey has recently joined a select group of states (California is a more-famous example) in which some recent, formal steps toward subdivision into two new states have taken place.

In November 1980 a nonbinding referendum was placed on the ballot in six South Jersey counties: Atlantic, Burlington, Cape May, Cumberland, Ocean, and Salem (see Figure 10.5). The governments of Camden and Gloucester counties refused to place the question on the ballot. The vaguely worded referendum sought approval to initiate a political process toward separate statehood. Voters in Ocean County rejected the referendum, but it was approved in every other county in which it appeared. A "State of South Jersey" does not appear imminent, however. No state of the United States has ever consented, as it constitutionally must, to a new state being formed from its territory (at the time West Virginia seceded from Virginia, Virginia was not, by its own proclamation, one of the United States).

The relative success of the referendum would seem to indicate widespread recognition within South Jersey that it is a distinctive region. There is a surprising degree of agreement on not only the characteristics, but the boundary of South Jersey. South Jerseyans, however, tend to be surprised at the lower level of regional consciousness among "northerners."

New Jersey's "split personality" dates back to its early history and the division into East Jersey and West Jersey discussed in Chapter 2. The seventeenth-century Lawrence Line (the surveyed boundary between East and West Jersey) roughly coincides with the *functional region* boundaries of the New York–oriented northeastern region of New Jersey and the Philadelphia-oriented southwest. The commuting boundary or daily-interaction-zone boundary between the metropolises would be at about Princeton, matching the Lawrence Line rather closely through the center of New Jersey and cutting at right angles through the heavily utilized megalopolitan transport corridor. The boundary between New Jersey's two telephone area codes generally follows this metropolitan bipolar orientation boundary also.

The political problems associated with interstate metropolitan areas are hardly unique to New Jersey. Interstate govern-

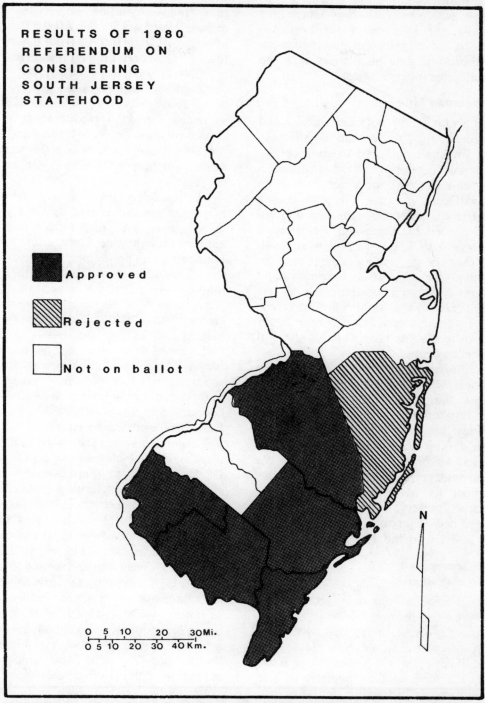

RESULTS OF 1980
REFERENDUM ON
CONSIDERING
SOUTH JERSEY
STATEHOOD

Approved

Rejected

Not on ballot

0 5 10 20 30Mi.
0 5 10 20 30 40Km.

N

FIGURE 10.5.   Only Ocean County's voters, with their orientation to New York rather than to Philadelphia and their historic association with East Jersey, rejected consideration of movement toward separate statehood for South Jersey.

ment authorities to manage specific sets of problems (the New York–New Jersey Port Authority; the Delaware River Port Authority) could be the forerunners of a rationalization of state boundaries, as some political geographers suggest.

The Freeman Line

The South Jersey boundary envisioned by "secessionist" leader and popularizer, Albert Freeman, followed existing county lines, separating the eight southern counties along the northern boundaries of Burlington and Ocean counties. Freeman, then a Mount Holly newspaper publisher and editor, launched his campaign for separate statehood in 1976; he was particularly outraged that the governor's cabinet and the executive staff of most state agencies and divisions had proportionately few (often, no) South Jerseyans. Many South Jerseyans share Freeman's belief that South Jersey does not receive its proportionate share of state expenditures.

"South Jersey statehood" received a major boost when the state determined to preserve and protect the Pine Barrens, one of the last "empty areas" of the northeast. The view popular in South Jersey is that South Jersey development is being restrained to preserve the purity of the groundwater reserve, which could someday be tapped for north Jersey's benefit. The Pinelands preservation controversy contributed new vigor to the secession movement and led to the 1980 referendum.

South Jersey as a Vernacular Region

The Freeman Line was accepted explicitly by the framers of the 1980 referendum. It is also substantiated by the general understanding of New Jerseyans, exemplified by a survey of New Jersey college students and an analysis of telephone-directory listings. In the latter technique, telephone-directory listings are scanned for explicit regional references, such as "South Jersey Gas Co.," "North Jersey Dental Labs," or "South Jersey Auto Club." Any business, voluntary organization, trade association, or service with a regional designation in its title was mapped by address listed in preparing Figure 10.6 (every telephone directory published by New Jersey Bell was used).

The other measure of the folk region of South Jersey was an open-ended questionnaire distributed to introductory geography classes at Glassboro State College and Trenton State College just before the secession movement surged forward in general consciousness.

The questionnaire was completed by fifty-eight "northerners" and forty-eight "southerners." All respondents had been advised that they need not follow county boundaries in bounding "South Jersey," though counties were shown on their base map for orientation. A large wall map of New Jersey was displayed for casual reference, but students had not previously participated in any discussion of South Jersey or of vernacular regions in general. Eleven northerners and seven southerners spontaneously followed the Freeman Line, and the overwhelming majority drew boundaries approximately east-west through Burlington and Ocean counties.

Respondents were also asked to describe identifying characteristics of South Jersey. Of 106 completed questionnaires (many with several characteristics volunteered), 46 mentioned differences in land use, stressing the agricultural south versus the industrial north as a popular, if not entirely accurate, perception. Comments related to population density ranked second (35 questionnaires), followed by a surprisingly strong association of the seashore environment, in both physical and cultural senses, with South Jersey, despite accompanying boundary lines that nearly always resulted in a "north shore" as well. Topographic differences ranked next in frequency of mention, with South Jersey typified (not entirely unfairly) as "flat." The perceptual association of South Jersey with the Pinelands, like the seashore, tended to ignore those same respondents' boundaries assigning at

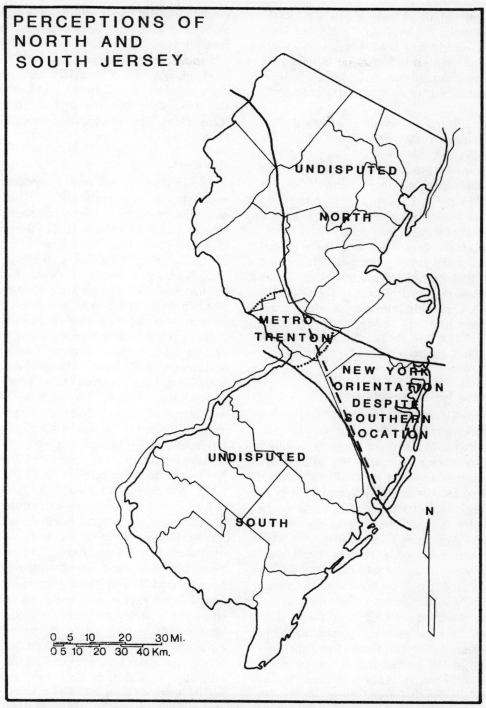

FIGURE 10.6. Curiously, the perceptions of north Jersey by those living in the New York–northeastern New Jersey metropolitan region seldom reflect awareness of the rural-exurban northwest. The common contrast of north and south is urban-rural; both of these regional pictures are overly simplified.

least part of the Pinelands to the north. Interestingly, the geologic "grain" of New Jersey, clearly northeast-southwest in orientation, had no reflection at all in either perceived functional boundaries (northwest-southeast) or folk boundaries (mostly east-west).

The cultural-economic interaction with Philadelphia rather than New York for South Jersey was noted by both northern and southern students (twenty) with the same frequency as observations of South Jersey's slower, friendlier pace, perceived as being less cosmopolitan and less frantic than that of its northern counterpart. Fourteen students observed differences in speech patterns and accents, while only a few noted South Jersey's lack of political clout. A few students explicitly accepted Bell Telephone's area-code boundary as the proper boundary of South Jersey, noting its coincidence with the Philadelphia–New York hinterland zones boundary.

Regional Self-Consciousness

Figure 10.6 summarizes that "folk region consciousness" as reflected in student perceptions and in telephone-directory listings. The much more frequent use of "north" or "south" compared to "east" and "west" would substantiate South Jersey as a popular regional perception. The north-south boundary is quite sharp, with no overlap at all. "West Jersey" identifications were less numerous (only twenty-three) than north or south, and East Jersey has almost disappeared from popular consciousness, with only a half-dozen references.

The results of the 1980 referendum (Figure 10.5) are not necessarily conclusive but are suggestive. Ocean County was the only county in the southern half of the state, below the Freeman Line and identified as part of the South Jersey vernacular region, to reject the referendum. Ocean County is also the only "southern" county that historically was part of East Jersey; its western boundary incorporates a portion of the Keith Line. Moreover, Ocean County, par-

ticularly its northern portion, has long been associated with New York as a commuting zone (Brush 1958, 23), and the whole county's shoreline traditionally has been a New York playground, whereas Philadelphians dominated the shore resorts south of Great Bay (the shore-hugging direct rail route from New York terminated near Beach Haven).

Summary

In summary, South Jersey appears to be a vernacular perceptual region with considerable regional self-consciousness, the southern and central remnant of the colony of West Jersey, and New Jersey's portion of the greater-Philadelphia metropolitan area. The ambivalence of Ocean County, the fastest-growing county in the state from 1960 through 1980, may be related to its historic heritage as a part of East Jersey, to its high proportion of recent in-migrants, and to its historic and contemporary orientation to New York. Thus, while other South Jerseyans perceive Ocean County to be "southern"—and indeed it is in the southern half of the state geographically and is "southern" in similarity of physical environments—Ocean County voters may behave more in a "northern" (New York–oriented) manner.

By combining all measures—political, cultural, and perceptual—an undisputed South Jersey, undisputed north Jersey, and transitional or ambivalent zone can be identified (see Figure 10.6). The indeterminate zone is most interesting as it can be subdivided into three sectors. In the center is the metropolitan area of Trenton (most New Jerseyans do not include their state capital in the metropolitan orbit of either New York or Philadelphia). South Jersey advocates firmly reject Trenton symbolically, as well as in their perception of South Jersey as a region. The northwestern sector is historically "West Jersey"; although included in north Jersey on perceptual maps, that area hardly fits the high-density, heavily industrialized, rather-polluted environment that is the popular image of north (East) Jersey. Finally, Ocean County, as noted, is southern in relative location, relative population density, and physical environment but apparently northern in its New York orientation.

The eight southern counties as a unit are the growth area of New Jersey. No southern county experienced a net loss of population, 1970 to 1980; five northern counties had such losses, totaling 242,554 (all data are from the U.S. Bureau of the Census, years noted.) The northern counties as a group had a *net loss* of 101,813, while the eight southern counties had a *net gain* of 266,509, giving the south a 17 percent population gain, 1970 to 1980. This gave the state a 2.3 percent gain despite heavy losses in the north. Even if Ocean County were shifted to the northern column, its 65 percent increase in population would barely give the north a net gain (of 33,665), while the south would remain a big gainer in percentage terms. This shift in population, while not of staggering numbers, represents a relative shift in political power that may be significant (see Figures 10.2 and 10.3). Although the eight-county South Jersey region is still very much in the population minority within New Jersey (23 percent of state population in 1970; 25 percent in 1980), its combination of growth and expanding, if not uniform, regional consciousness should enhance its clout somewhat. South Jersey is an unlikely state, but the region is a more vigorous defender of its regional interests as a result of its secession movement.

CHAPTER 11

PLANNING

Public enthusiasm for planning often is ambivalent. Planning is generally applauded when hazards and nuisances are zoned away from one's home, but planning becomes highly controversial when, as it often must, it infringes on private property rights. The basis of planning revolves around the inherent rights and interests of the society as a whole to direct and control the use of land and water for the benefit of all, even when individual rights are thereby limited. As an abstract, planning is, almost universally, a good thing; as a concrete limit on developing one's property, it becomes much less agreeable. When the state becomes an active land-use planner and zoner (in addition to local government, the traditional repository of zoning and planning powers and responsibility), the potential threat becomes serious indeed.

The right of private land ownership, long established as a keystone of individual freedom and of private entrepreneurship, has never been total. The interests of neighbors and of society in general have been recognized in the various forms of zoning, health, fire, and safety codes, and most importantly, in the concept of eminent domain. Health, fire, and safety codes establish minimum standards for use and maintenance of property. They are limits, however desirable and universally accepted, on the rights of private property owners. Zoning powers enable local, county, or even state governments to establish firm

limits on land use by private owners, in the interests of neighbors and of society. All but the supporters of the most extreme political viewpoints accept the concept of zoning. Your neighbors in a new suburban housing subdivision do not, for example, have the unchallenged right to do anything they please with their private property. They may not simply decide to transform their plot into an all-night gasoline service station, even though it might be in their economic interest to do so, because that would infringe on the property rights of their neighbors. For similar reasons, most citizens find zoning reassuring; if they object to a special instance of alleged improper or inappropriate zoning, it is objecting to a misapplication of the principle, not the principle itself.

The power of *eminent domain* is the power of government, or any agency of government, to take private property, with compensation, for some public use. It is a well-established power, tracing back through the English common law antecedents of U.S. civil law. The amount of compensation can be argued, but once the public need for that private land is established, eminent domain wins every time.

There is, then, a long-recognized, commonly agreed-upon assertion that there are several different strata of interest in, and control over, land. A private landowner, with legal title and not in default of any property taxes (or other taxes, for that matter), can be prevented from putting the property to certain uses and can be forced to sell the property to a public agency.

It has always been possible to subdivide economic rights to the land and to convey limited rights to others without selling or transferring the land outright. One can sell a utility easement, for example, to a public utility to lay a gas line under the surface, or an "air rights" easement to allow extension of high-tension lines over, but not touching, the surface. Relatively new applications of the "easement" principle are in recreation and conservation uses of privately held land. The British, for example, have developed the idea of "scenic easements." Rather than purchase all lands currently in farming within a scenic area designated a national park in Britain, outright purchase is limited to areas to be directly used by visitors—visitors' centers, parking lots, picnic areas, and the like. Scenic easements are purchased from landowners whose current uses of the land—pasture, for example—do not detract from, and even enhance, the scenic value of the land. Sale of scenic easements compensates landowners for no longer having the right to drastically alter their present use of the land. The purchase of "development rights" is a close cousin to scenic easements, and is now part of New Jersey law.

As in so many things, New Jersey is among the leaders in moving toward statewide planning. It is not coincidental that the states that have pioneered new responsibilities and powers in statewide zoning—Hawaii, Vermont, California, and New Jersey—all have significant tourist industries based on their natural amenities, and all contain (or are highly accessible to, or both) large metropolitan populations. In each state, mistakes have been made, in the past, that have helped spur a zeal for protecting what is left. In New Jersey, some of the most glaring examples of environmental mismanagement are in the seashore region, and the most controversial state

involvement in planning is the case of the Pinelands.

PRESERVING THE PINELANDS

"The New Jersey Pinelands, a million-acre forest expanse in the midst of the country's most densely populated region, have finally been recognized as one of the nation's premier environmental treasures." So opens, with a nicely provincial boast, the Draft Comprehensive Management Plan of the state's Pinelands Planning and Management Commission (State of New Jersey, Pinelands Planning and Management Commission 1979, i). The Pinelands are much more than a "premier environmental treasure," of course. Their 1,082,800 acres (438,534 ha), as officially designated in the federal government's national reserve, are home to more than a third of a million people. A good many of those people make their living in the Pinelands as well, in agriculture, forestry, boat building, wine making, and other traditional Pinelands occupations. Undoubtedly some landowners hoped to subdivide and sell at heavy profits as the Pinelands were encroached upon from both their Philadelphia metropolitan and seashore leisureopolitan fringes.

The first national reserve in the United States, the Pinelands is envisioned by both federal and state governments as a pioneering divergence from past governmental preservation and recreation management efforts. "The plan designates areas where public acquisition is deemed essential for preservation, but the major thrust of the planning effort has been directed toward developing ways to safeguard the Pinelands' resources while the land remains in the care of its traditional guardians, the people who live here (State of New Jersey, Pinelands Planning and Management Commission 1979, i). The management of the Pinelands as proposed thus attempts the difficult, perhaps impossible, equitable treatment of immediate land ownership and communal land stewardship.

The Pinelands is to be managed by a combination of different governmental powers and prerogatives, with limited outright purchase accompanied by heavy reliance on the restriction of private rights (see Figure 11.1). This management philosophy is both commendable and bursting with controversy. The already sizable proportion of lands in public ownership will be augmented by a further 100,000 acres (40,500 ha). The federal government now owns about 75,000 acres (30,375 ha) in this area, including Fort Dix, McGuire Air Force Base, the Lakehurst Naval Air Engineering Center, and wildlife refuges at Brigantine and Barnegat. The state owns 243,000 acres (98,415 ha) in parks and forests at Wharton, Lebanon, Island Beach, and Colliers Mills. State and federal ownership is about one-third of the total, with two-thirds remaining in private hands (Currier 1981, 2–3).

The 1.1 million acres (438,534 ha) of the federal planning area, the Pinelands National Reserve, involves all or part of fifty-six municipalities and covers about one-fifth of the state's total area (see Figure 11.1). This region currently produces about one-quarter by value of the state's agricultural production. It has a population of approximately 400,000 people in local jurisdictions whose average density ranges from 10 per sq mi to over 4,000 per sq mi (3.8 to 1,544 per sq km). Private land, even after completion of the planned government acquisitions, will still occupy 62 percent of the national reserve (Currier 1981, 2–3). Clearly, for the reserve to fulfill its conservation-recreation objectives, this private land must be controlled effectively. Comprehensive planning for the Pinelands is the responsibility of the Pinelands Commission, created by the 1979 Pinelands Protection Act, often called the strongest land-use legislation in the United States.

Private land is categorized into seven management types in an attempt to accommodate private use that is considered compatible with the long-range protection of natural resources. The strictest controls are placed upon the Preservation Area district of the central Pinelands, which generally lies northeast of the Philadelphia–Atlantic City corridor defined by the railroad, the Atlantic City Expressway, and U.S. routes 30 and 40; west of the Garden State Parkway; and southeast of the Fort Dix–McGuire Air Force Base tract. In this area, "compatible" cranberry and blueberry agriculture, forestry, recreation, and fish and wildlife management are permitted uses. In the less tightly controlled *forest areas,* permitted land uses add low-density residential and commercial development and resource extraction to the more-restricted list of the Preservation Area. *Agricultural Production areas* are those with larger, more-contiguous areas of conventional agricultural lands along with related commercial and residential uses. *Rural Development areas* are those that are already semideveloped and that can continue to develop at densities below 200 housing units per sq mi (77 per sq km). Municipalities are encouraged to designate *reserve areas* to accommodate future population increases. This is the "escape valve" for expected population increases, along with the *regional growth areas* category in which municipalities may regulate growth within average-density limits assigned by the commission. *Pinelands towns* are "traditional" communities that can shape future compatible land use within their urbanized areas. *Pinelands villages* are smaller settlements that, while not forced out of existence, will be allowed minimal growth.

Two fundamental problems are inherent in the comprehensive plan, and both excite intense criticism. The first is that not all the Pinelands, as customarily identified on maps of geologic and hydrologic factors and natural vegetation, are included. The omission is especially obvious in that no part of Monmouth County is within the official Pinelands, nor is that portion of Ocean County between Lakewood and

216

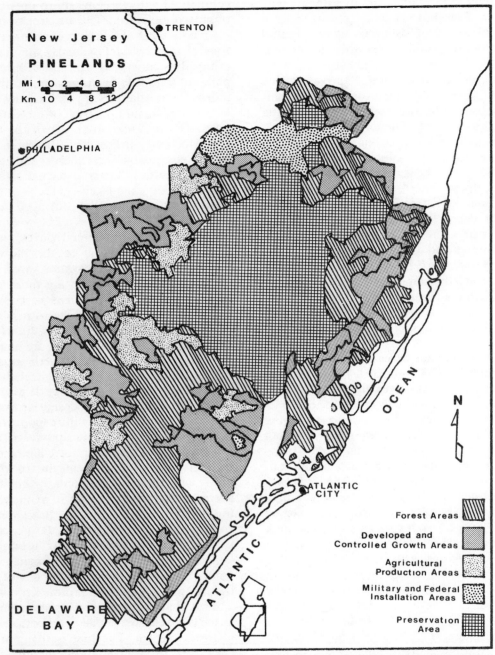

FIGURE 11.1. *The Pinelands as Seen by the Pinelands Commission.* All areas labeled on this map are part of the Pinelands National Reserve area, but the strictest controls on land use are exercised within the Preservation Area district. Note the two uncontrolled projections into forest lands to the west and southwest of Atlantic City. (State of New Jersey, Pinelands Planning and Management Commission, *Draft Comprehensive Management Plan.* New Lisbon, N.J.: New Jersey Pinelands Planning and Management Commission, 1979)

Toms River or even southeast of Toms River. Extreme southeastern Gloucester County and extreme northwestern Atlantic County are similarly absent from the "official" Pinelands, but generally included on any ecological map of the Pinelands. Two thick "fingers" of uncontrolled, unofficial Pinelands jut north and west from the metropolitan Atlantic City area; those generate unproven, perhaps unfair, speculation that powerful corporations with land holdings in these areas may have been favored by exclusion from the rigid controls of the reserve.

The other problem is that the Pinelands title is either an unfortunately misleading, deliberate broadening of the reserve to include within it some public lands that are clearly not pine forest or an indication that no one connected with the commission knows a pine tree from a salt marsh. The latter is most unlikely. Extensive salt-marsh and barrier-beach areas, though, are definitely within the forest areas category on the comprehensive plan. Clearly these areas *are* environmentally sensitive and should be protected. Just as clearly, though, Pinelands is an inappropriate umbrella term for "low-density Southern New Jersey growth control" area, perhaps a more accurate but politically unusable term.

The key to understanding South Jersey outrage at the Pinelands Reserve is the concern that the region's growth rate, especially its potential growth rate, is a perceived threat to north Jersey population (and voting power) supremacy. South Jerseyans are quick to point out that no comparably comprehensive and growth-restrictive plan has been offered for the Highlands of the north. South Jerseyans would understand the viewpoint of Alaskans who are resentful of what they regard as unreasonably large-scale "freezing" of Alaskan land and resource development by creation of huge national parks, forest, and other protected areas. A popular Alaskan belief is that the "locking up" of Alaskan resources unfairly retards Alaskan development. The zealous protection and preservation of the Alaskan environment has been carried out, it is asserted, more as collective penance for the much more ruthless exploitation carried out in the past in some parts of the "lower forty-eight." In a similar manner, South Jerseyans familiar with the unplanned, or at best poorly planned, urban-suburban sprawl of the northeast part of the state, with its embedded concentrations of noxious, polluting industry, wonder if the Pinelands preservation crusade is penance for earlier sins up north.

THE SEASHORE AND WETLANDS

As noted in Chapter 3, New Jersey's physical environments that are most vulnerable to the casual mismanagement born of ignorance and arrogance are the seashore and related wetlands. Both the increasingly densely urbanized beaches and the extensive wetlands bordering them have long been subjected to misuse. The tempo and scale of this misuse of both had accelerated between the end of World War II and the enactment of protective and regulatory legislation.

Whether we wish to call them "marshlands," "meadowlands," or "wetlands," these unique ecological environments where fresh water and saltwater intermingle along the tidal fringes of the state were highly vulnerable to being irretrievably altered by filling them in (see Figure 11.2). The very act of destroying them by fill was often referred to as "reclaiming" them, as if a hostile nature had dragged otherwise good, productive, and useful land into some dark limbo. In fact, the wetlands, as they were termed by the Wetlands Act, are extremely valuable in their natural, unfilled state. Each acre (.4 ha), it is estimated, produces about 5 tn (4.5 t) of marine food in the form of decomposing salt grass mixed with algae and supports a wide variety of life such as insects, crabs, snails, mullet, and menhaden that serve as food for many predators—fish, land animals, and birds. A great variety of life—finfish, shellfish,

FIGURE 11.2. *"Dredge and Fill" Activity on the Salt-Marsh Fringes of Barrier Beaches.* The practice of dredging small-craft boat channels and using the spoil to create housing lots in marshland has now been stopped by the Wetlands Act. This type of development destroys the breeding grounds of many shellfish and finfish and reduces the marshland's capacity to absorb flood waters. (Courtesy of U.S. Army Corps of Engineers)

and birds—feeds, breeds, and nests in the wetlands. Tidal marshes also function as biological and chemical oxidation basins, controlling pollution and returning pollutants to the food chain. They are also sedimentation basins, trapping sediments that otherwise would silt in river channels or harbors. Lastly, the marshes serve as a buffer to floodwaters, absorbing not only floodwater but also some wind and wave energy to further reduce flood hazard on the mainland. In recognition of these values, permits to use any wetland site (see Figure 11.3) must be granted by the commissioner of environmental protection. Thus, the Wetlands Act, together with the Coastal Area Facilities Review Act (CAFRA) and various pieces of legislation affecting tidal bays, rivers, and creeks, protects a high proportion of the state's environmentally sensitive areas.

The natural profile of the barrier beaches was generalized in Figure 3.5. Human mismanagement of these islands, along with the sand spit Sandy Hook (which has been an island and may become one again) and mainland beaches such as those at Asbury Park and Long Branch, is based on greed and a wistful and utterly unfounded hope that the ocean will cease its continual reshaping of the shoreline. Resort islands have disappeared before, and will do so again, given enough time for the powerful erosive and depositional forces of the ocean to act on the loose coastal sands. For example, Tucker's Island, or Tucker's Beach, now a shoal covered at high tide, was once the southernmost portion of Long Beach Island. Tucker's Island was detached at least twice in the last two centuries by the emergence of an inlet separating it from the larger island; once it was rejoined by natural buildup of sand. Below high tide by the 1950s, it may reemerge as the shoal broadens and the inlet shrinks. The saga of Tucker's Island does not make soothing bedtime reading for anyone owning real estate on a barrier beach. Old maps reveal many other examples of the maxim that here the ocean gives and the ocean takes away.

As if the natural reshaping forces were not enough to contend with, people have persistently and unwisely carried out their own reshaping. These efforts tend to increase the probability of floods and of storm waves surging right over the islands. The effect of efforts to increase the area of salable lots is to flatten the dunes that offer some protection against storm waves and to fill in the bay-fringing marshes that absorb flood water. Lowering the profile of the barrier beach by leveling dunes and using that sand to fill in bay marsh leaves not only the beach itself, but the mainland behind the marshes and bay as well, open to more effective attack by wind and waves. The relatively recent appreciation that dunes are invaluable "shock absorbers," soaking up the pounding energy of waves, has come rather too late, unfortunately, for many beach communities. Where the dunes have been leveled and built upon, it is difficult to regenerate them. Snow fences and bundled, discarded Christmas trees are used to trap sand and stabilize it; dune grasses are planted and protected. Some resorts pump sand from bay to beach front, as does Ocean City, but that is a temporary bandage, not a cure. Sand may in future be pumped to the beaches from submerged sand ridges off the coast.

In the meantime, the buildings constructed on loose fill in the bay-fringing marshes are settling as the moisture is squeezed from the underlying decaying vegetation. As the houses sink into the former marsh, they become even more vulnerable to floods. The seashore environment is inherently unstable in that change is normal and frequent; human mismanagement and greedy efforts to increase building lots and construct jetties to trap sand that otherwise might have replenished beaches at other locations have, in the long run, further destabilized the shoreline.

CASE STUDY: THE TOCKS ISLAND DAM

Any proposal to create or expand public recreation facilities normally can expect to

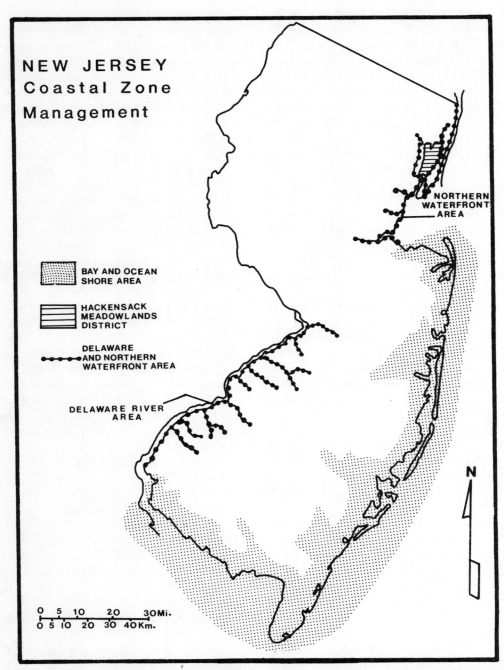

FIGURE 11.3. The State of New Jersey has been in the forefront of the national trend toward statewide zoning and control of lands and waters considered to be ecologically valuable and vulnerable.

FIGURE 11.4. In this most densely populated state, the pressures on recreational space frequently are obvious. State voters have approved several "green acres" bond issues to purchase and develop new parks, especially in the suburban fringes of metropolitan areas.

enjoy a politically unassailable status. It would be difficult to oppose a federally funded recreation project in a period of our national life so dominated by rising population, increasing mobility for recreation purposes, rising levels of disposable real income, and increasing amounts of leisure. The universal appeal of creating more public-recreation space and resources becomes especially tantalizing when the proposed recreation development would be within the already crowded, public-recreation-resource-poor Atlantic megalopolis.

In the northwestern Highlands region, the proposed Tocks Island Dam within the Delaware Water Gap National Recreation Area (DWGNRA) offers a case study of the complexities of such large-scale environmental engineering projects. Although defeated, the Tocks Island proposal is a good example of the need for *holistic planning* in New Jersey (and everywhere), that is, comprehensive planning that considers all aspects, and all future ramifications, of

any engineering project.

Programs of public acquisition of seashore lands and of scenic mountain lakes have not been able to keep pace with the rising demand for recreation space. The mountain and sea fringes of the Atlantic megalopolis are becoming, in a sense, the most remote suburbs of the cities. The "landscapes of leisure" are particularly vulnerable to the visual and ecological deterioration resultant from overuse by the ever-increasing hordes of vacationers.

The general enthusiasm that greeted the announcement of the Delaware Water Gap National Recreation Area, located conveniently close to the dominant northeast-southwest axis of the megalopolis, is thus easily understood. Located in an area of high scenic appeal that has long functioned as a summer resort, the DWGNRA would appear to be a politically ideal project—a project that will bring direct and lasting benefits to a large number of people who are acutely aware of its desirability. The

FIGURE 11.5. *The Delaware Water Gap in an 1874 Print.* More than a century ago, the Gap was a famed resort area, a function it retains as part of the national recreation area established by Congress in the 1960s. (William Cullen Bryant, *Picturesque America.* New York: D. Appleton and Co., 1874, p. 910)

controversy associated with the recreation development of the upper Delaware was limited to the proposed Tocks Island Dam and its reservoir and not to the overall DWGNRA.

Why a Tocks Island Dam?

The proponents of Tocks Island Dam deliberately intertwined the dam and the DWGNRA. Approximately half of the projected overall benefits anticipated for the dam and reservoir were based on their claimed recreation-resource functions. The Army Corps of Engineers assumed that about three-quarters of the projected 10.5 million annual visitors to the DWGNRA would be focused on the shoreline of Tocks Island "Lake." The recreation benefits claimed for the lake are delectable; unfortunately they might have proven to be

largely ephemeral. Tocks Island "Lake" would have been a multipurpose reservoir, one of whose major functions, it was claimed, would have been recreation. However, as a recreation resource the reservoir would have had limited appeal and use because of its other proposed uses. The other facets of Tocks Island dam-and-reservoir's multipurpose life would have been flood control, hydroelectric generation (pumped storage), and water supply.

Flood Control. The project later to be known as the Tocks Island Dam Project was first authorized by Congress in 1962, largely as the result of the 1955 flood on the Delaware that was triggered by the effects of the close-sequence onslaught of two hurricanes. Doubtless, the Tocks Island Dam would be capable of minimizing the downstream effects of a similar, highly unusual, flood crest if the level of the reservoir were kept low in the late summer and early fall. Almost forgotten is the fact that the ninety-nine persons who lost their lives in the 1955 flood perished in tributary valleys rather than on the main stream, and that most of the property damage resulting from the 1955 flood was downstream from Tocks Island to Burlington, New Jersey. A study conducted by the Sierra Club in 1970 of possible dam sites in the tributary valleys of the upper Delaware system estimated that 386 sites were feasible, of which only a small fraction are used. Since 1955, several dams have been constructed on major tributaries, including the Lehigh, Pohopoco, Neversink, and the Little Schuylkill. These dams should greatly reduce flood crests on the Delaware. Floods of the severity of 1955 are estimated to have a frequency of one in 500 years. A number of smaller dams on tributaries would appear to serve both the objectives of retaining floodwaters in those valleys, thus protecting lives there, and of reducing flood crests on the mainstream of the Delaware.

Hydroelectric Generation. The hydroelectric generating scheme associated with the Tocks Island Dam would have utilized the reservoir behind the dam as the lower storage reservoir for a *pumped-storage* system. Sunfish Pond, a glacial lake atop Kittatinny Mountain, was to become the site of the upper reservoir. The proposed utilization of Sunfish Pond, which would have destroyed its unique ecology, instigated much criticism when initially proposed, resulting in a retreat by the electric-power companies concerned. Pumped-storage facilities, such as that at Yards Creek, close by Sunfish Pond, do have certain inherent handicaps.

The basic appeal of pumped-storage projects to electric companies is that they are the only significant means of "storing" electrical energy that has been generated but is temporarily surplus to demand. Demand normally reaches a peak in afternoons, particularly during summer, and

ebbs to a low in the early morning hours. Rather than start, stop, and restart fossil-fueled steam generators, a time-consuming and expensive process, it is possible to utilize the temporarily "surplus" energy of the late evening–early morning hours to pump water up to a high-level reservoir. During the peak demand period for energy the water falls by gravity back through turbines to the lower reservoir, thus generating electricity.

The effect of the use of Tocks Island Reservoir as a lower basin for the pumped-storage facility would have been to create a daily fluctuation in water level of between 1 ft (0.3 m), when the reservoir was full, and 3 ft (0.9 m) when water level was low. Considering the total water demand placed on this proposed reservoir, the times when the level would be high would be infrequent. It is estimated that normal seasonal filling and drawdown on the planned reservoir would alternately cover and expose 3,253 acres (1,317 ha) of mud flats in a normally wet year and up to 8,845 acres (3,582 ha) under drought conditions.

Water Supply. The northeastern seaboard megalopolis is fast running out of fresh, clean water. Much of the fresh water available to the megalopolis, such as the once-magnificent Hudson as it flows past New York City, is in such polluted condition that its use is restricted to periods of extreme emergency. The upper Delaware, at present, is still considered a high-quality source for fresh water. The demands on it for municipal use are high and will clearly mount in the near future. At Montague, New Jersey, measured flow ranged from a low of 1,740 million gallons per day (mgd) to a high of 5,950 mgd in April 1969. On the basis of 1965 drought data extrapolated from Trenton upstream to Montague, drought flows at Montague would be in the range of 500 to 1,500 mgd, or about one-fourth normal. The minimum basic rate of flow at Montague is regarded as 1,130 mgd and the "design rate" is 1,710 mgd. The figures for 1969 were determined at a time when New York City was drawing

FIGURE 11.6.   Dramatic evidence of the growing problem of environmental pollution is this very explicit warning of contamination resulting from a chemical-waste dump near Pitman. The historic site marker refers to an amusement park that ceased operation here over fifty years ago.

mostly in the range of 600–700 mgd rather than the authorized 800 mgd permitted under the U.S. Supreme Court decree. New Jersey is currently allowed 100 mgd and in 1969 averaged a 65 mgd withdrawal rate. Bucks County, Pennsylvania, has requested permission to draw 200 mgd, and New Jersey has announced intention to seek 500 mgd limits. Clearly, utilization of the Delaware for municipal water in 1969 could have been increased under then-legal limits (Stansfield 1972, 29–33).

Undoubtedly, more municipalities will seek permission to draw still more water from the river in the future, and it cannot be assumed that users such as New York can continue to underdraw their allocation. The Delaware River Basin Commission has noted that "future growth in the Delaware Basin, coupled with projected water demands, dictates a flow and storage capacity vastly in excess of what is now available. The Tocks Island Reservoir would be the keystone of the water supply management program in the Delaware Valley without an alternative and the DRBC sees no alternative . . ." (Water Resources Association 1971, 4). The release of water at a minimum of 1,160 mgd to prevent salt-water intrusion into municipal water sup-

plies in the estuary area is necessary. Furthermore, minor losses should be expected from evaporation from increased surface area in the proposed reservoir and from leakage from the reservoir.

A further demand on the Delaware's flow is to prevent the increasing salinity of the Delaware estuary from ruining the Delaware Bay oyster industry. Increasing salinity due to diminished freshwater flow would encourage the predatory oyster drill. The Corps of Engineers committed the proposed Tocks reservoir to releasing all freshwater runoff entering the reservoir during the spring. The Tocks project would not have retained any additional water from April 1 through June 30, at which time flow is normally high. These multiple, often conflicting, demands upon the water of the Delaware could well have resulted in an abnormally slow filling of the reservoir once the dam was completed.

Recreation Drawback to the Proposal

Obviously, a great many demands exist for Delaware River water—the result of the dense urbanization of the megalopolis. Recreation, credited by the Army Corps of Engineers with the largest single share of benefits created by the Tocks Island Dam, unfortunately would have competed, at least occasionally unsuccessfully, with other, conflicting, uses. Multipurpose dams, such as that proposed for Tocks Island, are not new and are successful in many instances. Recreation development, however, is largely dependent on a relatively small fluctuation in shorelines and water levels. Drawdown-related problems formed the paramount objections to the Tocks Project from the recreation viewpoint. For example, *The Master Plan: Delaware Water Gap National Recreation Area,* prepared by the National Park Service's Planning and Service Center at Philadelphia in 1966, stated, "Maximum opportunity for visitors to attain an enjoyable water-related recreation experience requires maintenance of reservoir water levels and degree of fluctuation within reasonable limits during the recreation season. Otherwise, the public is faced with recreation facilities far removed from the water's edge, unsightly expanses of exposed bottom, etc." (U.S. National Park Service 1966, 20). The master plan further comments,

> with a possible drawdown under the ninety percent probability curve of sixteen feet between early June and late August even generally excellent shoreline can be expected to encounter bad local conditions . . . esthetic and public safety considerations suggest extensive work on the reservoir bottom prior to flooding. These include but are not limited to: removal of tree stumps, structures, and roads down to an elevation well below water surface during the period of May through November. Sculpturing of the form of the shoreline bottom will also be required to remove mudflats and dangerous shallows in active boating areas. This will ensure suitable drainage of the shorelines as the water elevation recedes, thereby avoiding objectionable stagnant water areas and marshes. (U.S. National Park Service 1966, 20)

Despite the necessity for extensive reshaping of the entire shoreline within the high- and low-water levels, the attractiveness and recreation aspects of the "lake" were dependent upon a relatively stable water level. Stability of shoreline was not a predicted characteristic of this reservoir. Daily fluctuation attributable to the originally proposed pumped-storage project would have been compounded by seasonal fluctuations that in drought years would have produced thousands of acres of exposed bottom, most of it unsightly as well as unusable. Hot, dry summers would contribute to the local electric-power shortage that plagues the Northeast, demanding maximum use of any hydroelectric facilities. Evaporation from the reservoir would reach a peak at that time. If the reservoir were otherwise capable of being filled for the summer maximum of recreation acticity, prudent management of the reservoir to allow storage of potential floodwaters such as those produced by hurricanes would

demand a level somewhat lower than peak capacity for the reservoir during the summer.

Changing leisure habits are extending the vacation season beyond Labor Day and initiating heavier use in May and June; winter sports are becoming more significant in resort economies. Those delights to commercial resort operators would only compound the problem of water-level management at Tocks reservoir, because the increasingly heavy visitation would spread progressively over longer and longer periods of the year. Vacationers would expect to use the Tocks reservoir well into September and October for boating and fishing. The maximum recreation level could hardly be maintained in the face of demands such as municipal water supply, which logically must have higher priority than recreation amenities in a serious drought.

For optimum operation as a recreation facility—in terms of water quality for swimming, stabilized shoreline for convenient utilization of beaches and related facilities such as bathhouses, aesthetic considerations of the shoreline's appearance, and conservation and encouragement of desirable fish species—little or no fluctuation in reservoir level is desirable. Municipal-water-supply withdrawal, evaporation and upper reservoir leakages associated with the proposed pumped-storage facility, flood-control considerations, dilution of pollution, maintenance of flow for the benefit of estuary municipal-water withdrawal, the dilution of the salinity that favors oyster drill incursions—all inevitably would have caused marked fluctuations and generally low water levels.

Logically, recreation as one reservoir management goal among many others could not consistently displace the other purposes of the reservoir. Other objectives would force decisions affecting water level that, by their timing and volume factors, would contribute to a poor-quality recreation facility. The Tocks project, if required to attempt the inherently impossible, would have failed to attain fully any of its goals.

Enthusiasm for the dam repeatedly obscured the real and potential recreation value of the area as it existed. The inundation of 12,000 acres (4,860 ha)—8,000 acres (3,240 ha) of which are classified as wildlife habitat—"would require the acquisition of approximately 880 acres of land for replacement," according to the engineers (U.S. Army Corps of Engineers 1970, 6). Even if the "replacement" land, an impossible function in fact, comprised 8,000 acres, would it not, if suitable to wildlife, already have such a wildlife population? How can we discuss "replacement" of something that clearly is not replaceable?

While not as dramatic as the Tocks Island Dam, many smaller dams on tributaries could contribute to the provision of a high-quality recreation environment. Land-based recreation in the area would be richer by the difference between the area to be drowned by the Tocks proposal and land used for many smaller dams and reservoirs. Thirty-seven mi (59.5 km) of free-flowing river are considered by many a resource worth conserving.

Conclusion

It appears unlikely that the proposed multipurpose dam at Tocks Island would have been able to serve all its announced objectives simultaneously and efficiently. We have not faced honestly the problems of increasing competition for land and water resources in the megalopolis: the Tocks proposal as a recreation project was a very dubious one, as it appeared to constitute a net deduction from present and potential quantity and quality of this scarce resource.

The Tocks Dam proposal was finally defeated by strong opposition from environmental activists, aided by political pressure from the "downstream" portion of the region—southern New Jersey, southeastern Pennsylvania, and Delaware—the areas most likely to experience negative effects from the dam. A later drive to designate the upper Delaware River a "wild

and scenic river" (permanently removing the possibility of a dam) was successful.

The Tocks Dam proposal, even though never constructed, served as a catalyst in the assembly and development of a sorely needed, market-oriented public-recreation facility. The Tocks proposal was withdrawn and "deauthorized" by Congress. It remains a dramatic example of resource competition in a crowded, heavily urbanized state.

FUTURE LANDSCAPES

An inexact science because it deals with so many human and cultural variables, geography nonetheless supports speculation on future spatial patterns. While it is not reasonable to rely entirely on the assumption that recent trends can be projected into the future, it would be just as unreasonable to ignore the recent past in attempting to predict future geographic patterns, problems, and potentials.

The number of inherently unpredictable variables involved in contemplating the future of New Jersey suggests a number of possible scenarios rather than one. Two crucial variables are the relative costs of energy, including vehicle fuels, and the future roles of government, particularly federal and state, in controlling and shaping land use. Among the dynamic factors to consider in predicting the future of New Jersey and New Jerseyans are:

1. Intrastate migration: Will southern New Jersey continue to gain population? Will northeastern New Jersey continue to lose population?

2. Interstate migration: Will the Sun Belt states continue to attract interstate migrants at the expense of the Frost Belt and Manufacturing Belt northeastern states?

3. Industrial location/relocation: Will outmoded industries be replaced by industries that are relatively nonsen-

sitive to raw materials and energy, but responsive to New Jersey's situational resources and to market accessibility?

4. Recreational space and farmlands: Will use pressures continue to mount for recreational resources, and will suburbanization continue to diminish the farmlands?

5. Suburban deconcentration and dispersal: Will galactic city continue to form or could there be a reconcentration of economic activity favoring cities as central places?

6. Cost of living and total tax burden: Will they continue upward, and will that trend contribute to relocation of people and of economic activities?

When each of two extremes is considered for each of the two major variables, there are four scenarios; these are not exclusive of one another but rather mutually influential. These are: (1) the "Limited-Mobility State," (2) the "Expanding-Mobility State," (3) the "Contained-Growth State," and (4) the "Sprawling-Growth State."

The Limited-Mobility State

In this scenario, a tempting assumption would be that central cities would revitalize as greater "friction of space" reduced the appeal of the suburbs and increased the desirability of centrality. If relatively cheap individual mobility dispersed urban functions and urban people, would not more-expensive or even erratically unavailable (due to fuel scarcities) mobility favor reconcentration? It must be remembered that about two generations of Americans have grown up with automobiles; old habits die hard, and Americans have demonstrated a willingness to devote a high proportion of their income to owning and operating cars. In addition, Americans have literally built a nation around the assumption that cars will continue to be virtually universally available. All of that fixed investment can-

FIGURE 11.7. *Inappropriate Attempts at Urban Rejuvenation, Newark.* Attractive new buildings such as this subsidized high-rise for senior citizens will fall short of their purpose if the entire surrounding neighborhood is not upgraded as well. The littered, weed-grown surroundings of this building testify to its tenants' perceptions of the outdoors as a hazardous, unfriendly place.

not be abandoned overnight. Most probably, the expansion of galactic city would be slowed, or even halted temporarily.

However, the inner cities and their residents could be affected more negatively than positively, as many inner-city workers commute *out* to the suburbs for work in factories, warehouses, and retail stores. If the office workers commuting to the central business district could pay the assumed higher costs of commuting, the inner-city workers could not. Furthermore, the existing public transit systems still funnel into the city center rather than connect inner-city people with the many scattered nodes of suburban economic opportunity. Without heavy subsidy of inherently expensive flexible public transit systems serving a relatively low-density metropolitan area, the intrastate effect of limited mobility could be an inner suburban ring of reconcentration along the interstate and freeway bypass routes, halting further outward movements but avoiding the old central cities as well. The Meadowlands devel-

FIGURE 11.8.   The urban core of northeastern New Jersey, in Hudson, Essex, and Union counties particularly, was long split by the Hackensack Meadows, a vast marsh that is a relic of glacial Lake Hackensack. Now the meadowlands are being extensively developed for the first time; development includes the sports complex. Also, for the first time, New Jersey hosts big-league teams that formerly were located within the great out-of-state metropolises due to the space demands of modern stadiums and their huge parking lots. (Courtesy of Meadowlands Sports Complex)

opment could be the prototype of "infilling" (see Figure 11.8).

The Expanding-Mobility State

In the Expanding-Mobility State, the two former fringes of the corridor—the northwest and the south-southeast counties— could be the major beneficiaries. Galactic city would continue its advance, drawing still more people and functions from the cities. The south would continue its faster rate of gain than north Jersey, as the whole megalopolis continued its southward and westward shifts. The interstate effects, however, would most probably feature a continued shift toward the Sun Belt as the post-industrial society abandoned the ob-

solescent industrial landscapes of the Manufacturing Belt, including most of New Jersey. The attractive landscapes of the mountains and the seashore would continue population growth at rates strongly influenced by the goals and powers of zoning and land-use control.

The Contained-Growth State

This scenario would be one of immediate frustrations to many landowners and would-be residents in the Pinelands, seashore, and mountain regions. Building permits would be either difficult or impossible to obtain in scenic and ecologically fragile protected areas. In the longer view, however, those general regions of the state would continue to attract people who would locate in the immediate periphery of the protected zones, particularly in a landscape influenced by a combination high-mobility and contained-growth scenario. The real estate values of existing houses, such as in traditional Pinelands villages, could soar beyond reach of the present inhabitants as "outsiders," lured by the surrounding preserved landscape, bid up prices for the privilege of living within it. The same could happen to seashore and mountain communities if further building were effectively frozen by rigid land-use controls. The ultimate beneficiaries of the Contained-Growth State would be, on a general level, everybody; on a specific, high-amenity residential level, the beneficiaries would be those wealthy enough to purchase homes in the narrow market of existing buildings. Many of the present "natives" could not afford to stay,

and fewer of their offspring could afford to establish their own homes there.

The Sprawling-Growth State

An ecological disaster could be a long-term result of the Sprawling-Growth State in tandem with expanding mobility. Low-density suburban growth would dominate the state beyond the aging cities, and state-owned lands would be open islands embedded within new subdivisions. Sprawling or nonchanneled growth would only be slowed by its concurrence with a limited-mobility situation.

Conclusion

We have no way of accurately predicting the future, but we can be absolutely sure of one thing. The actions that we take now, individually and collectively, will help shape that future. That the state will become

FIGURE 11.9. *Oysterboat at Shellpile.* The Maurice River Cove of Delaware Bay was the nation's most productive oyster ground in the late nineteenth century. Pollution, overfishing, predators, and disease combined to diminish the catch, although improved quality of the bay water has supported recent increases in the oyster catch. What effect could increased population density and diminished zeal for protection of the environment produce?

more deeply involved in channeling future land development to protect the physical environment would seem a safer assumption than any concerning relative energy costs. There appears to be broad-based support for the goals of such control, if not always agreement on specific areas and legal techniques of preservation. As with other aspects of "futurology" though, trends cannot be simply projected into the future, because people are responsive to changing conditions, new technologies, and new social and political concepts. There is a feedback mechanism working that can halt or reverse previous trends. The oil shocks of the 1970s led to declining oil consumption, at least temporarily, and we can expect similar feedback on such vital issues as statewide planning. If the voters conclude

that the Pinelands preservation was handled responsibly and responsively, for example, then the trend toward state controls will continue. Should the citizenry perceive the Pinelands preservation as a threatening incursion into private property rights or as lacking in genuine involvement of local people, then political support will diminish for any future extensions of state involvement in land-use planning.

New Jersey has an opportunity to help lead the nation in balancing private and societal interests in the management and planning of its landscapes. New Jersey has been a leader before in nationwide trends and experiences and will continue to be in the U.S. vanguard in its economic and cultural geographic interactions of land and people.

BIBLIOGRAPHY
Selected and Annotated

GENERAL NOTE

Fortunately for the serious scholar in any field of New Jersey studies, a great many interesting and informative books, monographs, and magazine and journal articles focus on New Jersey, place it in regional or national context, or significantly mention the state. Of course, some are more interesting, informative, and generally useful (sometimes all three) than others. It is the object of this bibliography to include all sources and references used and to list the better general sources, including some of historical interest and value, with some notations on their utility and enjoyableness. Scholarly research that goes beyond the limitations of this bibliography and the collective bibliographies of these sources is specialized enough not to need further help here.

In book citations, places of publication are in New Jersey unless they are in a generally recognizable city outside the state or otherwise noted.

THE SIX-AND-ONE-HALF-INCH SHELF

To begin with, the interested but uninitiated reader is directed to five books that together will reward the reader with a good background on New Jersey—its geography, history, and people. Individually, each book is delightful reading in its own way. These books, which will take up about six-and-a-half more inches in your bookshelf, are:

John T. Cunningham. *New Jersey: A Mirror on America*. Florham Park: Afton Publishing,

1978. Actually, if you only read *one* more book on New Jersey, this should be it. Cunningham writes gracefully and informatively, with a nice touch of humor. His books are notable for their many carefully selected and beautifully reproduced illustrations. As students of New Jersey quickly discover, he has written on most topics worth writing about in New Jersey; I think this is his best.

Federal Writers' Project, New Jersey: A Guide to Its Present and Past. New York: Viking Press, 1939. This is a sentimental favorite. Written during the depression by otherwise unemployed journalists, historians, geologists, sociologists, and other professionals, working mostly in the Newark Public Library, it is a reasonably balanced portrait of a state and its people just before World War II.

Frank Kelland and Marylin Kelland. *New Jersey: Garden or Suburb?* Dubuque, Iowa: Kendall-Hunt, 1978. A good, traditional, systematic geography of the state with a detailed survey of physical geographic factors. There are many good maps; an appendix provides maps of each county with all municipalities identified. Census data for counties and municipalities, 1960 and 1970, are included, along with an index map of New Jersey topographic sheets; all of this saves research time on New Jersey geographical topics.

Rudolph Vecoli. *The People of New Jersey*. Princeton: D. Van Nostrand Co., Inc., 1965. A fine social history of New Jersey's evolving ethnic and racial mix, this study relates changing economic conditions within the state to changing mixes of immigrants and interstate migrants. It is very nicely written if rather brief.

Peter O. Wacker. *Land and People: A Cultural Geography of Preindustrial New Jersey: Origins and Settlement Patterns.* New Brunswick: Rutgers University Press, 1975. A veritable model of historical cultural geography, this is a richly documented and meticulously researched study that is beautifully written as well. It ends too soon, but the good news is that a companion volume is planned—look for it.

SELECTED BIBLIOGRAPHY

Baer, Christopher T. *Canals and Railroads of the Mid-Atlantic States, 1800–1860.* Wilmington, Del.: Regional Economic History Research Center, Eleutherian Mills–Hagley Foundation, 1981.
Notable for finely detailed maps.
Bebout, John E., and Grele, Ronald G. *Where Cities Meet: The Urbanization of New Jersey.* Princeton: D. Van Nostrand Co., Inc., 1964.
Beck, Henry C. *Tales and Towns of Northern New Jersey.* New Brunswick: Rutgers University Press, 1964.
_____. *The Jersey Midlands.* New Brunswick: Rutgers University Press, 1962.
Bergman, Edward F., and Pohl, Thomas. *A Geography of the New York Metropolitan Region.* Dubuque, Iowa: Kendall-Hunt, 1975.
Boyer, Charles. *Waterways of New Jersey: History of Riparian Ownership and Control Over the Navigable Waters of New Jersey.* Camden: Sinnickson, Chew and Sons, 1915.
Delightfully chauvinistic view of the underhanded dealings of New Jersey's neighbors in controlling "shared" navigable waters.
Brush, John E. *The Population of New Jersey.* 2d ed. New Brunswick: Rutgers University Press, 1958.
An excellent geographic study.
Bryant, William Cullen, editor. *Picturesque America.* 2 vols. New York: D. Appleton and Company, 1874.
Burton, Ian et al. *The Shores of Megalopolis: Coastal Occupance and Human Adjustment to Flood Hazard.* Elmer: C. W. Thornthwaite Associates Laboratory of Climatology, 1965.
Carey, George W. *New York-New Jersey: A Vignette of the Metropolitan Region.* Cambridge, Mass.: Ballinger Publishing Co., 1976.
A first-rate study of the bistate region that holds most of New Jersey's population.
Carlino, Gerald. "From Centralization to De-

concentration: Economic Activity Spreads Out." *Business Review.* Federal Reserve Bank of Philadelphia. (May/June, 1982):15–25.
Christian, Charles M., and Harper, Robert A., editors. *Modern Metropolitan Systems.* Columbus: Charles E. Merrill, 1982.
Clawson, Marion, and Knetsch, Jack. *Economics of Outdoor Recreation.* Baltimore: Johns Hopkins Press, 1966.
Clay, Grady. *Close-Up: How to Read the American City.* Chicago: The University of Chicago Press, 1973.
Very interesting reading that will lead readers to a new way of looking at New Jersey's cultural landscapes.
Cranmer, H. Jerome. *New Jersey in the Automobile Age: A History of Transportation.* Princeton: D. Van Nostrand Co., Inc., 1964.
Cross, Dorothy. *New Jersey's Indians.* Trenton: The New Jersey State Museum, 1965.
Cunningham, John T. *Garden State: The Story of Agriculture in New Jersey.* New Brunswick: Rutgers University Press, 1955.
_____. *Made in New Jersey: The Industrial Story of a State.* New Brunswick: Rutgers University Press, 1954.
_____. *New Jersey: America's Main Road.* Garden City, N.Y.: Doubleday and Co., Inc., 1966a.
_____. *The New Jersey Shore.* New Brunswick: Rutgers University Press, 1958.
A personal favorite, with many interesting asides.
_____. *Newark.* Newark: New Jersey Historical Society, 1966b.
A lavishly illustrated "City Biography," its only flaw the overly optimistic view of the city's future (which is with us now).
_____. *Railroading in New Jersey.* Newark: Associated Railroads of New Jersey, 1951.
Currier, Wade. "Remote Sensing: A Tool in Delimiting the New Jersey Pinelands." A paper presented at the 1981 meeting of the Association of American Geographers, Los Angeles.
_____. "The Ports of Philadelphia." In *The Philadelphia Region,* edited by Roman A. Cybriwsky, pp. 200–216. Washington, D.C.: Association of American Geographers, 1979.
Cybriwsky, Roman A., editor. *The Philadelphia Region: Selected Essays and Field Trip Itineraries.* Washington, D.C.: Association of American Geographers, 1979.
Contains several essays and field-trip itin-

eraries for the Pinelands, Atlantic City, and the southern shore.

Dike, Paul. "Geology of New Jersey." Glassboro: Glassboro State College, 1967. (Mimeographed.)

Directions. The journal of New Jersey Council for Geographic Education, 1956 to present. Currently published by the Department of Geography, Glassboro State College, Glassboro, N.J.
Contains articles and book reviews of interest to New Jerseyans and geographers.

Flink, Salomon J., editor. *The Economy of New Jersey.* New Brunswick: Rutgers University Press, 1958.

Franklin, James, and Hughes, James. *Modeling State Growth: New Jersey 1980.* New Brunswick: Center for Urban Policy Research, Rutgers University, 1973.

Freegood, Seymour et al. *The Gateway States: New Jersey, New York.* New York: Time-Life Books, 1967.

Funnel, Charles. *By the Beautiful Sea: The Rise and High Times of That Great American Resort, Atlantic City.* New York: Alfred Knopf, 1975.
Delightful, breezy writing about the self-styled "Queen of the Jersey Shore."

Garreau, Joel. *The Nine Nations of North America.* Boston: Houghton Mifflin, 1981.
A journalist's best-selling popularization of what cultural geographers already knew; worth reading.

Gaver, Mary. *A Selected New Jersey Bibliography.* New Brunswick: Rutgers University Press, 1968.

Gesler, Wilbert. "North Jersey vs. South Jersey: A Population Geography Class Survey." *Journal of Geography* 80 (April/May 1981):124–129.

Gottmann, Jean. *Megalopolis.* New York: Twentieth Century Fund, 1961.
One of the few examples of a geographic term becoming a popular and widely understood descriptive term, *Megalopolis* holds special interest to anyone trying to understand contemporary New Jersey's recent background.

————. *The Significance of Territory.* Charlottesville, Va.: University of Virginia Press, 1973.

Hall, Peter. *The World Cities.* New York: McGraw-Hill, 1966.
Useful for its interpretation of the worldwide significance of the New York–New Jersey metropolitan region.

Hamer, Thomas. "The Casino Industry in Atlantic City: What Has It Done For the Local Economy?" *Business Review.* Federal Reserve Bank of Philadelphia. (January/February, 1982):3–16.
An excellent, detailed, and highly readable study.

Harper, Robert W. *John Fenwick and Salem County in the Province of West Jersey, 1609–1750.* Salem: Salem County Cultural and Heritage Commission, 1978.
A sympathetic study of one of colonial New Jersey's "Founding Fathers"; nicely done.

Kobbe, Gustav. *The Jersey Coast and Pines: An Illustrated Guide-Book with Road Maps.* 1889. Reprint. Baltimore: Gateway Press, 1970.

Kurath, Hans. *Word Geography of the Eastern United States.* Ann Arbor: University of Michigan Press, 1949.

Laccetti, Silvio R., editor. *The Outlook on New Jersey.* Union City: William H. Wise and Co., 1979.

Lane, Wheaton J. *From Indian Trail to Iron Horse: Travel and Transportation in New Jersey, 1620–1860.* Princeton: Princeton University Press, 1939.

McCormick, Richard P. *New Jersey from Colony to State 1609–1789.* Princeton: D. Van Nostrand Co., Inc., 1964.

McHarg, Ian. *Design with Nature.* Garden City, N.Y.: Natural History Press, 1969.
Includes an interesting discussion of the natural environment of the Jersey shore.

McPhee, John. *The Pine Barrens.* New York: Ballantine Books, 1971.
Superbly written with an obvious empathy for the Pinelands and its people.

Meinig, Donald, editor. *The Interpretation of Ordinary Landscapes: Geographical Essays.* New York: Oxford University Press, 1979.

Merrill, Leland G. et al. *A Plan for a Pinelands National Preserve.* New Brunswick: Rutgers University, Center for Coastal and Environmental Studies, 1978.

Morse, Jedidiah. *Geography Made Easy: Being an Abridgment of the American Universal Geography.* Boston: Thomas and Andrews, 1807.

Muller, Peter O. *Contemporary Suburban America.* Englewood Cliffs: Prentice Hall, 1981.

Of general interest to students of what might just as well be called the "Suburban State" as "Garden State."

————. *The Outer City: Geographical Consequences of the Urbanization of the Suburbs.* A.A.G. Resource Paper 75-2. Washington, D.C.: Association of American Geographers, 1976.

Muller, Peter O.; Meyer, Kenneth C.; and Cybriwsky, Roman A. *Philadelphia: A Study of Conflicts and Social Cleavages.* Cambridge, Mass.: Ballinger Publishing Co., 1976.
Includes some mention of the South Jersey portion of metropolitan Philadelphia.

Nelson, William, editor. *New Jersey Coast in Three Centuries.* 3 vols. New York: Lewis Historical Publishing Co., 1902.

New Jersey Economic Indicators. Trenton: New Jersey Department of Labor and Industry, Division of Planning and Research. Published monthly.

New Jersey Monthly. Princeton: Aylesworth Communications Corp. Published monthly since 1976.
With an understandable emphasis on north Jersey, this contains good articles on New Jersey life and phenomena, along with lots of gossip on the state's rather infamous crew of politicians.

New Jersey Writers' Project. *The Underground Railroad in New Jersey.* Stories of New Jersey Series. Newark: New Jersey Writers' Project, Work Projects Administration, 1939.

Norman, Thomas P., editor. *New Jersey Trends: Population and Economy; Natural Resources; Housing; Transportation; Energy.* New Brunswick: Institute for Environmental Studies, Rutgers University, 1974.

Office of Environmental Review. *Outdoor Recreation in New Jersey.* Trenton: State of New Jersey, Department of Environmental Protection, 1973.

Parsons, Floyd, editor. *New Jersey: Life, Industries and Resources of a Great State.* Newark: New Jersey State Chamber of Commerce, 1928.
A self-conscious "booster" view of the state near its apex of industrial power relative to the rest of the United States.

Pierce, Arthur D. *Iron in the Pines: The Story of New Jersey's Ghost Towns and Bog Iron.* New Brunswick: Rutgers University Press, 1957.
Interesting, popular recounting of New Jersey's "ghost towns."

Pomfret, John E. *The New Jersey Proprietors and Their Lands: 1664–1776.* Princeton: D. Van Nostrand Co., Inc., 1964.

————. *The Province of East New Jersey: 1609–1702.* The Princeton History of New Jersey Series. Princeton: Princeton University Press, 1962.

Porter, Glenn, editor. *Regional Economic History: The Mid-Atlantic Area Since 1700.* Wilmington, Del.: Eleutherian Mills–Hagley Foundation, 1976.

Price, Clement A. "The Beleaguered City as Promised Land: Blacks in Newark 1917–1947." In *Urban New Jersey Since 1870,* edited by William C. Wright, pp. 10–45. Trenton: New Jersey Historical Commission, 1975.

Radko, Thomas, editor. *Discovering New Jersey.* New Brunswick: Rutgers University Press, 1982.
A general guide to historical sites, recreation areas, and other attractions; a practical handbook of touring in New Jersey.

Regional Economic History Research Center. *Economy and Society: Philadephia and Its Hinterland.* Working Papers Series, vol. 2. Wilmington, Del.: Eleutherian Mills–Hagley Foundation, 1978.

Rose, Harold. "The All-Negro Town: Its Evolution and Function." *Geographical Review* 60 (1965):362–381.

Rose, Thomas. *Historical and Biographical Atlas of the New Jersey Coast.* Philadelphia: Woolman and Rose, 1878.

Schmidt, George P. *Princeton and Rutgers: The Two Colonial Colleges of New Jersey.* Princeton: D. Van Nostrand Co., Inc., 1964.

Schmidt, Hubert G. *Agriculture in New Jersey: A Three-Hundred Year History.* New Brunswick: Rutgers University Press, 1973.
An excellent, highly detailed study.

Singh, Harbans. *Paterson and Its Neighboring Communities.* Upper Montclair: Montclair State College, Department of Geography and Urban Studies Research Report, 1975.
An interesting study of urban growth and social characteristics of one of New Jersey's oldest and largest cities.

Sinton, John W., editor. *Natural and Cultural Resources of the New Jersey Pine Barrens.* Pomona: Stockton State College, 1979.
Valuable for the many fine essays it contains, notably Elizabeth Marsh's "Ethnic Archipelago."

Snyder, John P. *The Mapping of New Jersey.*

New Brunswick: Rutgers University Press, 1973.

Stansfield, Charles. "New Jersey's Ski Industry: The Trend Towards Market Orientation." *Journal of Travel Research* 11 (Winter 1973):6–10.

———. "The Tocks Island Dam Controversy." *Parks and Recreation* 20 (March 1972):29–33.

State of New Jersey. *New Jersey Agricultural Statistics, 1981.* Trenton: New Jersey Crop Reporting Service, 1981.

State of New Jersey, Pinelands Planning and Management Commission. *Draft Comprehensive Management Plan.* New Lisbon: New Jersey Pinelands Planning and Management Commission, 1979.

Statistical Almanac–New Jersey: A Compilation of Key New Jersey Facts and Figures. Union City: William H. Wise and Co., Inc., 1981. Issued periodically.

Stellhorn, Paul A., editor. *Planned and Utopian Experiments: Four New Jersey Towns.* Trenton: New Jersey Historical Commission, 1980.

Studley, Miriam V. *Historic New Jersey Through Visitors' Eyes.* Princeton: D. Van Nostrand Co., Inc., 1964.

Taylor, George, and Neu, Irene. *The American Railroad Network, 1861–1890.* Cambridge: Harvard University Press, 1956.

U.S. Army Corps of Engineers. *Tocks Island Reservoir Project, Pennsylvania, New Jersey and New York.* Environmental statement (preliminary draft). Philadelphia: U.S. Army Corps of Engineers, 1970. (Mimeographed.)

U.S. Bureau of the Census. *Census of Agriculture.* Washington, D.C.: U.S. Government Printing Office, various years.

———. *Census of Population.* Washington, D.C.: U.S. Government Printing Office, various years.

———. *Historical Statistics of the United States: Colonial Times to 1957.* Washington, D.C.: U.S. Bureau of the Census, 1961.

U.S. Department of Agriculture. *Climate and Man.* 1941 Yearbook of Agriculture. Washington, D.C.: U.S. Government Printing Office, 1941.

U.S. Department of Commerce, Weather Bureau. *New Jersey.* Climates of the States Series. Washington, D.C.: U.S. Government Printing Office, 1959.

U.S. National Park Service, Planning and Service Center. *The Master Plan: Delaware Water Gap National Recreation Area.* Philadephia: National Park Service, Planning and Service Center, 1966.

Veit, Richard. *The Old Canals of New Jersey: A Historical Geography.* Little Falls: New Jersey Geographical Press, 1963. A fine example of a historical geography of transportation routes and technologies.

Wacker, Peter O. *The Musconetcong Valley of New Jersey.* New Brunswick: Rutgers University Press, 1968.

Warner, Sam Bass, Jr. *Streetcar Suburbs: The Process of Growth in Boston, 1870–1900.* New York: Atheneum, 1971.

Water Resources Association of the Delaware River Basin. *Delaware Basin Bulletin* (September/October 1971).

Webster, Henry H., and Stoltenberg, Carl H. *The Timber Resources of New Jersey.* Upper Darby, Pa.: U.S. Forest Service, Northeastern Forest Experiment Station, 1958.

Whitehead, William A. et al., editors. *Archives of the State of New Jersey: Documents Relating to the Colonial, Revolutionary and Post-revolutionary History of the State of New Jersey.* First Series, vol. 2. Trenton: State of New Jersey, 1810.

Widmer, Kemble. *The Geology and Geography of New Jersey.* Princeton: D. Van Nostrand Co., Inc., 1964. A good but brief survey of the Garden State's geology.

Wilkerson, Albert S. *Minerals of New Jersey.* Trenton: The Geological Society of New Jersey, 1959.

Wilson, Harold F. *The Story of the Jersey Shore.* Princeton: D. Van Nostrand Co., Inc., 1964. A social and economic history by an unabashed fan of the Jersey shore.

Wright, William C., editor. *Urban New Jersey Since 1870.* Trenton: New Jersey Historical Commission, 1975. Contains several fascinating essays, including Clement Price's study of blacks in Newark (listed separately).

Zelinsky, Wilbur. "Generic Terms in the Place Names of the Northeastern United States." *Annals of the Association of American Geographers* 45 (1955):319–349.

———. "An Approach to the Religious Geography of the United States." *Annals of the Association of American Geographers* 51 (1961):139–167.

Zimolzak, Chester, and Stansfield, Charles. *The Human Landscape.* Columbus, Ohio: Charles Merrill, 1979.

INDEX

DATE DUE

MAR 1 6 1989		
APR 1 8 1989		
FEB 1 4 2000		

Demco, Inc. 38-293